MEDITATIONS

ON THE

LIFE OF CHRIST

BY

THOMAS A KEMPIS

TRANSLATED AND EDITED BY
THE VEN. ARCHDEACON WRIGHT, M.A.

AND
THE REV. S. KETTLEWELL, M.A.

BAKER BOOK HOUSE
Grand Rapids, Michigan

Reprinted 1978 by
Baker Book House
from the edition issued in 1892 by
E. P. Dutton & Company

ISBN: 0-8010-0123-4

Second printing, September 1981

PHOTOLITHOPRINTED BY CUSHING - MALLOY, INC.
ANN ARBOR, MICHIGAN, UNITED STATES OF AMERICA

Dedicated

TO THE MOST REVEREND HIS GRACE THE

LORD ARCHBISHOP OF CANTERBURY, D.D.

Primate of all England,

WITH PROFOUND RESPECT AND DUTIFUL

OBEDIENCE IN CHRIST.

CONTENTS

Contents.

Contents

PART II

ON THE PASSION OF CHRIST UNTIL HIS RESURRECTION, ACCORDING TO THE FOUR EVANGELISTS

(7)

Contents

Contents

PART III

ON THE RESURRECTION OF CHRIST AND HIS SEVERAL APPEARANCES

Contents

Contents

PART IV

ON THE ASCENSION, PENTECOST, AND CERTAIN OTHER MATTERS

PREFACE

THE full title of this work is, "De Vitâ et Beneficiis Jesu Christi Salvatoris Nostri Meditationes et Orationes." In the table of contents for the third volume of Sommalius's "Opera Omnia" of Thomas à Kempis[*] it is simply spoken of as "De Vitâ Christi Meditationes"; and so at the headings of the pages— on the one side we have "De Vitâ Christi," and on the other, "Meditationes."[†] It is found in the second edition of the above work. It occupies rather more than a hundred pages with an index at the end; and is placed at the begin-

[*] 2d Ed., Antwerp, 1607, small 4to.

[†] Other titles are given, viz. :—

1. "Liber Orationum De Vitâ Domini": MS. of Contemporary Biographer, and end of 15th Century.

2. "Meditationes in Vitam Christi": the Buxheim MS.

3. "Orationes in Totam Vitam Christi": 1626, Cologne.

4. "Oraciones y Meditaciones de la Vida de Jesu Christo, N.S.": 1661, Brussels. But all refer to one and the same treatise.

ning of the third volume, double columns, small type. It does not appear in the first edition, and, after its appearance in this second edition, it disappears altogether, in a strange and most unaccountable manner, without any explanation, in all future editions. This has tended in no small degree to discredit the work. To this subject some reference will shortly be made.

But the first and principal question that will be asked is, How do we know that this "De Vitâ" was written by Thomas à Kempis What other evidence, besides its appearance in this edition, is there that he was the author of it? It is important to give an answer on this point before we proceed further, because it may be said, "Its appearance in only this one edition is slight ground to build upon, and unless you have some more satisfactory and decisive proof to produce, you are not justified in so deliberately speaking of the 'De Vitâ Christi Meditationes' as the work of Thomas à Kempis."

Happily we have, quite apart from Sommalius, far more certain evidence to depend upon, to assure us that Thomas à Kempis was undoubtedly the author of it. A contemporary but unknown writer, soon after the death of Thomas, gives a short biography of him; from which it is evident, that, whether the contemporary lived on Mount St. Agnes with the Kempen, or in the mother-house at Windesheim, not many miles distant, or only intimately knew some of the Brethren, he was evidently well acquainted with what Thomas did, and *what he wrote.* He it is who gives us that pleasing anecdote about him, that, when a wave of fervent devotion came over him, he would ask leave of the Brethren, with whom he might be talking, to withdraw, under the plea that some one was waiting for him in his cell. He retired to hold communion with his Saviour. This writer of his life then adds, that we have the result or fruits of this frequent and sacred intercourse with Jesus in some of the books and treatises which he wrote.*

This gives the contemporary writer occasion to say in conclusion that, as few knew what Thomas had written, he would put down very specifically a catalogue of his works. Having told us that this devout Father died in the year 1471, he continues :—" Et quia multos Tractatus scripsit et dictavit in vita, et pauci sciunt, quomodo intitulantur vel vocantur, ideo tabulam de ejus Tractatibus et Libris hic intitulare et scribere intendo, ut omnes qui legunt, vel audiunt, possint scire, quot sunt."

* See Eusebius Amort, *Moralis Certitudo pro Ven : Thoma Kempensi,* 4to, Augusta Vindelicorum, 1764, p. 145.

And in the " Tituli Librorum et Tractatuum " given, we have at No. 34 the very book now under consideration, named and specified. It is mentioned and set forth in these words :—

" Liber Orationum De Vita Domini. *Domi-nus Deus meus, laudare te desidero.*"

The latter words in italics are those with which the book begins, and are given to make it clear that it is the identical work alluded to, so that there might be no mistake. It is in this manner that the biographer indicates the books of the " De Imitatione Christi," which are found separately noted, after this form :—

" 5. Libellus sententiarum et verborum humilis Jesu. Alias vocatur de Imitatione Christi, scilicet ; *Qui sequitur me.*"

" Secundus Tractatus. *Regnum Dei intra vos est.*" The words in italics being those with which the first and second books of the *Imitation* begin.*

The writer of these sacred colloquies with Jesus, whilst desirous that pious Christians should have the benefit of the precious thoughts contained in them, wished, nevertheless, to remain hidden from the world : a line of conduct thoroughly in accordance with the humble character of Thomas à Kempis ; who, whilst

* See Eusebius Amort, in his *Moralis Certitudo*, pp. 144–147.

striving to point out the beauty of holiness, and to set forth its perfect and Divine Exemplar in all His loveliness, would shrink from the idea of making it known to the world, that he himself it was who held this personal intercourse with the Saviour. This, doubtless, at the first prevented his attaching his name to what he wrote; so that some persons at a distance, who were unacquainted with Thomas and his writings, speculated as to who was the author of them; and in one or two noticeable instances erroneously attributed them to other famous men.

The value of the testimony just produced should be well considered, for it is of the highest character, and such as one who is desirous of getting at the truth of the matter would like to have. It is not the witness of some one at a distance, in another country, who could know but little or nothing of the life and writings of Thomas à Kempis but by hearsay; it is not given by one who lived fifty or a hundred years after the death of this devout Father; it is written by one who lived during the lifetime of Thomas à Kempis, and, we may presume, at no great distance from the monastery of Mount St. Agnes. Possibly he belonged to that house, or to the mother-house at Windesheim. However that may be, this is certain, the writer shows, in the hagiographical sketch given by him, that he had an intimate and thorough knowledge both of the life and writings of the pious author.

It is this kind of testimony, I repeat, that is so valuable. It comes from one who is well qualified to give us authentic information. The work is clearly indicated; and the record assures all men that Thomas à Kempis is the author of the "De Vitâ Christi Meditationes." If there had been any mistake about the matter, we might have expected that some notice of it would have been taken, and that it would have been corrected at once. If it had been attributed to any one else, it is certain that some one would have made the claim known; but as there is no other account to be found in that age or country, the testimony of this contemporary biographer is most important, and may be taken as conclusive.

There is, moreover, other contemporary evidence to show that this book—the "De Vitâ Christi Meditationes"—was in existence *at the time* of the death of Thomas à Kempis in the year 1471. It arises in a very singular and undesigned manner, which helps to confirm the testimony already advanced, and is therefore of great worth. Eusebius Amort is not defending the authorship of the "De Vitâ Christi Medita-

tiones," but that of the " De Imitatione Christi."
And, in doing this he brings forward an ancient
codex, containing several works—some more
ancient than others—found in the Carthusian
monastery of Buxhaim or Buxheim, Suabia, Germany, in which another amanuensis, contemporary with Thomas à Kempis, gives, at the end of
two of the works bound up in the codex, the dates
when they were copied; which is an evident
proof that these dated manuscripts must have
been known at the time named. The Carthu-
sians, as well as the Brethren of other Orders,
were familiar with, and were held in much
esteem by the Windesheim community, to
which Thomas à Kempis belonged. He alludes
to them, it will be remembered, in book i.
chapter xxv. of the *Imitation*. Hence a frequent interchange of fellowship and kindly
actions passed between them; and that of lend-
ing valuable manuscripts to be copied out was
one of them. By this means, doubtless, a copy
of the " De Vitâ Christi Meditationes" was to
be found in the Monastery of Buxheim.

And of so much worth does Amort regard
the codex in which it is found, that he is very
particular in giving the account he received of
it. *First*, it is in folio; *secondly*, the material
of the paper is throughout wholly of a papyrus
nature; *thirdly*, the character of the writing is

the same throughout from the beginning to the end; *fourthly*, the contents or names of the books in the codex are put down. And here it should be noted that, after naming a few of them in the list, there comes this:—

"Item Meditationes in Vitam Christi."

And then, further down the list still, mention is made of the *Imitation* in these words:—

"Item liber de Imitatione Christi, qui continet in se quatuor libros."

In the *fifth* particular, Amort gives a more special account of the "De Imitatione Christi," for this is the object with which he is most concerned; and, after alluding to the several titles of the four books, he states other things, such as, that each chapter begins with a large capital letter, etc.

In the *sixth* particular he notices the subscription to these books. And here the copyist remarks, that the writer of the *Imitation* was "quidam Frater Thomas" of the St. Augustinian Order of the Canons Regular at Mount St. Agnes, in the Diocese of Utrecht, A.D. 1471. He states, however, that others attribute the *Imitation* to John Gerson, Chancellor of Paris.

The *seventh* particular is with regard to the *age* of the codex; where it is stated, that it was written in the fifteenth century, that one of the books is dated as copied in the year 1470, " qui annus subscribitur Meditationibus Vitæ Domini nostri Jesu Christi "; the very work now engaging our attention. And the year 1471, it is to be noted, is subscribed to some short and useful works on penitence.

The eighth, ninth, and tenth particulars relate to the binding of the codex, the present possessor of it, and the name of the individual who sends these particulars to Amort, with the attestation of a public notary attached to them.*

Here then we have certified evidence, that a copy of the " De Vitâ Christi Meditationes " had been written out in the year before Thomas à Kempis died, and that it was found in close connection, or bound up with his most celebrated work, the " De Imitatione Christi," bringing both works up to the lifetime of Thomas. It will be observed that the latter work was attributed by some persons to the Chancellor Gerson. But that question has been, we may hope, settled forever, and certainly need not occupy our attention. But, as far as we are aware, there is, and has been, no such dispute about the " De Vitâ Christi Meditationes." Its authorship is directly and from the first assigned to Thomas à Kempis. And, until some definite evidence to the contrary can be produced, we claim the work on behalf of this devout Father.

* See Amort's *Moralis Certitudo*, pp. 152–154.

Another curious piece of evidence is before me. I have lately received from Amsterdam an old volume with the first two Parts of the "De Vitâ Christi Meditationes" printed in large legible Gothic type; followed by another work which will be noted later. But, as might be expected, no name is attached to the former. It was only likely that they, who first printed the "De Vitâ," would pay some respect to the wishes of the author, who desired to remain unnoticed and unknown; especially when printed at one of the monastery presses. This was the case with his most famous work, the "De Imitatione Christi." Several editions of it appeareed before one was published with his name. Hence, later on, other names were attached to it; until at length the upholders of the Kempen deemed it their duty to vindicate his right to the authorship. There were not many writers who desired to be hidden from the world as Thomas did; so that this very singularity became rather a mark of his writings in that part of the world; especially among the piously disposed, and the members of his confraternity, scattered in various brotherhoods. Hence, naturally, we find no name attached to these two parts of the "De Vitâ" now under consideration. This omission, so far is it from being an objection to the Kempen's authorship of the treatise, is distinctly in favor of its having been written by him. There are, however, certain peculiarities about the volume, to which attention must be drawn, that confirm the view that this evidence is in favor of Thomas à Kempis.

Several points show that the volume must have been printed in the first years of printing in Germany. No name of the author is attached to the "De Vitâ," neither is there any proper title-page appended to it. Only the titles of the two works contained in the volume are put in the upper corner of the first page, in a similar type to that of the book itself. There is no publisher's name, no year when it was printed, no place, town, or even habitation, where copies could be obtained. The capital beginning each chapter is a large red letter, which has evidently been written, not printed, by a good penman, generally called the "rubricator." The pages are not numbered, but instead the leaves are, yet after a different form to that which was afterwards generally adopted. In one corner, at the bottom of the front page, you have the usual signature, followed by some numerals; the first signature *a* is taken, and is continued in numerals up to viii.; then the signature *b* is taken, and is also continued up to viii., and so on. Moreover, there is no *per-*

mission given for leave to print the book, as is
mostly found in religious works, even before
A.D. 1500, and was after that date required.
All these points prove that the printing of
books was then in its infancy.* But these particulars seem to indicate something more. It
is thought, and not without reason, that this
volume proceeded from one of the printing-
presses of the Brothers of Common Life. It is
known that they were deeply interested in the
new invention; for the subsistence of very
many of that community depended upon copying books for sale.† Moreover, they were very
early in the field as printers. And no wonder,
for they at once perceived, that, by this marvellous invention, they could speedily multiply
their publications; whereas, previously, they
had spent months of labor in copying each one
out by hand. Glad indeed must they have

---

* The volume was sent up to the British Museum for
further information, and, singularly enough, the author-
ities possess another similar copy, to which the date
A.D. 1475 is conjecturally assigned. This is the year
after Caxton printed his first piece at Westminster, on
"The Game of Chesse," A.D. 1474.

† Vide Buschius, *Chronicon Windesemense*, Antverpiæ,
1621, 8vo, vol. i. cap. ii. pp. 6, 7; à Kempis, *Chronicon
Sanctæ Agnetis*, also Antverpiæ, 1621, 8vo, cap. iii. p. 11;
and à Kempis, *Vita Gerardi Magni*, cap. ix. 2, 3. *Opera*,
1607, p. 771.

been to avail themselves of this new instrument to produce books more readily, and to any extent.

Schaab, in his *Erfindung der Buchdruckerkunst,* Mainz, 1831, intimates that one of the Brother-houses in Maryvale probably had a printing-press with type for themselves as early as A.D. 1468. And Delprat mentions several other Houses of the Brothers, that shortly after set up their presses. They did their work remarkably well, and what books they sent out were greatly valued. Neale in his *Jansenist Church of Holland,* p. 100, says, "Among the most valuable volumes to be found in the *incunabula* of German libraries, the Canons of Windesheim have their full share."

But what would further lead a bibliographer, in addition to what has been said, to regard this remarkable volume as issuing from the printing-press of one of the Brotherhoods of Common Life is, that the two books it contains are by two celebrated men of that devout community. Bearing in mind, then, that the contemporary biographer of Thomas à Kempis put down the "De Vitâ" in the catalogue of the works he wrote; that it was well known by the various members of the Brotherhood in many places to be by him; and that not a single instance is known of the authorship being

attributed, in its early days, to any one else; it
is not unreasonable to ascribe this devout
treatise to him, who was recognized as the great
ornament of the Brotherhood. They paid all
the greater reverence to his writings, because
he sought not for this world's fame, but rather
despised it; and this he did the more, that men
might know and follow Jesus for Himself. The
Brotherhood had probably been the first to
print that most precious book, the "De Imitatione Christi," and it is a pleasing fact to note,
that they were probably the first to print the
chief parts of another like precious book, the
"De Vitâ," written by their much revered
Brother.

The other work that follows this in the
volume, called "De Spiritualibus Ascensionibus," is by another remarkable member of the
community, Gerard of Zutphen, an ardent student and lover of God's Word, who preceded
Thomas à Kempis. The latter gives a sketch
of Zutphen's life. Gerard's example kindled a
flame of enthusiasm in the life of Thomas, then
a young man in the community. Gerard was
a great advocate, in those early days, for the
Bible being translated into the language of the
people, and in his treatise brings forward many
cogent arguments. In another treatise he pro-
posed also that the Prayers of the Church

should be said to the congregation in their mother-tongue * The "De Vitâ," then, thus early was clearly associated with another chief work of a former member of the Brotherhood, noted for his learning and spiritual influence; and was even placed before the "De Spiritualibus Ascensionibus," as if it were accounted of more importance.

Now, who more interested in publishing these two works, or more likely to print them, than members of the Brotherhood, in one or other of their Houses, as it would be a great saving of time and labor in not having to copy them out; and as they were the kind of books they would at first be most anxious to multiply? It is therefore probable, that the "De Vitâ" was at the first printed in one of the houses of the Brotherhood. But be this so or no, the great point to draw attention to is, that the work was printed and made known within four or five years of the death of Thomas, and thoroughly recognized as his among the Brethren in the country and neighborhood where he lived. And it is at once a testimony of their deep regard for Thomas à Kempis, and how much they valued the work on account of its supreme worth.

* See Kettlewell's *Thomas à Kempis, and the Brothers of Common Life*, 1882, vol. i. pp. 296–306.

It may be asked, why were only two parts printed, and the remaining parts left out? Though it may be difficult to answer such questions, unless one is directly acquainted with the particular circumstances, yet it may be observed, that the "De Imitatione Christi" was treated in a similar way. Sometimes we find the first book alone printed by itself, sometimes only three books, when four were considered to be its complement. Moreover, if you look at the "De Vitâ," in this volume, you will perceive that the first two parts already take up about half of a thick two-inch book; and had they continued the remainder of it, the printers would not have been well able to get in Gerard's work. Besides, it was probably considered most profitable for readers to ponder over the parts they had so far printed, since they referred to the Passion and Death of Christ.

Thomas à Kempis, in the earlier period of his long life, is known to have copied out the whole of the Bible in four large volumes. What more likely than, when he came to the Holy Gospels, he should frequently and deeply ponder over the wonderful and beneficent life of Christ? To this his mind would often return, as most worthy of his life-long attention: and, taking the several portions of that Divine history from time to time as they recurred to

him, he would make them the special subjects
of meditation and prayer. It is evident that he
was a man who lived much upon his knees;
and that he held continual intercourse, in deep
abasement and profound reverence, with the
blessed Saviour. The words and thoughts of
these gracious moments spent with Christ were
very precious to him—carefully noted and
treasured up. And it seems that afterwards he
had gathered them together, and formed them
into one connected treatise, for the benefit and
help of other religious persons. This he did to
show them, by an example, how they might
make use of the Holy Scriptures to their everlasting welfare. Not only by reading and
hearing them, not only by taking heed to the
preaching and comments upon them, but by
praying over them. They could then turn the
words into devout meditations, and, in each
separate and distinct portion, make a grateful
acknowledgment of particular instances of the
Divine favor and goodness to uswards.

Nor is all this simply conjecture. When he
began to write his immortal work, the "De
Imitatione Christi," he seems to have had before
him the design of such a work as *The Meditations.* For, on turning to the first chapter of
the first book of the former work, we read these
words :—" To meditate on the Life of Christ (in

vitam Jesu Christi meditari) should be our chief
study. His teaching surpasses all that the
Saints have taught; and he that has the Spirit
will find in it 'the hidden manna.'" Observe
how this devout writer brings in the very title
of the book, as it were, which he afterwards
adopts; pointedly advocating the use of such
meditation, and showing what a blessing is to
be derived from such an exercise of devotion.

And it would seem strange if, in the many
years the Kempen lived after he had completed
the "De Imitatione Christi," he did not write
such a work as that "De Vitâ Christi Meditationes," when it would appear to have been the
very desire of his heart to do so. There are
very few, even of those who seclude themselves
from the world for the sake of religion, qualified to produce such a sacred treatise; but
from the records of his life, and the peculiar
excellency of the "De Imitatione Christi," we
may judge that he was eminently fitted to write
such a volume. It appears then only reasonable to conclude that Thomas à Kempis was the
author of the "De Vitâ," especially when we
take into consideration the external evidence
that has been produced; which early attributed
the work to him—evidence given by those
grown up at the time of his death, and who

were fully able to supply information that might be depended upon.

The internal evidence also seems much in favor of Thomas à Kempis being the author of the "De Vitâ Christi Meditationes"; for one who is familiar with his writings would say, "Well, if it is not his, it must be by one of the Brothers of Common Life." But since we have external evidence of the best kind that asserts Thomas à Kempis to be the veritable author, an examination of the contents of the book will serve to establish still more the authenticity of it. Though there may seem a difference in character between the *De Imitatione Christi* and the *De Vitâ Christi Meditationes*, it is more because the two must necessarily be treated differently, than in anything else. The latter does not differ from the *De Imitatione Christi* more than do the other undoubted works of Thomas à Kempis.

The "De Vitâ Christi Meditationes" is of an ascetic character, like the "De Imitatione Christi"; and he who would find fault with the exalted pitch of the former, must find fault also with the latter for the same reason. Both bid us aim at the highest ideal of the Christian life; and in the use of one as well as of the other, the feeling that will pervade the mind of the earnest Christian, who is diligently seeking after the welfare of his soul, will be, *first*, that he comes vastly short of what he should be; and this must lead him almost to despair of attaining to higher excellency; *secondly*, it will cause him to feel more than ever his great need of the Saviour, willing and able to redeem him; and that he must truly fly to Him for help and salvation; and *thirdly*, it will incite him to daily endeavors to become like unto Christ, and to follow in His blessed footsteps. This, we must remember, is the only right way to attain the Christian life; not to tone down the standard of our life to our earthly desires and imperfections, but to set before us and strive to follow the noblest and most perfect example of our humanity. For this is what the Gospel of our salvation bids us aim at, when we are told :—" Be ye *perfect*, as your Father which is in heaven is perfect." "Be ye holy, for I am holy."

Besides, the peculiar character of theology which is found in one work is the same as in the other. The doctrine and views of religion in both are from the same school of divinity, if not from the same pen. There was in those days a strikingly earnest and awakening application of Gospel truth prevailing among a number of devout souls, of which Thomas à Kempis was the representative and exponent.

Moreover, there are several peculiar modes of expression, sentences, phrases, and words which are common to both works. The form of the sentences in the "De Imitatione Christi" is short, terse, admonitory, and complete; and so is that in the present work. Many instances of these several points might be readily adduced, but the fear of lengthening this preface prevents us from doing so. It is worth while, nevertheless, for those who are interested in the question respecting the authorship of this treatise, to follow out these points, as it will serve to establish the evidence already brought forward, that the "De Vitâ Christi Meditationes" was written by Thomas à Kempis.

It will be asked, however, "How is it that this important work of Thomas à Kempis has been so long lost sight of, and unrecognized by the public? Why has it not been noticed before, and brought forward for the benefit of the Christian world?" The reason appears to be chiefly on account of the treatment which the book received. This brings us back to Sommalius, who published three editions of Kempen's works. He did not print the "De Vitâ Christi Meditationes" in his *first* edition, it appears in the *second*, disappears from the *third*, and is never again found in any of the other many editions published under his name.

Hence serious misgivings and doubts have arisen, whether it were really written by the venerable and esteemed author of that devout and heavenly book, the " De Imitatione Christi." And some have concluded, though on insufficient grounds, that it was left out by Sommalius because he had found that Thomas à Kempis was not the author of it. And this opinion has the more prevailed because of the general ignorance of the positive and original proofs that the work was written by him. Might there not, however, be some other reason?

The exclusion of the " De Vitâ " from so many editions will in no small measure account for its being so long lost sight of by the public, and almost forgotten, except by a few; as well as for the doubts thrown on its authorship. It must be remembered that Sommalius gives not the slightest reason why it is expunged. He leaves his readers altogether in the dark as to this, after having assured them that it had been written by Thomas à Kempis, and was one of his works which he had discovered. There is something mysterious about this, to say the least; and thereby hangs a tale, which it may be difficult to unfold, for it leaves us in some perplexity.

It is asked, " Why did Sommalius omit the work from his *first* edition? Had he then any

doubts about it? Then why does it appear in
his *second* edition? and again, why is it excluded
from his *third*, and from all other editions? Is
there not some other more likely reason than
that which has generally been received, why it
had been suppressed? As to the first point, it
may be assumed that at the time when Sommalius published his first edition he was un-
aware of the existence of the "De Vitâ Christi
Meditationes." He had probably made use of
former copies of the collected works of à
Kempis, edited by other writers; diligently
comparing them with the autograph copies of
Thomas à Kempis, to be found in the Royal
Library at Brussels in the two codices dated
severally A.D. 1441 and 1456, and with the
manuscripts of some of his other works depos-
ited in St. Martin's monastery at Louvain; and
as the "De Vitâ" was also not found in either
of these collections, Sommalius was at first
ignorant of its existence. Afterwards, however,
some friend or antiquarian scholar may have
informed him of the existence of this work, and
where a copy of it was to be found. This, we
may be sure, he examined into with great curiosity and delight, and obtained forthwith a
copy for his second edition. Such seems the
most likely account of its appearance in this
second edition. But why does it disappear in

the next edition, and in all others afterwards?
And what reason can be assigned for leaving it
out, seeing Sommalius gives none?

The conclusion generally arrived at is not
unnatural, and one that would at once strike
the casual reader. He, without giving much
consideration to the subject, would be inclined
to conclude that, upon further investigation,
doubts arose in the mind of Sommalius as to
whether there was sufficiently clear evidence
that the work was indeed by Thomas à Kempis,
and it had consequently been excluded. As to
his complete silence regarding its being left
out, it might be said that Sommalius would not
like to confess that he had been in error, and
therefore he quietly omitted it in his next edition, the *third*, without saying a word as to the
reason why he did so.

But, after all, this is only a conjecture, not
resting upon any sound foundation. Observe,
Sommalius does not give this as a reason; it
is only those who are puzzled by his leaving
the "De Vitâ" out without giving any explanation, who jump to this conclusion. When we
come to make further research into the matter,
and look more closely into various particulars,
we shall see reason to doubt whether this is the
right conclusion, and be led to seek for some
other; especially when we take into considera-

tion the positive proofs we possess of Thomas à Kempis being the real author, and the manner in which Sommalius acknowledges this when he introduces the "De Vitâ" into his second edition.

Sommalius is said to have been born A.D. 1534, and to have died A.D. 1619. His *first* edition of the "Opera Omnia" appeared in 1600—about a hundred and twenty-nine years after the death of Thomas à Kempis. His *second* edition came out in 1607; and the *third* in 1615—about four years before his death. To all three there is a dedicatory epistle, and an address to the "Pious Reader." But upon critically examining the latter in all three editions, although they seem to read alike, we find that there are just a few words added in the 1607 edition—that in which the "De Vitâ" first appears—which do not occur in the 1600 edition, but do so in the 1615 edition; showing that the 1607 edition was used as a copy for the third edition. Sommalius rejoices that he has had both the health and some little leisure afforded him opportunely to supply those things *which were wanting in the first edition* (quæ in primâ editione defuerunt). Now the "De Vitâ" is the only considerable addition made to this *second* edition, and consequently he must chiefly refer to this work, and the absence of

which in the first edition he considers made it
defective. The passage given in Latin has been
continued in other editions printed in the name
of Sommalius after his death, and no remark
made in its place, in any of them, accounting
for the omission. Hence the only allusion to
the "De Vitâ" made by Sommalius in the 1607
edition is certainly in favor of its being written
by Thomas à Kempis.

Nor can we imagine that he introduced the
"De Vitâ" into the *second* edition of the "Opera
Omnia" without giving to it great consideration
and research. In his address "Pio Lectori," in
all the three editions, he tells us how anxiously
and diligently he had labored to produce only
what he had well authenticated, and compared
with the manuscripts or autographs of Thomas
à Kempis. He informs us, that like a bear he
had licked, and like an ostrich had gazed upon
the writings of his beloved author. He had
been as a *bear* to them, "quæ frequenter lam-
bendo expolire atque efformare consuevit."
He had been as an *ostrich*, "quæ non incu-
bando, sed fixis oculis ova diu multumque
intuendo pullos excludit . . . *tam sæpe auto-
grapha vidi, legi, revolvi, et cum priori editione
tam sedulò contuli ; adeo ut sperem me ad eam
perfectionem omnino castigationem adduxisse, ut
meritô animo conquiescere debeam.*"

All this implies searching examination and close deliberation; so that this learned man was not likely to have admitted the "De Vitâ" among the works of Thomas à Kempis, unless he had well assured himself that it had been written by him. Moreover, when he so satisfied himself as to the authenticity of the work he was at the ripe age of seventy-three, the judgment then being mature, and he was in good health. Nor can we believe that he ever went back from an opinion which he had so carefully formed. Why the "De Vitâ" disappeared from the third edition, that of 1615, without a word being said by the learned editor, will, we trust, be made clear as we study more closely this interesting question.

The suggestion of this silence given by those who would make it out that he excluded the "De Vitâ," because he afterwards doubted its authenticity, and was ashamed to confess his error, is putting forward a motive altogether unworthy of so learned and conscientious a man as Sommalius seems to have been. We might surely have expected that, if he had been a free man, he would have endeavored, at the first opportunity he had, to correct the mistake he had fallen into, that he might not mislead those who trusted him. Such a course an upright and honorable man would have taken.

But no; he does not make any correction or retractation. He would not enter upon the open avowal of such a thing, after what he had already said and done. And yet it is evident that there was some secret reason why the "De Vitâ" was excluded from the third edition, and no explanation whatever given. It is this view of the matter—together with the evidence we possess that it was written by Thomas à Kempis—that leads us to look out for some other reason for its disappearance—some other solution to the inquiry, Why was it left out and never after appeared?

It has been asked whether there is anything *heretical* in the work that caused it to be rejected. The work has been carefully looked over to ascertain whether this is the case or not. And though there are several passages, as in the *Imitation* (but more in number), which the members of the Reformed Church would not allow or consider sound, yet is there nothing that the Romanist, or the dominant authority in the Church, at the time when the "De Vitâ" first became known, would consider to be heretical. This, then, cannot be the reason for its rejection or exclusion.

But though there may be nothing openly heretical in the "De Vitâ" according to the teaching of the Church a hundred years before the Reformation, still we cannot but suspect that, when Sommalius published the "De Vitâ" in his second edition, it did not meet with favor in certain quarters; and it was therefore intimated to him, or to the printers, that permission would not be given to publish it again; and that it must be quietly withdrawn, without rendering any reason for the omission of it. Sommalius was one of a religious Society who was required to pay implicit obedience to the direction of his superiors; and if the conjecture offered be correct, then the publication of the works of Thomas à Kempis, being entirely in the hands of those bound to obedience, the "De Vitâ" was left out, without the least hint as to the reason for doing so. Silence about it would rather further the object of those who desired its exclusion; for the withdrawal would not only hinder it from becoming generally known, but would also throw doubts on its authenticity, and incline those who did know of it to question whether it was written by Thomas à Kempis. And the manner of its withdrawal seems to have had this effect. It is otherwise difficult, we repeat, to account for the silence of Sommalius when the work did not appear again in his next edition, after his unequivocal acknowledgment of it as one of the Kempen's works.

If he had given a reason for its withdrawal,

under the circumstances alluded to, that would in a great measure have defeated the object of those who wished to exclude it; for such a course would have drawn all the more attention to it at the time; and others, not under obedience, might have been greatly induced to publish this work by itself, in opposition to those who wished to expunge it without any noise.*

But this is not all. It is certainly a curious fact that, between the death of Thomas and the year 1607, there is only a single printed edition of a part of the "De Vitâ" known to have existed. There are, as we have already seen, three distinct manuscript copies of it referred to, which in themselves clearly direct us to Thomas à Kempis as its author. But they formerly must have been very rare, and now scarcely a manuscript of the work can be found.

* Some ill-informed critics have stated that the "De Vitâ" was written by S. Bonaventura; others have attributed it to Ludolph of Saxony, the Carthusian of the fourteenth century. The reader is referred to the Meditations put forth by those holy and learned men. They have not the slightest resemblance to the treatise of the Kempen: in matter and language they are altogether inferior. (See *Opera Omnia* of S. Bonaventura, Moguntia, 1609; *Meditationes de Vitâ Christi*, in the sixth vol., fol. 334–401; Ludolphus de Saxonia, *Vita Christi*, Strasburg, 1474, fol.; and *Meditationes de Vitâ Jesu Christi*, Nürnberg, 1473, fol.)

How then can you account for the early exclusion of it from public use?

It would appear, from the analogous title it bears to the "De Imitatione," and from its division into four parts, making it like the four books of the *Imitation ;* as also from what à Kempis says in this inimitable work respecting the worth of such a book as the "De Vitâ," that it was his earnest desire to have the Meditations accounted as a proper sequel or companion to his *chef-d'œuvre.* Moreover, from the two most important parts of the "De Vitâ" being *printed* in the very infancy of the art, and so soon after the death of its author, as well as from the Kempen character of the book itself, we cannot fail to perceive the esteem in which the "De Vitâ" was held.

From these considerations there is reason to conclude that, next to the *Imitation,* the devout writer of it valued the "De Vitâ" more than all his other works; and would have all those who admired the former to make a diligent use of the latter. And it is not too much to say that, like the *Imitation of Christ,* the *Meditations on the Life of Christ* are calculated to prove an equal blessing to the Christian world. We may rightly believe, then, the author would ardently wish that copies of it might be multiplied; and this, too, would be the wish and effort of those who in its early days loved the *Imitation*. But, strange to say, there seems to be, on the contrary, an unaccountable scarcity of the treatise.

On what grounds, then, can we reasonably conceive that it was kept back from the public, unless it had been suppressed by some one in authority after the death of Thomas à Kempis, so that it should not be again printed, or any more copies of it written out? As the Brotherhood were sworn to obey those that were over them, the injunction, we may be sure, was yielded to without any question or disturbance. The public would know little or nothing as to the cause of its disappearance; and it would soon be generally lost sight of and forgotten. This seems to be the only reasonable ground on which to account for its singular scarcity, why so little is known about it, and why in these days it comes as a surprise upon the public.

That some books were suppressed in those days, and in many instances lost sight of, is well known to the student of history. As early as A.D. 1486, Berthold, Archbishop of Mentz, forbade the printing and sale of books without license through the whole of his province, and certain books were not allowed to be published. But, even previous to this time, in England the manuscript copies of Wycliffe's version of the Scriptures had been condemned and suppressed

by Archbishop Arundel. Many of them were
of small size, and so escaped destruction, since
"they could easily be hidden and made the
constant companion of the owners." And in
1501, Pope Alexander VI. issued a Bull, de-
nouncing, in certain provinces, the printing of
books "containing various errors and perni-
cious doctrines, even hostile to the Christian
faith"—as the views and sentiments of the
Reformers were at that time considered. The
Pope's order was, that nothing should be printed
for the future except with the archiepiscopal
license.

And in those days it was accounted no light
thing, it must be remembered, to disregard or
set at naught the mandates of the Pope, or
of the Archbishops acting under him. What
more likely, then, that the "De Vitâ" was early
suppressed by authority, because it seemed to
favor the views of the Reforming party in the
Church, who were so eager for the revival of
true and earnest religion—a revival Thomas à
Kempis had much at heart, and by his works
so zealously promoted? It is well known also,
that certain rulers of the Church, especially in
the fifteenth century, not only opposed the Reforming party, but were intent upon excluding
them from the Church and her sacred ordinances; so that a large number of pious souls,

which the Church ought to have retained, were
driven by unwise treatment to combine and
provide religious services and communion for
themselves. And it is not unlikely that these
said rulers would suppress and keep back from
publication, as far as they were able, all works
that furthered the movement of the Reforming
party.

And the "De Vitâ" might well be classed
among such works, not only from the character
of the book, but inasmuch as it was at the first
printed with a treatise by Gerard de Zutphen;
who publicly contended, that an open Bible
should be allowed, and the prayers of the
Church said in the vulgar tongue.

There were, be it observed, many Romanists
who greatly esteemed Thomas à Kempis and
his works; and at one time there was a hope,
and even a promise made, that he should be
canonized. There was also, and is now, a party
among the Pope's followers much opposed to
him; and from one cause or another, whether
it be on account of their knowledge of the suppression of one of his works by some one in
authority, or that he is considered to have for-
warded the Reformation movement by his pious
writings, no Pope has as yet been prevailed
upon to place him in the rank of Saints.
Thomas à Becket and Thomas Aquinas have

both been *Sainted;* but for some reason left
unexplained no such distinction has been ac-
corded to Thomas à Kempis; though so many
individuals, through the reading of the *Imitation*, have been led to live the saintly life. This
much, however, is certain: the celebrity of his
honored name has not suffered much through
this omission or slight.

Supposing that our view of the early suppression of the "De Vitâ" be correct, it must
have been well effected; as Sommalius, a hundred years after the death of à Kempis, appar-
ently knew nothing of the treatise when he
published his *first* edition of the *Opera Omnia*.
And that the suppression was secretly and very
quietly carried out is further supported by the
fact, that Sommalius introduced the "De Vitâ"
when he published his *second* edition. For had
he known that it had been forbidden in high
quarters, so true a son of the Church of Rome
would have been the last to place it promi-
nently among the works of à Kempis. And
that Sommalius, when informed of the suppression, and forbidden to publish the treatise any
more, paid implicit obedience to the direction
of his Ordinary we may readily conjecture,
from his leaving the "De Vitâ" out of his *third*
edition without the least explanation. This no
honest and consistent man of learning would

have been inclined to do of himself, after having once published it as the work of Thomas à
Kempis, and thoroughly satisfied himself that
it was by him.

Not only did Sommalius, after careful consideration, acknowledge the "De Vitâ" as the
production of Thomas, but he evidently had a
special regard and value for this particular
work, as one specially fitted to promote the welfare of souls by drawing them to Jesus as their
Saviour. Fully to support this statement, we
have simply to refer to the commendatory notice which he placed on the title-page to this
effect :—

> "This little book, concerning the life and
> loving kindnesses of Christ, will be service-
> able to those who are accustomed to pray
> aloud, and even to Pastors and Preachers,
> who from hence may (if they please) draw
> forth pious, devout, and spiritual concep-
> tions, which they may advantageously set
> forth to their hearers."

This is certainly to draw attention to it in a
very marked way.

In addition to this, he prefixed the small
preface, which, though not written by him,
since it is found in the earliest edition of the
"De Vitâ" *cir.* A.D. 1475, was certainly approved

by him, as showing how serviceable the work would be to earnest-minded Christians.

Beginning with a title—

"On the Utility of the Life of Jesus and His Passion,"

it proceeds :—

"If thou desirest to be perfectly cleansed from corruption; to be nobly endowed with virtues; to be eminently enlightened with the knowledge of the Scriptures; if thou desirest to triumph over thy spiritual enemies; to be abundantly comforted in adversities; to have a devout conversation on earth; to frequently feel compunction on your bed; to weep sweetly in prayer; to be fervently inflamed in meditation; to persevere in good works; to be replenished with spiritual joy; to be carried up in a holy rapture of mind; to enjoy the secret things of God; to die happily at the last; to reign eternally in heaven—exercise thyself in the life and sufferings of Jesus Christ, the Son of God, whom the Father sent into the world that He might show forth to all men a glorious example of perfection, and bring His followers to an everlasting Kingdom. Therefore love Christ; follow Jesus; embrace the Cross."

Though Sommalius's name is attached to the
Opera Omnia of Thomas à Kempis, not only in
the three editions published during his life, but
in those issued after his death, we are disposed
to think that it was not of his own judgment
that the "De Vitâ" was excluded from the *third*
edition. Our firm belief is, that, apart from
Church authority, he held, to the end of his
days, that Thomas was the author of it. In
pursuance of this idea, it has been suggested
that the interests of the publication had passed
out of the hands of Sommalius into those of
the printer or bookseller. But it is to be
doubted whether this is an adequate reason, or
so likely to be the case, that we may fasten the
responsibility on them. For, merely on com-
mercial grounds, it would not commend the
sale of the work to put forth an incomplete
edition of the *Opera;* for Sommalius himself,
in his second edition, had stated that the *first*
edition, which did not contain the "De Vitâ,"
was defective. And to publish the *third* edition
without the work would not be likely to bring
it into favor with the public. No; it rather
intimates that there were some behind the
scenes, who, for their own purposes, carried out
their design irrespective of the convictions that
others held; and would not permit, or give their

sanction to the " De Vitâ " being again printed in the *Opera Omnia*.

And this is the more likely when we consider the religious controversy which was then beginning about the authorship of the " De Imitatione Christi." To this we must give a moment's attention. A party had sprung up eagerly bent upon defrauding Thomas à Kempis of his claim to be the author of this much valued work; and it is in keeping with their design to throw doubt also on his authorship of the " De Vitâ "—a work which not a few thought to favor the Reformation. John Gerson, Chancellor of Paris, who flourished a few years previous to Thomas; and then, Joannes Gersen, Benedictine Abbot of Vercelli, who lived about two hundred years before him, were boldly put forth as claimants of the authorship of the *Imitation*. D. Cajétan had started the claim for the latter, on the most flimsy grounds; and the Benedictines at first smiled at the audacity and absurdity of such a thing. But afterwards, when it was thought that much glory and credit would accrue to their Order, they, as a body, took up the cause, gave him all the support they could, and countenanced the claim he had made. In 1616, Cajétan published at Rome a copy of the *Imitation*, and attributed it to the Abbot Gersen, for he was not at first quite certain about the name. Then, in 1621, F. Rosweyde published his *Vindiciæ Kempenses*, and afterwards brought out other treatises in defence of Thomas à Kempis. D. Cajétan and the Benedictines were, however, irrepressible; and in 1638 obtained permission from the Congregation of the Index to print the *Imitation* under the name of Gersen. The controversy waxed very fierce, and almost set Europe in a flame. The Parliament in Paris undertook, with the help of the learned, to thoroughly sift and examine the vexed question; and after two years they ended, by forbidding the printing of the *Imitation* under the name of Gersen, and permitted the Canons-Regular to publish it under the name of Thomas à Kempis.

This slight reference to the events which caused so much excitement must suffice. But it must be observed, that as the opposing party were frustrated in overthrowing the rights of Thomas à Kempis with regard to the "De Imitatione Christi"; so were they also defeated, to some extent, in their attempt to damage his credit, with respect to the authorship of the "De Vitâ Christi Meditationes," by excluding that work from the *Opera Omnia* of the Kempen Brother.

It has generally been thought that no action had been taken by the Kempenists to defend the right of Thomas, or reassert his authorship to this last work; after having been thus unjustly, and without any reason or assignable ground, deprived of it. But such was far from being the case. At first we may suppose the defence was confined to verbal discussions. In due time, however, more active measures were taken; and in 1626 a small volume, containing 516 pages of the " De Vitâ," was duly published at Cologne, and authorized by ecclesiastical license, having the name of Thomas à Kempis as its author. The title of the book is a little varied from that in the *Opera* by Sommalius, A.D. 1607; but upon examination it is found (word for word) the same work. It is as follows:—" Orationes in Totam Vitam Christi. Auctore Thoma à Kempis. Ex antiquis manuscriptis, Thomas Gratianus, Provinciæ Col. Ord. F.F. Eremit. S. Aug. Diffinitor eruebat." The " Librorum Censor," in giving his *Approbation* of these " Orationes," says, " Neque quidquam Christianis moribus et dogmatibus contrarium habeant." Hence the Roman Catholic authority, in another province to that in which the *Opera Omnia* was published, asserts that there was no heresy in it, nor anything contrary to Christian morals, as we have before intimated.

But it is desirable to notice the date of this valuable book, for it seems to tell a tale. We have already implied that certain persons were annoyed by the suppression of the "De Vitâ" in the third edition of Sommalius, 1615. Hopeless of redress, they naturally determined to print the treatise by itself. It is supposed that at first some remonstrance was made by the supporters of Thomas à Kempis, and they entertained the idea, that in the next edition of the *Opera Omnia* the "De Vitâ" might be restored. If so, great must have been their disappointment; for in 1625, the fourth edition appeared, and they found that the "De Vitâ" was still left out; and never likely to be printed again by those who had power over the *Opera Omnia.* No time was then lost, for before the next year was out, *i.e.* in 1626, this little volume of which we are speaking, was printed and published as the work of Thomas à Kempis, with the full consent of the Church in the province of Cologne. This was done, we presume, not only as a protest against the action of those who had expunged the "De Vitâ" from the *Opera Omnia*, but also to declare before the world the authenticity of the work—that it had been written by Thomas à Kempis; desiring that he should be fully acknowledged as its author. This struggle then, to maintain his

right of authorship to the "De Vitâ," should
only enhance its value to us, and lead us to regard it as some precious gem recovered for our
use : just as the contention, which continued so
long and warmly, between those opposed to
Thomas and those in favor of his claim to the
Imitation, led to its being held in higher estimation than ever.

It should here be noticed also, that a translation of the "De Vitâ" was made and printed
in Paris, A.D. 1664, by Thomas Carre, Confessor
to the Canonesses Regular of the Augustinian
Order, who attributes the work to Thomas à
Kempis. This Thomas Carre had published an
able work during the great controversy, to
show that Thomas à Kempis was incontestably
the author of the *Imitation;* and then before
long he proclaims that the same saintly Father
was the author also of the "De Vitâ"; and of
this he assures the devout sisters, for whose
use he had printed it, by affixing the name of
Thomas à Kempis to it.*

Thus, whatever may have been the cause for
the sudden and extraordinary expulsion of the
"De Vitâ" from the *Opera Omnia* of Thomas à

---

* As Carre's translation was made expressly for Eng-
lish Nuns in Paris, only a few copies would be printed.
The work is now very rare. Carre's real name was
Miles Pinkney. He died in 1674.

Kempis, in 1615, it is a very remarkable fact, that, shortly afterwards, there were those, as the representatives of a large party, who stoutly supported the rights of Thomas to be its author. We have just noticed the valuable little edition of the " De Vitâ," published entire at Cologne, in 1623, by Thomas Gratianus. Then we have the edition printed in Paris for Thomas Carre in 1664, both claiming the work as the production of Thomas à Kempis. And now we bring forward another edition, in Spanish, published three years before Carre's edition. It is a rare and valuable book in fine quarto, containing the whole of the " De Vitâ" in 320 pages, translated by the great Don Francisco de Borja, who ascribes it directly to Thomas in these marked words : " Compuesto por el Venerable Thomas de Kempis, Canonijo Regular de la Orden de San Augustin. MDCLXI "; which further shows that, though the treatise received such ill-treatment at the hands of a certain school, there were nevertheless able and learned men, who still regarded the " De Vitâ" as the undoubted work of Thomas à Kempis, and recognized it as one of his chief and most valuable writings.

Moreover, it is necessary to notice that a translation of the " De Vitâ" was made into English by Henry Lee, LL.B., in 1760. But in this case, so much of the translator's reflections

and other references to Scripture are added,
that it is difficult to tell what really is Lee's and
what belongs to Thomas à Kempis, to whom the
whole volume is inscribed. It is most desirable, therefore, that a new translation be made
of the "De Vitâ," in which rarely is any word
given but what has been written by the devout
author himself. This is as necessary as the
re-authentication of its real author; that the
public may have some confidence that they are
using a most precious and veritable treatise by
the author of the *Imitation*—Thomas à Kempis.

Though the story of the blessed Gospel is
now so familiar to the minds of the humblest
reader, through the free circulation of the Holy
Scriptures, yet it may not come with that fresh-
ness and delight, and eager desire to know
more about the things revealed to us, as it did
to many in the days previous to the actual
Reformation. Nevertheless, we may conceive
what a boon the "De Vitâ" must have been at
that time to earnest Christian souls, just emerg-
ing out of the darkness with which they
had been encompassed. This priceless volume
would be as a little Gospel to them, to enlighten
their minds, to press home to their consciences
its deep importance. It would be to them like
a guide, who, being well versed in the sacred
story, would lead them through it in some

orderly manner. The touching pages point
our attention to the various scenes of the Divine Life of our Master on earth as they happened, and tell us about each one of them—the
particulars and the holy words He spake from
time to time—that we may become deeply interested in each event, and learn holy lessons from
them all.

Even in these days, though it may be said
that we are living in the full blaze of Gospel
light, the "De Vitâ" has a definite value *for
us*. It must be remembered, that there is still
a knowledge and interest in the life of Jesus to
be obtained over and above the common, or, as
Thomas would call it, the *exterior* reading or
understanding of the Gospel. We are enabled
to gain from it something far more valuable
than the mere outward sense of the words—
even a saving knowledge of Divine Truth. In
heart and life we are drawn to Jesus with a
deeper love and attachment, and become one
with Him to our infinite delight. Hear what
Thomas à Kempis says in the *Imitation* to im-
press this truth upon us :—

"Remember the profession you made, and
set always before your eyes the image of the
Crucified."

"You may well be ashamed as you contemplate the life of Jesus Christ, when you see how

little you have endeavored to make your own life like His—long as you have walked in God's way.

"A religious person, who earnestly and devoutly gives himself to the contemplation of the most holy life and passion of our Lord, will find in it abundance of all that is profitable and needful for him ; nor will he require to seek out of Jesus for anything better.

"O, if Jesus crucified could enter into our hearts, how quickly should we learn all that is necessary" (book i., chapter xxv.).

Or again, as it is rendered in the rhythmic version :—

"Your thoughts must be with God on high,
Your prayers unceasingly must go straight up to Christ.
And if you know not how to muse on high and heavenly themes,
Rest your thoughts on what Christ suffered,
And let them love to dwell upon His holy wounds ;
For if you hurry with good thoughts
To Jesus' wounds and to the precious nail-prints,
In your trials you will feel great comfort ;
You will think but little of the scorn of men,
And with ease you will endure detracting words."
Book ii., chapter i.

Thomas à Kempis thus, once more and again, recommends to us the use of such a work as the "De Vitâ." It was his great and longing desire to lead men to Christ Himself, to learn of Him : that, however excellent, comprehensive, and engaging were the words of His servants, and the sayings of His Saints, it was better to come ourselves to the Master Himself, and be taught "from the simplicity that is in Christ Jesus." His life, simply, truthfully, and touchingly told, is still the best book for learning the true life of a Christian.

There is, we may be sure, a wonderful power in the sacred exercise this book brings before us; the influence of which is not sufficiently comprehended, and consequently will not be so diligently sought for as it should be. We know, even in ordinary life, how it occasionally happens that, when a person constantly associates with another individual living on a higher level than he himself has hitherto done, how gradually and insensibly he is lifted up above himself, and becomes like to him whose whole conversation he so justly admires ; so that in a few years a remarkable improvement of character takes place. And so, only in a greater degree, is it with those earnest souls who live much with Jesus; having His life constantly before them, daily and hourly learning from Him. By more intimate acquaintance with Christ, they are not only drawn nearer to Him, but are drawn to love Him more deeply, to trust in Him more entirely, and become more like Him in their daily living.

This may be said of prayer in general, but the result to which we allude is more fully secured, when our prayers and devotions are especially directed to the life and loving-kindnesses of the Lord Jesus. The contemplation of the sorrows and inconveniences, the shame and desertion, the Cross and Passion, and the horrible death, which the Lord willingly endured for us, should teach and beget in us the spirit of self-sacrifice and self-denial, a readiness to live and lay ourselves out—our means and abilities and gifts—for the good of others. The soul becomes steadily centred on Christ, until His image is stamped upon it. A marvellous and transforming influence is wrought in those who, day by day and year by year, constantly have His life before them, and prayerfully mark His blessed footsteps. In time this most sacred exercise will manifest itself even in the outward appearance, so that men will take "knowledge of them that they have been with Jesus." This will happen to them, of which St. Paul speaks: "We all, with open face beholding as in a glass the glory of the Lord, are changed into the same image from glory to glory, even as by the Spirit of the Lord" (2 Cor. iii. 18).

A few observations must be made about this undertaking before concluding. As in some of the former editions of the *Imitation* it was found desirable to omit certain passages, so also has it been felt advisable to do so, even to a greater extent, in the "De Vitâ." Any words sanctioning Mariolatry, and the Invocation of Saints or Angels, or any occasional allusion to some corruption or error prevalent in the Pre-Reformation Church, are carefully excluded. Indeed, three entire chapters are left out : two in the second Part, which, to a certain extent, repeat what had gone before; the other chapter is in the third Part, founded on Christ's appearance after His Resurrection to the Virgin Mary. That appearance has no authority in Holy Scripture, or in the primitive Church, and can only have been imaginary or conjectural.

The initial words of almost all the chapters —viz., "I bless and give Thee thanks," etc., together with the various titles of our Lord Jesus Christ, are carefully retained, as suitable to the opening of fresh points in our Saviour's life. The reader must not look for a full historical narrative, or any critical account of the life of Christ, but rather for graphic and impressive pictures of the great scenes or outlines, drawn by the pen of a most devoted and loving follower of our Lord. In these the most noticeable circumstances of His life are severally, in the *first* place, unfolded to our view, and made the subject of fervent thanksgiving. Then, in the *second* place, each is enlarged upon by way of meditation. Thus our affections are sweetly drawn to Christ, and kindled into a holy flame of zealous love for Him. And *thirdly*, after the heart is thus devoutly exercised with the warm recognition of all that Christ has done and suffered for him, the reader is led to make an earnest supplication that he may enjoy the fruits thereof, and be made thoroughly conformable to the blessed steps of His most holy life.

S. K.

EASTBOURNE, 1891

PART I

FROM THE INCARNATION OF CHRIST TO HIS PASSION

CHAPTER I

A MEDITATION OR PRAYER CALLING ON US TO
PRAISE GOD FOR HIS EXCELLENT GREATNESS

O LORD my God, I desire to praise Thee,
for to that end was I created. Open
Thou my mouth in Thy praise, that I may sing
to the glory of Thy Name. Rouse my heart to
Thee, keep from me all weariness, infuse grace,
kindle in me love, that I may pay Thee the
due tribute of grateful thanks.

Take away the iniquity of Thy servant,
cleanse me from all pollution of flesh and spirit,
that my lips may worthily honor Thy holy
Name.

But who can fully declare the profound dignity of Thy Majesty—who can fully utter its
praise? Lo! all the powers of heaven, all the
holy Angels cannot attain thereto. How infi-
nitely less then frail man, who is corrupt and
but a worm! All creation, all reason, every
tongue and language, cannot duly praise Thee.

What then? Because I cannot worthily
praise Thee, shall I close my lips? Because I

know that I am unclean and insufficient, shall I therefore be silent as one altogether dumb?

Far from me be that ingratitude, when reasonable man, whom Thou hast endowed so plenteously, should above all Thy creatures sing to Thy glory.

O Thou Father of mercies and God of infinite goodness! I know, indeed, and with all my heart confess, that I am before Thee a sinner most unworthy; and ought, with downcast look and with tears and sighs, to plead for pardon, rather than with polluted lips laud and make mention of Thy most holy Name.

Yet, trusting in Thy tender mercy and inherent sweetness, I desire, from the very depths of my soul, to laud Thee; praying Thee with the bowels of Thy compassion not to despise me as vile and corruptible, nor to hold me back from praising Thy glorious Name; but so to quicken and move my inner soul, that with devout and joyful voice I may gladly honor Thee.

Thou, O Lord God, art Thine own praise, neither canst Thou be praised with befitting dignity, save by Thyself, who art the Maker and Controller of all things; from whom all things have their beginning, their virtue, and their operation, tending to the glory and honor of Thy Name.

Thou art, therefore, ever to be praised and

magnified throughout all creation. But Thy Name far transcends all utterance. Tongue cannot utter all Thy praise, when the mind, contemplating Thy Majesty, would fain extol Thee as Thou art, according to Thy excellent greatness.

Let therefore Thine own incomprehensible Essence, O my God, Thine inexpressible Omnipotence, Thine unsearchable Wisdom, Thine unutterable Sweetness, Thine immeasurable Holiness, praise Thee.

Let Thy pre-eminent Goodness, Thy boundless Mercy, Thine everlasting Strength, Thine ineffable Majesty, praise Thee.

Let Thine infallible Truth, Thine unchangeable Equity, Thy never-failing Light, Thy most perfect Knowledge, and Thine inviolable Substance, praise Thee.

Let Thy most righteous Justice, Thy most profound Decrees, Thy calm and loving Government, and Thy resistless Power, praise Thee.

Let Thy wondrous Majesty, Thy supreme Loving-kindness, Thy most benign Good-pleasure, Thy most fair Beauty, and Thy most tender Compassion, praise Thee.

Let every title that can show forth Thy greatness, every word that can be uttered in proclaiming Thee, praise Thee and magnify Thee for ever.

Let the whole Court of Heaven unceasingly and for ever extol Thy divine Majesty.

Let the thousand thousands of Angels, serving Thee with due reverence, sing aloud to Thy Name their songs of infinite thankfulness.

And let the heavenly citizens, ten thousand times ten thousand, who for ever stand before Thee, praise Thee with boundless joy, and adore Thee with the deepest reverence.

And on my behalf, let all this most blissful assembly of the celestial Court salute Thee with the most devout and acceptable salutation, praising and glorifying Thee for ever.

Let also the pure and bright aspirations of the Saints, and all the mellifluous eloquence of the Doctors, every distinct virtue, every perfect desire exercised in honor of Thy Name, with the universal melody of all creation, bless Thee to the utmost, and throughout all ages extol Thy glorious Deity.

And let all Thy Saints and Thine Elect, whose names are written in the Book of Life, laud and glorify Thee with perpetual praise.

Blessed Lord God, I entreat Thee for the full remission of my sins, for a good death and a peaceful departure. May I escape the bitter pains of eternal punishment, and enjoy the beatific vision of celestial glory. May I in

Christ, be found worthy to dwell in Thy presence for ever.

CHAPTER II

ON THE CREATION OF THE FIRST MAN, AND HIS MISERABLE FALL

I BLESS and give Thee thanks, O Holy Trinity, and inseparable Unity—Father, Son, and Holy Ghost—Thou One true omnipotent God, who, to declare the unspeakable bounty of Thy Goodness, didst in the beginning create the heavens and the earth, the sea, and all that in them is; and hast raised man, by a peculiar honor and dignity, above Thy other creatures, to Thy image and likeness, by making him powerful in dominion, wise in reason, and innocent in life.

I praise and glorify Thee, for the lavish bounty with which Thou didst honor man in Paradise with delights flowing to him on every side; that, possessing them all to Thy perpetual praise and glory, he might have the fruition of things above, and the government of those below.

I praise and magnify Thee, O most holy God, for Thy excellent mercy and unutterable compassion, in sparing man from irreparable con-

demnation, when he with base ingratitude for-
gat all Thy benefits; banishing him for his sins
from the delights of Paradise, that he might
be led to penitence.

For, although by his transgression he merited
eternal punishment, being totally undeserving
of pardon, yet Thou didst not inflict the full
severity of Thy justice, but rather didst display
the sweetness of Thine ineffable mercy; by
placing him under the yoke of a fitting penitence, and extending to him in due season the
soothing balm of Thy long-desired pardon.

And this was so done, that the rational being,
who wilfully fell through his own iniquity,
might be saved by Thy grace. Hence all faithful souls ought ever to render thanks to Thee,
and not trust in their own strength, nor glory
in their own righteousness.

For we are Thy creatures, O my God; we
subsist by Thy goodness, and of Thy bounty
receive what we have. Yet, by our proneness
to evil, how quickly we slip and fall. And,
unless we were again raised up and established
under the safeguard of Thy mercy, we should
for ever be transgressing, and so pine away in
our iniquities.

Therefore, O most gracious God, we implore
Thy compassion, we call to mind the abundance
of Thy loving-kindness. With sweet accents we

announce Thy gentleness, and tell it out with gladness.

Yea, now with grateful hearts we offer to Thee the sacrifice of holy praise for the multitude of Thy favors, which Thou hast so plentifully showered on us Thy children, sold under sin.

CHAPTER III

ON THE RECOVERY OF MAN, AND THE PROMISE OF CHRIST'S ADVENT

O LORD GOD, Almighty and Merciful, Whose nature is love, Whose will is power, Whose property it is ever to have compassion, I bless Thee and give Thee thanks for Thine infinite pity and gracious goodness, with which Thou didst hasten to recall man, deceived by the guile of the devil, and prostrated by contact with deadly sin, from his manifold transgressions and defilements, by the way of penitence, to a state of well-doing. For, through the quickening promise of Thine Advent, Thou didst grant unto him the hope of pardon, Thou didst abundantly bestow upon him the comforting prospect of salvation.

And, lest man should at any time make ignorance a plea for his ill-doing, Thou hast guarded him from error by frequent admonitions, by revealing Thy Law, by inflicting plagues, by open judgments on sinners, by abundant signs, by promise of future blessings; so that all might be without excuse, who are not converted to Thy worship and to the knowledge of the Truth.

For, during the five ages of Patriarchs, Judges, Priests, Kings, and Prophets, from righteous Abel unto John the Baptist, Thy Forerunner, Thou didst not cease by signs and oracles wonderful and many to foretell, promise, and prefigure Thy desired Advent; that, by so many witnesses preceding Thee and declaring Thy mysteries, Thou mightest stir up our minds to receive the Faith, and ardently inflame our dull affections by the lively examples of so many ancient Fathers.

CHAPTER IV

ON THE REDEMPTION OF THE HUMAN RACE THROUGH THE MYSTERY OF THE INCARNATE WORD

I BLESS and give Thee thanks, O Lord God, Thou Creator and Redeemer of mankind, for Thy exceeding great Loving-kindness, whereby Thou wouldest that man, wonderfully created, should be the more wonderfully restored.

For, when we were yet Thine enemies and death had long exercised an evil power over the whole family of man, Thou didst call to mind Thine abundant mercies and look down from the sublime habitation of Thy glory into this vale of tears and misery.

Forasmuch as Thou sawest on earth the great affliction of Thy people, the grievous burden of the sons of Adam; inwardly moved by the sweetness of Thine inherent love, Thou didst, in Thy wisdom, devise peace and redemption for us.

For, when the fulness of time was come, Thou, the Day-spring from on high, camest to visit us, and didst fulfil the desires of the Prophets by manifesting Thyself in Thine assumed flesh, and appearing among men—very God and very man.

I bless and praise Thee, O Jesus Christ, our Saviour, for Thy exceeding great humility in deigning to choose as Thy Mother a lowly maiden; whom also Thou didst cause to be espoused to the poor carpenter Joseph—a man truly just and devout.

I bless Thee for the glorious Annunciation of Thy Incarnation, and for the holy Angelic

Salutation, with which the Angel Gabriel did hail the Blessed Virgin Mary, declaring to her the divine mystery, that from her the Son of God should be Incarnate.

I praise and glorify Thee for the wondrous faith of the Virgin Mary, for her firm assent and the lowliness of her answer; for all her virtues specially manifested when thus obediently she responded to the glad tidings of the Archangel:—"Behold the handmaid of the Lord, be it unto me according to Thy Word."

I praise and glorify Thee, O Eternal Wisdom of the Father, for the amazing descent of Thy unattainable Majesty into the common prison-house of our mortal nature, and for Thy sinless Conception by the Wonderful co-operation of the Holy Spirit. For in the virgin womb of Mary, the ineffable power of the Most High overshadowing her, Thy sacred and adorable body was formed from the flesh of an undefiled virgin. For Thou, the true God, consubstantial with the eternal Father, wast made one flesh with us without the contagion of sin; that Thou mightest make us one Spirit with Thee through the adoption of the Sons of God.

I praise and magnify Thee for the spontaneous emptying Thyself of Thy glorious fulness, and lovingly taking upon Thee our sufferings, our lowliness, our weakness, and our mortality; that Thou mightest replenish us by emptying Thyself, heal us by Thy sufferings, exalt us by Thy lowliness, strengthen us by Thy weakness, and by Thy mortality bring us to a glorious immortality.

I praise and highly exalt Thee, that Thou, who in Thy Divinity hast neither times nor years, but hast ordained to every operation of nature its proper season and order, didst await the due time of birth, and for nine months wert hidden within the narrow limits of a Virgin's womb.

O what loving and wondrous condescension, that Thou, who art endless and essential Glory, shouldest not abhor being made a despised worm; that Thou, Who hast created all things by Thy word, shouldest for our deliverance willingly bear our sorrows!

O most sweet Jesus, the brightness of Eternal Glory, the lower Thou madest Thyself in humanity the more didst Thou show forth to me Thy goodness; the more Thou becamest vile for me, the more art Thou precious to my soul.

CHAPTER V

ON THE NATIVITY AND POVERTY OF JESUS

I BLESS and give Thee thanks, O Lord Jesu Christ, the Only-begotten of the Father, unutterably born before all worlds, that Thou didst vouchsafe, in Thy great humility, to be born in a cattle-soiled stable, that from love of holy poverty Thou didst find lowly rest in a manger.

I praise Thee, O most loving Jesus, for Thy transcendent origin, for Thy glorious Nativity from the Blessed Virgin Mary, for Thy poverty and humble repose in so small and so mean a cradle.

Who can worthily meditate on the most high God becoming so low for the sake of man. O, what cries of gratitude should he raise unto Thee, Who, for his redemption, didst choose the narrow manger.

O boundless mercy! O marvellous sweetness! O most comforting love! God, born as a little child, wrapped in swaddling clothes of little worth, placed in the narrow crib among the brute creatures of His hands. O Humility incomprehensible! that the Lord of all Lords should deign with His servants to be a fellow-servant.

But, O Lord God, little was it to Thee that Thou, who art my Creator, shouldest be my Father, and deign also to become my Brother, as very man—my flesh, yet without its corruption.

O Nativity, above nature, yet for the restoration thereof! surpassing all ordinary births by the majesty of the miracle; and by divine virtue comforting man in his sad entrance into life.

O how blessed and most lovely was Thy Nativity, most sweet Jesus! Thou Child of the excellent Virgin, Offspring of Thy Blessed Mother Mary, Who dost repair the flaws of man's birth, renews his condition, cancels prejudice, blotting out the handwriting against him. Thus, when distressed as born a child of wrath from the stock of Adam, he can rejoice in Thy undefiled Nativity, well assured that by Thy grace he is most happily regenerate.

I give Thee thanks for Thy freely-bestowed and glorious Nativity, O Jesus Christ, Thou Only-begotten Son of God, through whom we have access to this grace, wherein we stand and trust; looking hopefully for the glory of the sons of God, promised anew to us from Heaven.

Thou art the pledge of our Redemption.

Thou art the eternal hope of all. To Thee as suppliant sinners we flee for refuge, for Thou didst search us out, when as yet we had no knowledge of Thee.

O holy and sweet Childhood, which infusest true innocency into the heart of man, by which every age may return to a blessed infancy and be made like unto Thee, not in littleness of body, but by humility of the senses and godliness of conversation.

Grant unto me, O benign Jesus, to follow the holy steps of Thy lowliness and poverty; Who, to give unto all men an example of holiness and the remedy of eternal salvation, wast willing to be born of the Virgin Mary in the hour of midnight.

Bid me, with the Angels and all the heavenly host, whom Thou madest the joyful heralds of Thy Nativity, devoutly to sing, with grateful heart, thanks and praise to Thee. Amen.

CHAPTER VI

ON THE TRIALS AND WANTS OF JESUS IN POVERTY

O LORD JESU CHRIST, I bless and give Thee thanks for Thy gracious endurance of many trials, even at the very beginning of

Thy nativity, and for Thy harsh taste of ex-treme poverty.

For, when Thou, O God, wast born into the world, Thou didst choose the night season for privacy, and the cold of winter for Thy delight.

Nor didst Thou seek a brilliant palace meet for Thy royal dignity, but a small crib to pro-tect Thy tender infancy.

O poverty most poor, in that Thou, Who rulest the universe and didst for Adam make a coat of skins, and with a wondrous variety adorn the heaven with stars, the earth with flowers, and the cattle with hairy hides, hadst scarcely coarse clothing enough to swathe Thee!

O holy poverty of the Son of God! more precious far than all the riches of the world; who, in its fulness can approach thereto? Who of the family of man hath e'er endured such straits? What record, what tongue, what ex-ample tells of Saint of old, who, when life began, suffered misery so early?

Therefore, to Thee, O Jesu, glorious King, Thou lovely Child, do I most heartily present my fullest praises; beseeching Thy sweetness, that Thou wouldest grant me lovingly to em-brace the gifts of Thy holy penury, and by Thy grace to endure such trials with a patient spirit.

Thou didst come down from Heaven that

Thou mightest make poverty our delight; and becamest poor by assuming what attaches to man, although, in that which is Thine Own, Thou art ever rich and abounding.

I highly extol Thee for the assumption of our poverty and weakness, for to Thee were we so dear, that Thou, by a participation of our frail nature, having laid aside Thy royal diadem, didst humble Thyself to be numbered as one of the sons of Adam, yet ever utterly free from every stain of sin.

CHAPTER VII

ON THE CRIES OF THE INFANT JESUS

O LORD JESU CHRIST, Thou joy of Angels, Thou Consoler of the miserable, I bless and give Thee thanks for the tears and cries of Thine infancy, by which Thou didst sorrowfully bewail the sins of the sons of Adam.

Wondrous truth, stupendous condescension! That God, whom Angels laud in heaven, should cry as a cradled infant; that He, who dispenses life, and sustains all, should, as a mortal being, draw a mother's breasts; He, who speaks by thunder, and waters the earth with showers, should be held in the hands and carried in the arms as a helpless infant.

Behold how the lowest things are joined together with the highest; things human with those that are divine! Therefore the weepings of Thy wailing infancy purify me, and Thy tears deplore my sins.

To Thy sorrows then, O Lord, am I the more indebted, in that I have been redeemed, than to Thy works that Thou hast created me.

O how much ought I to grieve for my sins, since Thou, O Lord, didst never cease to bewail them!

O how deep were the wounds of my soul, that Thou shouldest for their healing pour forth Thy tears so plenteously!

Yet it is not wonderful, nor is it against reason, to think that in compassion Thou shouldest so sorrow; seeing that Thou camest to shed Thy most precious Blood, to cleanse us from our every sin.

Therefore I praise Thee, O beloved Jesus, and evermore will I extol Thee for Thy most tender compassion on me, a miserable sinner.

CHAPTER VIII

ON THE NURTURE OF THE INFANT JESUS

O LORD JESU CHRIST, Thou never failing Fountain of life, I bless and give Thee thanks for Thy receiving nourishment from the breasts of the Blessed Virgin Mary, with whose sacred milk Thou wast fed: Thou, who Thyself art the Feeder of all—the food and sustenance of Angels.

O the ineffable sweetness of divine condescension to man! Who can worthily estimate the greatness of the Sacrament, and the favor to man, in that God Himself draws the breasts of flesh, and is nourished by a Virgin's milk?

O Lord, who didst stoop to the necessities of human frailty, with what tenderness of love art Thou united to me.

O great and tremendous mystery, that Thou, one and the same Person, art declared to be God of God the Father, and very man of a virgin mother; and believed to be One and the same, the Son of a woman, and the Only-Begotten of the Father's glory. One and the same, Thou art made a partaker of man's nature, and art worshipped as the Lord of Angels.

Wherefore I bless Thee and praise Thine ineffable sweetness, that Thou didst in lowliness draw Thy Mother's breast; showing clearly that Thou didst derive Thy fleshly nature from Thy Virgin Mother.

O Thou, who feedest all things, and wast content with such moderate provision, feed my soul with the food of Thy Holy Word; and grant me to serve Thee with thanksgiving, so long as I dwell in this my poor frail body.

CHAPTER IX

ON THE PAINFUL CIRCUMCISION OF THE INNOCENT JESUS

O LORD JESU CHRIST, Thou Saviour of the world, Thou Fountain of purity, Thou Protector of perfect innocence, I bless and give Thee thanks for the painful circumcision of Thy flesh; to which Thou, free from all pollution, didst subject Thyself, keeping in every way the tradition of the Law of Moses.

I praise Thee for the first shedding of Thine innocent blood, which on this day Thou didst pour forth for us.

O most meek Lamb of God, how deeply are we indebted to Thy love, how great the virtue of Thy patience; when, at so tender an age, Thy sacred and spotless flesh did suffer.

I have sinned, but Thou payest the penalty of my transgression. I was conceived and born in sin, but Thou, that art ever sinless, endurest for me the brand of vengeance.

Because I could not make to Thee satisfaction for mine offences, Thou didst in mercy come to my succor, and apply, through the Circumcision of Thy flesh, a cleansing remedy to my soul.

Neither still is it marvellous, for Thou wast ready to be slain for all. Since wholly wast Thou given for me, wholly also for my benefit hast Thou been expended.

O good and most gracious Jesus, who in Thine innocent Body didst suffer for me, purify my every member, and, according to Thy holy Life, direct all my doings and regulate my whole nature.

Whatever Thou findest in me that is carnal, cast it utterly away. Remove from me all that Thou seest unclean in me. Keep down with Thy strict discipline all that is vain and light in me; that, being inwardly cleansed from sin and adorned with the beauty of holiness, I may have a perpetual love of Thy holy Name, and be found a meet partaker of Thy heavenly kingdom.

CHAPTER X

ON THE GIVING THE MOST SWEET AND SAVING NAME OF JESUS

I BLESS and give Thee thanks, O Lord Jesu Christ, for the new, saving, and adorable Name that was given to Thee—that Thou wert called Jesus.

This Name was first announced by the Angel to the Virgin Mary; afterwards revealed to St. Joseph in a dream; and on this day made Thine by Thy parents.

O most sweet Name of Jesus, blessed beyond every Name in heaven above and on earth below! According to Thy Name Jesus, so be Thy praise to the ends of the earth.

Praised be Thy Name from the rising up of the sun to the going down thereof; most worthy is it to be glorified from this time forth for evermore.

To Thee by the Father, from everlasting, was this most holy and blessed Name made Thine, and in due season manifested unto men.

"For there is none other Name under heaven given among men whereby we must be saved."

Just is it, therefore, that "at the Name of Jesus every knee should bow, of things in heaven, and things in earth, and things under the earth"; and every tongue should confess Thy holy Name, in that Thou art Jesus Christ our Saviour and Redeemer.

O most sweet Jesus, how excellent is Thy Name in all the world! For Thy Name is magnified far above the name of Solomon, yea above all kings that were before him, or shall be after him.

All kings of the earth, therefore, shall fall down before Thee; all nations and languages shall serve Thee; for Thou art the Lord our God, the King and Saviour of all who follow Thee, and love the Name of Christ.

O sweet and saving Name of Jesus, which heals all diseases, enlightens our minds, inflames our hearts, dispels sadness, softens anger, yields peace and concord, nourishes love —yea, turns our very sorrows into joy.

This most lovely Name an Archangel brought down from heaven to earth. Apostles preached it throughout the world, and for it the Martyrs suffered.

This Name Confessors have proclaimed with no uncertain sound; holy virgins have tenderly loved it; old and young have sung its praises, and thousand thousands of the faithful have chosen death, rather than deny the sweet Name of Jesus.

This saving Name kings and princes now adore; Priests and Doctors declare it; all the faithful in Christ, renouncing the world and the devil, hold It in special reverence and love; on It they rest their hope of Salvation, for Jesus is the Saviour and Protector of all who, as His, with a firm and loving faith, abide in Him.

O sweet Jesus, my one, my only Saviour! write Thy blessed Name on my heart, not in the letter but in spirit, there to remain so indelibly engraven, that no prosperity, no adversity shall ever move me from Thy love.

Be Thou to me a strong tower from the face of the enemy, a comforter in tribulation, a counsellor in doubt, a deliverer in distress, a very present help in trouble, a guide in behavior, a reclaimer from error, and a faithful leader to the courts of heaven through the many temptations and dangers of this life. Amen.

CHAPTER XI

ON THE MANIFESTATION OF JESUS, AND THE DEVOUT OFFERINGS OF THE HOLY KINGS

I BLESS and give Thee thanks, O Lord Jesu Christ, Thou Prince of the rulers of the earth, for Thy glorious Manifestation to the three Kings.

For when Thou wast born in Bethlehem of Judæa, Thou didst forthwith reveal Thy Majesty to men of a far-off land. Leading them by a heavenly light to Thy miserable dwelling-place, Thou didst manifest to them Thy state of holy poverty.

O God, great and wonderful! Thou alone orderest all things, and doest great works in heaven above. Thou wast not ashamed to appear before so many kings and nobles, poor and unadorned—an example of lowly indigence.

For, neither the place nor the habit assumed for us didst Thou change for aught more splendid; in one and the same way before shepherds and kings didst Thou manifest Thyself.

I praise Thine ineffable compassion for the first-fruits of the Gentiles, for Thy call of the Heathen; whom from the far-off East Thou didst, by secret inspiration, draw to the light of the Gospel.

There are not found in Israel among her princes those who, with so much glory and faith, hasten to search out the place of Thy Nativity. The faith of these strangers was brighter far—their devotion far more fervent.

I glorify Thee for the marvellous enlightenment of the Gentiles. So gloriously didst Thou shine into the dark minds of these men of the

East, that, with undoubting faith, they followed over wide regions the heaven-shown sign.

With the holy Magi I reverently adore Thee; longing so to walk in their footsteps, that I may offer to Thee, with devout affection, the three precious gifts, which in themselves contain the high mysteries of the faith.

Falling down before Thee they presented *gold* in token of Thy royal dignity; *frankincense* in veneration of Thy divine majesty, and *myrrh* to tell of Thy assumed mortality.

Wherefore, O Lord most merciful, King of Kings, O Jesu Christ, Thou Ruler of the universe, accept from the hand of Thy unworthy servant the mystical offering, that I, in the spirit of these holy Kings, this day devoutly present unto Thee.

I offer to Thee, now and for ever, first, a sound faith, a firm hope, and a pure love. I believe Thee to be the Ruler of all things in heaven and on earth. I adore Thee, Very God, the Only-Begotten of the Father. For my Salvation I confess that Thou didst take of the Virgin Mary a mortal body.

Further, accept, I pray Thee, three other gifts, containing within themselves a sweet-smelling savor. Lo, I present unto Thee that which I received from Thee; I relinquish, out of love for Thee, all my worldly goods. I wish not in this life to call anything my own. My desire is to be content with plain food and simple clothing. In this lies the true oblation of precious gold.

I also add the gift of frankincense, by which is signified the incense of devout prayer for my own sins; pleading with sighs and tears, thanking Thee for many mercies, and grieving for all who are afflicted or distressed. This is the burning of sweet frankincense, so acceptable unto Thee.

I offer unto Thee also the spices of myrrh, in memory of Thy most bitter Passion, longing, by a stern self-denial, to go on unto perfection.

For as often as I, through love of Thee, call to mind Thy cruel sufferings, I present unto Thee acceptable incense.

And, when I overcome my evil desires and renounce mine own will, then do I bruise fragrant myrrh in my heart, that from thence a fitting sacrifice may be prepared for Thee.

O how happy should I be, could I offer to my Jesus plenteous myrrh, by gathering together all the labors, the sorrows, and the bitterness of Thy Passion!

For, by such a mingling of myrrh and frankincense, the faithful soul is moved to ardent amendment, to deeds of penitence, and crucifying of the flesh.

O Jesu Christ, I give Thee thanks for the profound sanctity of this day, adorned as it was by Thee with three glorious miracles. On this day, by the guidance of a star, Thou didst lead the three Kings to Thy manger; to-day Thou wast baptized of John in Jordan; on this day Thou turnedst water into wine at the marriage feast, clearly in all proving Thyself both God and man.

I, therefore, pray Thee, O lowly and gracious Lord, that Thou wilt not suffer me to be led astray by Herodian delusions, by the honors of the world, and the allurements of the flesh, but so guide me with the blessed Magi in the right way to the heaven of heavens, that I may be found meet to behold Thee in everlasting glory.

CHAPTER XII

ON THE PURIFICATION OF THE BLESSED MARY, AND ON THE PRESENTATION OF THE CHILD JESUS

I BLESS and give Thee thanks, O Lord Jesu Christ, author of purity, for Thy lowly presentation in the Temple of God; where, with sacrifices and gifts, Thou wast offered by Thy parents as one of the sons of Adam, and redeemed with five pieces of silver, as it were some slave set forth for sale.

I bless Thee, most holy Redeemer of the world, for Thy meek submission to the divine Law. Free from the debt of transgression Thou didst show Thyself to us an example of perfect obedience; in that Thou madest Thyself in all things subject to the Law.

I glorify Thee for the exceeding great humility of Thy blessed Mother, and for her willing attention to the precept of the Law. Ever a holy Virgin, nevertheless she refused not the cleansing rite of Purification.

O grateful oblation! O sweet satisfaction! for it was voluntary—yea, it was complete and free from all fault.

What shall I offer, what shall I render unto Thee, O Lord, for all the benefits Thou hast bestowed on me? A poor sinner, helpless and contemptible, what can I give unto Thee? I can but entirely resign myself, body and soul, into Thine hands.

O how needful for me is purification—the cleansing from my sins! Fitting satisfaction necessary for mine offences, sinner as I am, defiled with pollutions innumerable.

Therefore, to Thee I look, most benign Lord Jesu Christ, and pray that Thou wouldest vouchsafe to make satisfaction for me, and by a perfect oblation of Thyself wash away all my sins; so that, cleansed and purified, I may be deemed worthy to enter the Temple of Thy heavenly habitation, there to praise Thy blessed Name for ever.

I offer unto Thee a pair of turtle-doves—a double compunction of soul; I bewail my sins and my negligences, and then long for joys eternal.

I also gladly present, as an offering to the Lord, two young pigeons, to preserve within me a twofold honesty of heart; desiring to render unto no man evil for evil; and, what is more, to overcome evil with good.

Which do Thou most graciously vouchsafe to me, O kind Jesus, who wast on this day presented in the Temple by the lowly Virgin Mother, and taken up with joy into the arms of love by the just and truly devout Simeon. Amen.

CHAPTER XIII

ON THE PERSECUTION OF JESUS, AND THE FLIGHT INTO EGYPT

I BLESS and give Thee thanks, O Lord Jesu Christ, Thou exalted King of Kings, for the persecution and tribulation wrought on

Thee in Thine infancy; when Thou fleddest from the face of most impious King Herod, and wert forced, as an exile and wanderer, to go forth from Thine own country, and enter privily the land of Egypt; from whence, in former times, Thou leddest forth the children of Israel with a mighty hand.

I praise and glorify Thee for that painful journey and long wandering, endured by Thee in a strange land, where, for seven years, Thou didst dwell among a barbarous people, with men unlike indeed to Thyself.

O cruelly impious, to aim at the death of the Author of life; to thrust out from His own country the very King of Heaven!

What rivers of tears would have flowed had one beheld a child so lovely and so fair, with the Virgin Mother all so delicate, fleeing, 'mid the darkness and secrecy of night, to a region utterly unknown to them.

At this time of persecution how truly marvellous the patience! How should it teach all Christ's faithful servants to look for persecutions many at the hands of the wicked.

I praise and glorify Thee, O Lord Jesu, for that blessed return from Egypt; for Thy journey back again to Thine own land; for Thy social dwelling with Thy parents in the city of Nazareth; where Thou didst hold sweet converse with friends and neighbors, and in poverty dwell in sweet fellowship with Thy Mother and the saintly Joseph.

Grant to me now, O beloved Jesus, that I may, if only in some small degree, imitate this Thy walk of patience; that I murmur not when injuries are done to me, but rather humbly give place to the wrath of man.

Should any one mock me, or speak evil of me, or in any way assail me, give me grace to endure it; let me not burn with hatred against the offender; rather let me fervently plead for his salvation, and impute all his sin to Satan, who provoked it.

Give me grace to live at peace with all my brethren; willingly to yield to them, and patiently to endure with them poverty of this world's goods however severe, to the praise of Thy Name. Amen.

CHAPTER XIV

ON THE HOLY INNOCENTS, SLAIN BY HEROD FOR THE NAME OF JESUS

I BLESS and give Thee thanks, O Lord Jesu Christ, Thou hope of babes, Thou glory of the lowly, Thou crown of all the Saints, for the deaths of so many thousand innocent children, slain for Thy Name's sake.

I praise and glorify Thee for the first-fruits of the Martyrs. Free from actual sin they suffered. Clean in heart and pure in body Thou didst take them from this evil world to Thyself; yea, Thou gavest the crown of martyrdom to babes, who knew not yet the use of reason.

I adore the righteousness of Thy judgments, so wonderfully seen in all Thy works; for Thou didst exalt the humble and innocent to eternal glory, but the proud Herod and his associates Thou didst cast down to hell in utter confusion.

I earnestly beseech Thee of Thy goodness, most innocent Jesus, so to guide me, that I may in heart and mind follow the innocence and simplicity of these little ones. Having laid aside all bitterness and pride, may I henceforth, in my daily walk with my fellows, be found more meek, more pure, more lowly, more patient, and more cheerful.

Nor let any carnal wantonness defile me; rather let a perfect mortification of the flesh keep me from all that is hurtful.

CHAPTER XV

ON THE FINDING JESUS IN THE TEMPLE

I BLESS and give Thee thanks, O Lord Jesu Christ, Thou Master of lowliness and profound Teacher of eternal truth, for the example of Thy amazing humility, and for the ray of Thy hidden wisdom manifested to man; when Thou wentest up to Jerusalem with Thy parents to keep the Feast; offering for us to God the Father the sacrifice of praise and sacred prayer. Sitting in the midst of the Doctors, Thou, when only twelve years of age, didst draw on Thee the eyes of all beholders, by Thy childlike attention and Thy discreet questioning.

I praise and magnify Thee with deep devotion, for Thy reverential obedience, manifested to Thy parents; when, after long and painful searching, they found Thee. Renouncing at once Thine own will, Thou, the great Ruler of the Universe, didst humbly become subject to them. Although they understood not the words spoken to them, yet didst Thou go down with them from Jerusalem to Nazareth, and there show Thyself the obedient son of a most excellent mother.

O sweet Jesus, Thou most lovely Child, Thou mirror of all holiness and virtue, teach me to keep down all perverseness of self-will, and readily to heed the advice of my elders; devoutly to visit the House of God, and there attentively to hear the preaching of Thy Word; to reverence the Teachers of Thy Church; humbly to obey those set over me in the Lord; and joyfully to serve Thee in perfect subjection all the days of my life.

CHAPTER XVI

ON THE HOLY AND HIDDEN LIFE OF THE LOWLY JESUS

I BLESS and thank Thee, O Lord Jesu Christ, for the spotless sanctity of Thy Life, which, for a long period, Thou leddest privately with Thy Parents in Nazareth. From Thy twelfth to Thy thirtieth year, in great poverty, humility, and obedience, didst Thou abide with them.

I praise and magnify Thee with boundless love, for Thy lowly and hidden Life among men and Thy fellow villagers. Never manifesting any sign which might have led to a recognition of Thy Godhead, Thou deignedst to be called and to be considered the son of a carpenter.

O the humility of Christ! How dost Thou confound the pride of my vanity, and with what a bright example dost Thou admonish me to shun all vain show, to avoid the crowds of the outside world, to choose a life of obscurity; desiring to be known of God alone, taking heed above all things to my own salvation.

Suffer me not to thrust myself rashly before men for the sake of edification; may I rather, with diligent endeavor, study the Word of Life, until the voice from heaven shall call, "Bring forth fruit."

Help me, sweet Jesus, Thou good Master, to examine with all watchfulness the manner of my hidden life, and inwardly to dedicate myself to Thee. May I ever love contempt of the world and a hidden retreat, and be very silent as to the things of this life. May I embrace eagerly all that concerns Thee and things divine; and, within the deep recess of my heart, keep closely the book of Thy holy conversation.

CHAPTER XVII

ON THE BAPTISM OF JESUS, AND OUR SANCTIFICATION IN WATER

I BLESS and give Thee thanks, O Lord Jesu Christ, Thou fountain of goodness, and source of all virtues, for Thy lowly reception of holy Baptism, so fulfilling all righteousness; and for the voluntary submission of Thyself under the hands of Thy forerunner; by whom Thou didst deign to be baptized in Jordan, consecrating to our use the waters of Baptism.

In which Thou hast given an example to all about to be baptized, both young and old, that, if they desire to enter the mansion of Thy heavenly Kingdom, they must humbly receive the Sacrament of Regeneration, that bringeth salvation.

In Thy baptism we indeed were washed. This sanctification was profitable to us, not to Thee, Who haddest no spot of sin.

I praise and magnify Thee, most high and adorable Head, object of holy awe even to Angels, for humbly descending into the Jordan, and bending to receive its waters for the washing away of our sins.

I bless and glorify Thee for the revelation of heavenly mysteries, for the clear manifestation of the presence of the most glorious Trinity, for opening the entrance to eternal Life, for the miraculous enlightenment of Thy blessed Forerunner, John the Baptist, and for his humble response and ready obedience.

O Jesu, most exalted King, how didst Thou this day abase Thyself for me, the vilest of sinners; what great gifts of divine grace didst Thou declare unto me. Mercifully look upon me and forgive me all my sins, which, in various ways, I have committed both openly and secretly.

I pray to be baptized by Thee with the Holy Ghost and with fire, for in many things I have offended Thy goodness. "Wash me thoroughly from my wickedness, and cleanse me from my sin."

For no one on earth is free from defilement, not even the babe a day old: none other but Thou, O Christ. Thou alone art pure, and the only Purifier: Thou alone art holy, and the only Sanctifier; Who, according to the multitude of Thy mercies, hast power to forgive men their sins.

I pray Thee, O Lord, let my soul live by Thy favor. O remember not against me my former iniquities, but renew my youth like the eagle's.

Forgive the past, make me to walk circum-
spectly for the time to come, and pour into me
fresh grace; that I may attain the full fruition
of the eternal glory of Thy Godhead.

———————

CHAPTER XVIII

ON THE FASTING AND TEMPTATIONS OF THE INVINCIBLE JESUS

I BLESS and give Thee thanks, O Lord Jesu
Christ, for Thy sacred fast of forty days
and forty nights, which Thou didst undergo
alone in the desert, a pattern of abstinence for
Thy people.

Where, as a hermit, Thou wast with the wild
beasts, away from the solace of men, but with
Angels ever near unto Thee; setting forth
thereby to all who love Thee a great example
of retirement from the world.

I laud and honor Thee, O Jesu Christ, Thou
food of Angels, and refection of men, for Thy
many and long watchings, for Thy holy prayers
and devout meditations, accomplished in the
vast wilderness.

I praise and highly exalt Thee for ever, for
Thy mighty conflict with the devil; for the
many vexations of the wicked tempter; for the

scorn of all his evil suggestions; for meeting his proposals by fitting answers taken from the Word of God; and for the glorious victory over the three great vices, achieved by Thee; to the perpetual confusion of Satan, and the strengthening of our infirmity.

With the holy Angels duly honoring Thee, I meekly on bended knees laud and magnify Thee; seeking from Thee, so long as I dwell in the desert of this world, daily food, the upholding power of Thy grace, comfort in tribulation, courage when tempted, and protection from the wiles of the enemy.

I believe and confess that Thou art the Christ, the Son of God, God and Lord of Angels, Creator of mankind and Redeemer, clad in the infirmity of our flesh; proved and tried in all things, that Thou mightest have pity on us; and compassionating us, Thou mightest heal us of the diseases of our sins.

O holy Jesu, Thou most valiant combatant, Who for me didst so strictly fast, so bravely fight and conquer; give unto me to fight manfully against the world, the flesh, and the devil; and, with a determined heart to repel every temptation that shall assail me.

As a comfort in my exile, send to me Thy holy Angels, ministers of light and peace, that they may ofttimes visit me, watchfully guard, powerfully help, kindly solace, and abundantly bless me ; and, when this life is ended, may they safely conduct me with joy and gladness to Thee, my Lord Jesu Christ.   Amen.

<h1 style="text-align:center">CHAPTER XIX</h1>

ON THE HOLY PREACHING AND SALUTARY DOC-
TRINE OF JESUS

I BLESS and give Thee thanks, O Lord Jesu Christ, Thou good Shepherd and faithful Guardian of Thy sheep, for Thy loving care, for Thy salvation of souls, and for Thy burning desire to proclaim to the world the glad-tidings of God's Word.

For, on leaving the wilderness, Thou camest to preach the Kingdom of Heaven, sounding the trumpet of salvation throughout all Judæa ; calling upon all to repent, to despise the world and its follies, and forthwith to seek diligently for treasure in heaven.

O sweet Jesus ! with what diligent care didst Thou go about the villages and streets, the towns and fenced cities to convert sinners, to heal the broken-hearted, and to grant forgiveness to the truly penitent.

I praise and magnify Thee, from the very

depths of my heart, for Thy comforting doctrine, and for Thy fervent preaching throughout all Galilee and Judæa; and for Thy glorious renown, proclaimed far and wide among the Gentile nations.

Blessed be Thy sacred lips and most gracious tongue, with which Thou didst so often express the delight of the heavenly Life, and commend to us the counsels of eternal truth; announcing distinctly to the whole world, that Thou Thyself art the true and marvellous Light.

Grant me, most loving Jesus, Thou best of Masters, that I may, with a holy thirst, drink from the streams of Thy saving teaching. May I diligently study, wisely understand, sweetly taste, peacefully enjoy the sacred words of Thy mouth, and carefully fashion all my discipline according to their guidance.

For nowhere do I so readily and so clearly find the way of perfection as in the bright mirror of Thy Holy Gospel, laid open to me and all men for our study.

O Lord, in Thee, the fountain of eternal wisdom, the light of life, and the fulness of all sweetness abound and endure for ever.

"Incline therefore my heart to Thy testimonies." Open mine ear to the words of Thy mouth. "Turn away mine eyes lest they behold vanity, and quicken Thou me in Thy way."

For, although the words of the Gospel Story
appear simple and plain, yet are they both profound and deep; and so full of heavenly mysteries, that the whole world could not contain
them.

CHAPTER XX

ON THE GLORIOUS MIRACLES AND BENEVO-
LENCE OF JESUS

I BLESS and give Thee thanks, O Lord Jesu
Christ, Thou Power of God and Wisdom
of the Father, for Thy glorious signs and
mighty miracles, by which Thou didst most
nobly enlighten the world, and draw to Thy Gospel the minds of unbelievers; so clearly showing Thyself, by open proofs and radiant wonders, to be the Son of the living God, and that
Thou camest upon earth to redeem lost man.

I praise and give Thee glory for Thy boundless love in manifesting Thyself so generous
and so kind to all people. The poor and feeble,
even the vilest sinners, feared not to draw near
unto Thee. Thou didst permit them freely to
speak unto Thee and to touch Thee.

Blessed be Thine eyes, brighter than the sun,
which Thou didst mercifully lift up on the
multitudes that came to Thee; for whom Thou

didst so tenderly care, that Thou wouldest by no means suffer them to go to their homes fasting; but didst, on two occasions, with a few loaves and small fishes, by a great miracle, more than abundantly satisfy thousands.

Blessed be Thy venerable hands, which Thou didst gladly stretch forth over sick and suffering poor; and by the touch of Thy sacred body didst at once drive from them every infirmity and disease.

Blessed be Thy most beautiful feet, which often, soiled with dust, and weary in work for the salvation of souls, bore Thee hither and thither up the mountain side, and along the valley path, as Thou sowedst plenteously the Word of Life.

Thou didst also, in proof of Thy sacred doctrine, ofttimes work miracles, causing the paralyzed to stand up, the blind to see, lepers to be cleansed, devils to be cast out, and the dead, through God, to rise again.

O illustrious Jesus, Light of the world, Salvation of Thy people Israel; our life, our strength, and our glory, look favorably on mine infirmity, and cast from my heart every evil desire. Enlighten the eyes of my mind, that they may see the light that cometh from on high; open the ears of my understanding, that I may hear, O my God, what Thou sayest unto me.

Raise me up from the bed of sloth, that I may go on ever increasing in virtue. Make me to walk straight in the way of Thy commandments, and strengthen my enfeebled hands unto diligent labor.

Cleanse me from the leprosy of the flesh, heal me of all burning wrath, assuage in me all proud boasting, deliver me from all that moves to envy; guard me against gluttony, drive far from me the plague of covetousness, and stay within me all impure desires.

For these trying passions of a diseased soul, the secret workings of devils, by Thee, O Lord Jesu, are to be healed—to be cast out only by the word of Thy power.

For none can heal these spiritual wounds and work the inward signs of holiness, but Thou alone, O Lord God Omnipotent. Thou speakest, and immediately it is done: Thou commandest, and straightway Thy word is accomplished.

Say therefore to my soul, "Be clean," and it shall be cleansed; charge the unclean spirit, which so often tempts and vexes me, "Go out of the man and enter no more into him."

Say to my soul in its every tribulation: "I am thy Salvation. Fear not." Speak the word only, and my soul shall be healed.

CHAPTER XXI

ON THE EXAMPLE AND HOLY CONVERSATION
OF JESUS, AND ON HIS TRIBULATION IN THE
WORLD

I BLESS and give Thee thanks, O Lord Jesu
Christ, Pattern of holiness, Rule of conduct, Flower of virtue, sweet Savor of life, Perfection of patience, for all Thy virtues and
sweet manners; for Thy singular gentleness
and perfect examples, openly shown before Thy
disciples and all Israel; thereby gently inviting
to Thy love the hearts of the lowly.

But, further, Thou hast, by the tenderness of
Thy words, moved the hard hearts of sinners
to repentance. To the learned also, in all Thy
works and all Thy teachings, Thou hast afforded
an edifying example.

I praise and glorify Thee for all the priva-
tions and trials of the body endured by Thee
on earth; which Thou, being made flesh, from
Thy very birth even to Thy crucifixion didst
graciously deign to suffer for us dying worms;
ofttimes enduring hunger and thirst, cold and
heat, labor and weariness, sorrow and disquietude—and that with all meekness of heart.

I praise and give Thee all honor, for the many and grievous persecutions, the malicious artifices, and undeserved blasphemies ever being plotted against Thee by Scribes and Pharisees; also for the great ingratitude and envious revilings exercised against Thee. Sad return indeed for the innumerable benefits and wondrous miracles gloriously wrought by Thee among the people!

I praise and give to Thee all glory for Thy work of unbounded love, exercised for the conversion and salvation of all men; for Thy long and frequent nights spent in prayerful watching; for Thy groans and tears, fruits of Thy compassion; for the joy and congratulations of all the godly, converted to the faith; for their unbounded thankfulness and inward uplifting of their minds; for the many wondrous works meetly wrought by Thee, to the praise and glory of Thy heavenly Father.

O most adorable Jesus, the world's brightest mirror! grant to me, Thy poor servant, hitherto alas! most unruly, to piously contemplate Thy most noble and sweet manner of life, and to fashion all my acts and conduct according to the pattern thereof—that I may learn to be meek and lowly of heart.

That I may be temperate in diet, simple in dress, modest in look, circumspect in my walk, tranquil in mind, given to silence, cautious in action, on my guard within and without, watchful in prayer, devout in meditation, diligent in labor, patient when corrected, prompt in obedience, docile for all that is good; not slothful, not careless, never peevish, not turbulent, not a gossip, no brawler, but holy, calm, joyful, and discreet.

CHAPTER XXII

ON THE FEAST OF PALMS, AND THE LOWLY RIDING OF JESUS INTO JERUSALEM

I BLESS and give Thee thanks, O Lord Jesu Christ, Saviour of the world, the gracious and merciful Redeemer of mankind, for the manifestation of Thy wondrous humility, and for the magnitude of Thine ineffable piety; which, as on this day, Thou didst in lowliness show forth, when, with feet all bare and seated on a mean ass, Thou didst in the midst of a vast multitude, and with songs of little children, enter the holy city Jerusalem.

I praise and glorify Thee, O excellent Jesus, Thou Son of David, for the solemn reverence this day offered Thee by the people of Israel; as with loud Hosannahs they acknowledged and proclaimed Thee the great King and Prophet.

I praise and honor Thee for the wondrous love and unwearied tenderness which led Thee, meekly and of Thine own free choice, to come unto murderers, by whom Thou knewest Thou Thyself wouldest soon be put to death; for whose sins and wickedness Thou didst pour forth abundant tears, when foretelling to them what terrible evils would ere long follow their momentary joy.

I praise and glorify Thee for Thy fervent zeal against evildoers. Having entered the Temple, Thou didst at once drive from the House of Thy Father those who bought and sold therein, making as they did the House of Prayer a den of thieves.

On the one hand, how severe wast Thou against the unjust and covetous—sellers of their own souls; while, on the other, how gentle and merciful towards the poor and feeble, lovingly dispensing to many the word of doctrine and the help of healing.

O inexpressible power of Christ! O the all-surpassing goodness of the Son of God! "Who can express the noble acts of the Lord, or show forth all His praise?" Remember me, O Jesus, in Thy good pleasure, and visit me with Thy Salvation.

Come, beloved Jesus, and lead me into the Holy City, Jerusalem; not that which killeth the prophets, but Jerusalem which is built in the heavens, where celestial citizens dwell in perfect unity.

Ride upon the foal of an ass, by holding in check with the bridle of continence all light and wanton motions of my flesh.

It is good for me to bear, my Lord, and to be subject to Thy law; never to kick against the precepts of obedience, but with patience and meekness to bear the burden laid upon me.

Nor must I ever cease from labor and spiritual progress. No other way than this must I go. I must advance in holy purpose, until, under Thy aid and guidance, I come to the Jerusalem which is above, where there is peace for evermore.

Therefore, to Thee with the Hebrew children do I devoutly cry, "Hosanna to the Son of David, Salvation in the Highest."

Hail, Lord of the Universe! Hail, Thou Saviour of the House of Israel! Whose coming the Prophets foretold from the foundation of the world; whom the Jews, as on this day, gladly received with loud songs of praise.

I adore Thee, I glorify Thee, who, in the name of Thy Father, camest to redeem us from the hand of the enemy, and with Thy most precious Blood to reconcile us to God the Father.

I beseech Thee, also, O Lord Jesu, to enter the temple of my heart, and to purge out and drive far away from me whatever Thou shalt see there polluted and profane.

Cast out from Thy Tabernacle all that is of this world, all tempting regard for places and persons. Overturn the money-tables, lest the love of riches prevail against me. Take away all cattle and doves, and the noise thereof, lest the abundance of earthly things stay my desire for things that are heavenly.

Seize the scourge, made from the small cords of the fear of Thee, and with firm zeal drive out from me all evil fancies and foul suggestions; with which the devil, that vilest of traffickers, is ever ready to tempt me, even at prayer-time in the very House of God; lest my soul, being sorely tried and enticed by vain delusions, be led into compliance, and suddenly destroyed.

Help me, O most valiant Jesus, and suffer me not to be taken by the snares of the devil, and by my own wicked heart. Preserve me from evil and strengthen me in all goodness; that, having escaped the dangers of eternal damnation, I may enter with Thee into the everlasting habitations of the heavenly Jerusalem.

CHAPTER XXIII

I BLESS and give Thee thanks, O Lord Jesu Christ, Thou Bread of Life, and Fountain of healing water, for Thy most holy Feast of the last Supper with Thy disciples, which Thou hadst so long and ardently desired to celebrate.

Thou, O Lord, the King of heaven and earth, didst then eat at the same table, and out of the same dish, with those Thy poor disciples; among whom was the wicked Judas; and during Supper, whilst sweetly uttering words of holy exhortation, didst study, by gentle admonition, to turn that same Judas from his base design.

I praise and glorify Thee, for the wondrous bounty of Thy surpassing charity; when, after eating the Paschal lamb to terminate the old Law, Thou didst first institute the Sacrament of Thy most precious Body and Blood, in remembrance of Thy Passion and perpetual love. With Thy blessed hands, and with a passion of singular devotion, Thou didst deliver the same

to all Thy disciples to eat and drink thereof;
and, at the same time, showing to them, and
the Priests their successors ordained by them,
the form of Consecration, Thou didst give them
full authority to celebrate this Holy Sacrament
henceforth, even unto the end of the world.

O singular and admirable exhibition of love!
O the exceeding liberality of divine goodness!
Where the Giver comes into the gift, and what
is given is inwardly one with the Giver.

O worthy and never to be forgotten memorial, in which the faithful soul recollects its own
death as dead in Christ's death; and finds everlasting life in the Beloved, whom that soul re-
ceives!

O wonder above all wonders, and sweetness
transcending all sweetness, to have God truly
though mystically present, veiled under this
marvellous Sacrament!

Whom the holy Angels adore, as exalted far
above themselves in heaven, appearing to them
all in glorious Majesty.

That I may worthily partake of this Holy
Sacrament, grant unto me, O most loving Jesus,
a heart deeply sorry for my sins, a pure conscience in confessing them, a mind lifted up in
prayer, a firm faith, a fervent hope, an ardent
affection, a devotion stirring to tears, reverence
with love, a bright gladness with fear; also a

profound inclination telling of increased thanksgiving, proceeding from a real lowliness of heart, to appease the excellency of Thy divine Majesty.

CHAPTER XXIV

ON THE WASHING THE FEET OF THE DISCIPLES, AND THE HOLY DISCOURSE OF JESUS AT SUPPER

I BLESS and give Thee thanks, O Lord Jesu Christ, Thou most exalted King of Saints, for that very great example of deep humility and servile submission, shown and left to us for our imitation; when Thou, the Most Holy God, didst condescend with Thy blessed hands and on bended knees most tenderly to wash, wipe, and kiss the feet of the poor fishermen, Thine own humble servants.

Nay more, Thou didst not omit, with like loving condescension, to wash the feet of Thy most perfidious betrayer; although he, unthankful for such vast benefits, foul and unwashed within, did, with all obstinacy, persist in his wickedness.

O marvellous and great gentleness towards a disciple so hardened! O the bending love of a gracious Lord towards a servant so base—yea, so utterly hardened, that neither the familiar bearing during supper, nor the kindness of lowly service, nor the sweet and pleasant discourse, could hold him back from his unholy design!

I praise and glorify Thee, for the long continuance of this most sacred last Supper; at which so many acts of love were wrought by Thee. Verily no times, no moments could ever suffice for their worthy commemoration.

I praise and glorify Thee, O Jesus, Thou best of Comforters, Thou sweetest Instructor and most powerful Upholder, for that last, long, and heavenly discourse, full of the fire of love and the sweetness of the honeycomb; which, after the washing of the feet and the withdrawal of the traitor Judas, Thou didst, with voice most clear, deliver to Thy disciples. Thus didst Thou study to strengthen and comfort their sad hearts, when tribulation was very nigh at hand.

By many very lovely discourses Thou didst promise the sure hope of the Resurrection, the upholding their faith by the coming of the Comforter, and their assumption from this exile into Thy Father's heavenly mansions.

And, at last, when closing this sacred address, Thou didst most lovingly commend them equally to Thy Father, in true union of heart, saying: "Father, I will that they all may be one, even as We are One."

Then didst Thou with Thy disciples enter a garden, away from the noisy world, and so fitted for secret prayer; and didst there make ready for the beginning of sorrows and Thy sacred Passion, saying, "Tarry ye here and watch with Me, while I go yonder and pray."

I beseech Thee, O most loving Jesus, my Lord and Master, that Thou wouldest grant me, a sinner vile indeed, unworthy to be called Thy servant, devoutly and deeply to meditate on this so divine a subject; and to study closely the lively examples of Thy all-holy doings.

More especially, I pray Thee, grant that I may heartily bow down my stiff neck, and so completely conquer all proud shame, that I may readily enter upon deeds of humility and lowly obedience. And may I learn to do works of love, not only to devout brethren and to my friends, but also to those who are morally or bodily offensive to me.

Let me not deem it hard to seek pardon for my shortcomings, since Thou, my God, wast not ashamed, in the presence of Thy disciples, to bend Thy holy knees when Thou wast in the act of washing.

Moved as I am by Thy example, may I, by Thy aid, do what I hear and read of Thee. But altogether imperfect as I am, and defiled by so many evil affections, vast is my need of a thorough cleansing, that my sins may be washed away.

To Thee, therefore, I stretch forth my hands and humbly bend the knees of my heart, praying that Thou wouldest in mercy thoroughly wash not my feet only, but my hands and my head; for in many things have I offended Thee by thought, word, and deed—yea, and by duties many left undone.

Wash me, therefore, O Jesus, from my every defilement; cleanse me from all filthiness of the flesh and spirit; that, being fully purged, I may be meet to have part with Thee in Thy eternal blessedness; which Thou hast promised to all Thy beloved, who continue with Thee in Thy temptations.

Open Thou also, I pray Thee, the understanding of my heart, that I may fully apprehend the sweet discourse from Thy mouth, which Thou didst deliver at the Supper; for they are words of burning love, of delightful consolation, and of wisdom most excellent.

Write the new commandment in my heart, that my soul may burn with a twofold love; uphold me in my every tribulation; and, in place of worldly delights, pour Thou into me the sweet comforting of Thy Holy Spirit.

Grant me the true peace of heart, which the world cannot give. Send to me "the Comforter, the Spirit of truth, whom the world seeth not, neither knoweth."

Come, O Lord Jesus, and vouchsafe to make Thy abode with me; that, Thou in me and I in Thee, we may dwell together in one. Amen.

PART II

ON THE PASSION OF CHRIST UNTIL
HIS RESURRECTION, ACCORDING
TO THE FOUR EVANGELISTS

CHAPTER I

ON THE SELLING OF JESUS BY THE PERFIDIOUS TRAITOR JUDAS

I BLESS and give Thee thanks, O Lord Jesu Christ, Goodness Supreme and Majesty Eternal, Thou who wast unjustly sold by Thine own disciple, for so vile and mean a price as thirty pieces of silver.

I praise and glorify Thee for Thy gentle sufferance of one so treacherous. No anger didst Thou show; no word of hard reproof; no exposal at once to the brethren of his unholy plot; after so foul a deed no suspension from his office and sacred communion; although Thou foresawest that he was hastening to betray Thee.

O most loving Lord Jesus, how wonderful Thy patience! how great my impatience!

Alas for me! that I can bear so little from my brother, when he has said or done aught against me. For a small injury how soon am I moved to anger—how many are my plans to avenge or excuse myself; whilst Thou didst calmly bear with Judas, Thy disciple, even at the very moment he was about to sell and betray Thee.

Where then are my meekness and patience? Help me, O good Jesus. Implant Thy gentleness more abundantly in my heart, for, 'mid the many vexations of this life, I cannot secure the blessing of quiet, without Thy special grace and guidance.

CHAPTER II

ON THE SORROW AND DREAD OF JESUS BORNE FOR US

I BLESS and give Thee thanks, O Lord Jesu Christ, Thou Creator and Redeemer of all believers, for the painful entering on Thy most bitter Passion; for Thy great sadness of soul, for Thy anxiety and dread through the weakness of the flesh, taken voluntarily by Thee for us.

As the hour of Thy betrayal drew nigh, Thou didst begin to be heavy and sore afraid, and very sorrowful. Nor wast Thou ashamed to confess the same in the ears of Thy disciples, saying, "My soul is exceeding sorrowful, even unto death."

O the wondrous dispensation of God! Thou

Lord of all power, Who, a little before, hadst strengthened Thy disciples for the struggle, dost now bear Thyself like unto one helpless, as if destitute of all strength and courage.

This Thou didst to benefit and comfort us, weak and faint-hearted as we are; lest perchance some one, sorely tempted, should despair of pardon or salvation; if he, less cheerfully disposed to endure or undergo some things contrary to the flesh, should be found timid and sad. Yes, this Thou didst that he might say, what we read Thou didst say:—"Nevertheless, not My will, but Thine be done."

I beseech Thee, O most loving Jesus, my only hope in every trial and affliction, enable me, with a heart full of compassion, to examine diligently into the sorrowful beginnings of this Thy blessed Passion; and from thence gradually ascend to the prayerful contemplation of the more bitter parts thereof; that, in every step of Thine Agony, I may be able to discern a saving remedy for my soul.

Grant me, for the glory of Thy Name, patiently to suffer whatever afflictions await me; that I may never despair because of my many tribulations, but wholly resign myself to the good pleasure of Thy eternal purpose.

CHAPTER III

ON THE THREEFOLD ·PRAYER OF JESUS; ON THE
BLOODY SWEAT; ON THE ANGELIC COMFORT-
ING; AND ON RENOUNCING HIS OWN WILL

I BLESS and give Thee thanks, O Lord Jesu
Christ, Thou Sustainer of Angels, Thou
Refuge of the helpless, for Thy sorrowful plead-
ings and for Thy lowly prostration; when
thrice, with bended knees, Thou didst, from the
very depths of Thy soul, entreat Thy heavenly
Father, "If it be possible, let this cup pass
from Me"; yet ever adding, "Nevertheless, not
My will, but Thine be done."

I praise and magnify Thee for Thy mighty
struggle with the terrors of death, and with the
rendings of Thy most bitter Agony; when burning love so prevailed, that Thou couldest cast
out all human fear.

I praise and give Thee thanks for the large
effusion of Thy bloody sweat, when, being in
an agony, Thou didst pray more fervently; and
from Thy Body, contrary to nature, poured
forth great drops of blood.

I adore and give Thee glory for Thy lowly
acceptance of angelic comforting, which Thou,

the Creator and Ruler of the heavenly host, didst not scorn to receive from an Angel, for the strengthening of man's weakness; teaching us, Thy feeble creatures, not to rest on transitory comforts, but steadily to look heavenward for aid.

O sweet Jesus! with what burning love didst Thou love me, when, moved thereby, Thou couldest pray so fervently, that, in Thy firm resolve to suffer, Thou didst, beyond all nature, sweat warm drops of blood, flowing forth even to the ground.

I praise and glorify Thee with perpetual honor, Thou greatest lover of my soul and singular exemplar of my life, for the full resignation of Thyself, for utterly renouncing Thine own will, and all that ready sensitiveness, with which Thou didst naturally shrink from pain and death; and yet, when the hour of suffering was come, Thou didst, at once and without a murmur, resign Thyself to the will of Thy Father, saying, "Father, not My will, but Thine be done."

In those words Thou didst indeed highly glorify Thy Heavenly Father, amply and effectually benefit us, and beat down Satan under Thy feet; showing most clearly to all the faithful the beauty of Thy perfection, the symbol of our salvation, and the way to the highest virtue.

O Jesu, ever to be remembered and adored! grant, I earnestly beseech Thee, that I may enjoy the fruit of Thy thrice-repeated prayer, and with a perfect heart imitate the example of Thy self-denying love.

Grant me also grace manfully to subdue the stubborn flesh to the spirit, to cast aside all carnal fear, ofttimes to kneel in prayer, and watchfully continue therein.

May I devoutly hope for Thy help, and confidently commit all my doings to Thee; entirely renouncing my own will, and having my mind always prepared patiently to endure whatever Thou shalt be pleased to lay upon me.   Amen.

CHAPTER IV

ON THE VOLUNTARY GOING FORTH OF JESUS TO HIS PASSION, AND HIS GREAT MEEKNESS IN THE HOUR OF HIS BETRAYAL

I BLESS and give Thee thanks, O Lord Jesu Christ, our Saviour and Deliverer, for Thy voluntary readiness to suffer. Having offered to God the thrice-repeated prayer, Thou, on the coming of Thy most cruel enemies, with the base traitor Judas and a great multitude in the dead of night, with swords and staves, torches and lanterns, as if to take a thief, didst at once freely go forth to meet them, saying, "Whom seek ye? I am He. If, therefore, ye seek Me, let these go their way." At this first word of Thy power, all their proud daring was stayed, and brought to utter confusion.

For immediately "they went backward and fell to the ground." What then would have come to pass, if at Thy bidding twelve legions of Angels had appeared? But Thou, who camest to suffer, wouldest not so use Thy divine power; but rather show Thy tender forbearance. By a single word didst Thou make manifest what Thou couldest do, by the full exercise of Thy will.

For a season didst Thou permit the ungodly to prevail against Thee, and despitefully entreat Thee; showing that of Thine own free will Thou wouldest suffer, that the work of our redemption might be accomplished, and "the Scriptures of the Prophets might be fulfilled."

I praise and glorify Thee, Thou most innocent Lamb of God, Jesus Christ, for Thine ineffable meekness and the invincible power of Thy gentleness; that Thou wert not moved with anger against the basest of traitors, nor didst Thou indignantly turn away from his presence. Nay, rather, with Thy wonted goodness, Thou didst condescend to kindly words,

calling him " Friend "; and didst lovingly in-
dulge him—one most unworthy—with the sweet
kiss of Thy mouth, saying, " Friend, wherefore
art Thou come ?" His rashness and impious
treachery Thou didst gently reprove :—" Judas,
betrayest Thou the Son of Man with a kiss ?"

Alas! how more than sad! He, who had
shared companionship with the Apostles, now
stands forth the leader of a band of miscreants.
Unawed by Divine justice, unsoftened by loving-kindness, he held not back his hand from
the direst of deeds, but gave the sign, saying,
" Whomsoever I shall kiss, that same is He;
hold Him fast."

O thou wicked disciple of the most loving
Master! O base servant of the most faithful
Lord! Most gentle Jesus, how wonderful is
Thy goodness, how excellent Thy patience!
Amidst such persecution and shameful treachery Thou didst not forget Thy sweet friendship
of the past; but, in return for injury most
gross, Thou didst graciously exercise Thy power
of healing.

For, with a touch of Thy sacred hand, Thou
didst restore the ear of the High Priest's servant, which Thy disciple had cut off; and didst
withhold Peter, Thy defender, from resisting
Thy assailants, saying, " Put up again thy
sword into his place. The cup which My

Father hath given Me, shall I not drink it?"
For thus it must be.

And here, O my God, I beseech Thee, give
unto me, a frail reed, more abundant patience in
my hours of trial. When mine enemies rudely
insult me, or when false charges, of which I
know myself innocent, are brought against me,
let not sudden anger overcome me, nor a spirit
of revenge urge me to return evil for evil.

Grant that I may not fear mine accuser, but
receive with gentleness his reproaches. May I
regard as a friend the man who harshly reviles
and oppresses me. Let no indignation arise at
any cruelty shown me, nor the remembrance of
a wrong done me rankle in my breast.

But, may Thy most loving endurance of evils
strengthen me to suffer with cheerfulness; and
willingly to bear still greater trials, for the love
of Thee.

CHAPTER V

ON THE APPREHENSION, THE BINDING, AND THE
LEADING AWAY OF JESUS TO ANNAS THE
HIGH PRIEST

I BLESS and give Thee thanks, O Lord Jesu
Christ, Thou hope of the Saints and their
tower of strength in the day of tribulation, for

the violent seizure of Thee by hateful enemies;
for the audacity of Thy captors in laying unholy hands on Thee; for their fierce and angry
looks, and the threatening shouts of those arrayed against Thee; for Thy rough and cruel
binding and Thy close and savage detention;
for the hasty and wild hurrying of Thee onward; and that foul treatment, when, with
insulting blows and wild clamor, Thou wast
dragged to Thy death by a vile and vulgar
rabble; whilst Thy dearest disciples fled in dis-
may, and with heavy sorrow and sadness gazed
on Thee from afar.

O Lord, Thou King of Kings and Ruler of
all creatures, who alone among mortals art
free; wherefore didst Thou suffer Thyself to
be thus violently seized by wicked hands, and
basely carried away by men whom Thou didst
create, and whose well-being had ever been Thy
care?

Alas, how grievous was the sin against Thee!
How madly insulting to Thine Almighty Power,
to bind the very Deliverer of souls with the
cords of a malefactor, to lead away captive the
sinless One, as if the vilest robber.

But Thou, most excellent pattern of all virtues, most gracious Jesus, wast willing to suffer
thus patiently for us, to be our perfect example
of meekness, that the clear saying of Esaias the

Prophet might be fulfilled:—"He is brought as a Lamb to the slaughter, and as a sheep before her shearers is dumb, so He openeth not His mouth." He was offered up because it so pleased Him.

Dwell now with compassion, O my soul, upon the sorrow and captivity of thy loving Lord God; Who, of His own free will, endured all these things for thy sins. Deeply lament and let thine eyes pour forth tears plenteously, in that the Only-Begotten Son of God was for thee so unworthily treated.

Behold what these shameless wretches, the impious Jews, did. Lo! they held Jesus captive, and led Him bound to Annas and to Caiaphas, the High Priest. Yet, when He is taken, He resists not; when He is bound, no murmur is heard; when He is led forth, no resistance is offered; when He is hurried away, He utters no reproach. He goes on in meekness, silent as a lamb; as innocent He follows, and humbly suffers.

And now, I beseech Thee, O my God, that the bitterness of this Thy sad captivity may ofttimes enter into the inmost thoughts of my heart.

Every morning may it move me to the fervor of holy prayer, driving away all slothfulness, making me zealously and watchfully persevere in Thy praise. Thus, by earnest service, day by day may I show forth some return for Thy love; for wast not Thou born for me in the night season, for me in the night season wast Thou not betrayed, captured, and bound with cords?

Therefore, in the night season will I remember Thy Name, O Lord, pondering deeply how bitterly Thou hast suffered for me, the vilest of sinners. Let Thy hard bonds secure me true liberty, restrain me from profitless wandering, and, by a firm discipline, keep me true to Thy service.

Let it be no heavy task for me to break and cast from me all self-will, but readily to walk the path of obedience, guided thereon by those set over me in the Lord. May I not fear being led whither I would not, provided the course directed be acceptable to Thee.

Let rebellion and strife, and boldness and clamor be far from me; rather may I be God-fearing, obedient, ever ready and glad to keep Thy Commandments; and may I never cease devoutly to observe all the rites and ceremonies of Thy Holy Church. Bow down my neck to settled ordinances, and bind my hands to holy labors.

May I ever deem it unworthy of me to go mine own way, and waste my time in indolence.

May I ever earnestly desire to live under strict rule, to keep down my own bad passions—so highly desirable to my hard and untamed self; and may I in some degree, however small, by inward conformity exhibit something of the spirit of Thy capture and binding. Amen.

CHAPTER VI

ON THE LEAVING JESUS IN THE HANDS OF HIS ENEMIES, AND ON THE FLIGHT OF THE DISCIPLES

I BLESS and give Thee thanks, O Lord Jesu Christ, Thou good Shepherd and benign Master, for Thine utter desertion and abandonment in the hour of Thy direful necessity; when, forsaken by all Thy disciples and friends, Thou wast left alone in the hands of Thy most cruel enemies.

For Thy brethren and Thy most familiar friends, who had vowed to lay down their lives —to die for Thee; alas! in the testing hour of need, they all forsook Thee and fled.

I praise and honor Thee for that painful compassion of Thy heart, when grief so heavily sat on Thee, beholding, as Thou didst, the offence and flight of Thy fear-stricken disciples. When the Shepherd was in the midst of wolves,

Thine own, the sheep of the flock, as thou hadst foretold, were scattered to their own homes.

O what great sadness, what grievous pangs were there in the hearts of Thy disciples, when they beheld their Lord and Master—to follow whom they had left all—torn from them so violently and dragged to death!

But Thou, Lord, who knowest all things, and permittest nothing to be done save for a wise end, didst in Thine Elect allow this so great a weakness, that through it, in time, greater good should come.

In short, from this fall it was they learnt their own frailty, and so became more gentle to other weak brethren; and, ever after, moved by greater caution and fervor of spirit, they bore themselves lowly and reverently.

O vast the blessing to me that I very diligently study this portion of God's Word, and presume nothing great of myself!

For, although at times, when praying, new fervor is present with me, still I cannot tell how long it will endure, nor what may befall me when temptation sets in.

For if the pillars of heaven, the Apostles of Christ, were thus shaken in the hour of trial, what then is to be expected of a poor frail worthless creature, when but a slight temptation shall come upon him?

And yet, O Lord, how severely do some censure the holy Apostles, that they so basely deserted Thee; and, broken down by fear, sought to escape. But such critics little perceive how readily they themselves are daily turned from the truth, as love or hatred may act on them.

I beseech Thee, therefore, O dearest Lord, keep me from that madness of heart, which would lead me to turn from the holy purpose to which I have put my hand; in life or in death may I follow Thee whithersoever Thou goest.

Restrain me, that I wander not far from Thee in the hour of adversity; let me not consent unto sin, following my own evil desires. May I rather, for the love of Thee and with a hearty yearning to do Thy will, manfully endure all labor and difficulty; lest, through my own slothfulness, I lose Thee, the Supreme Good.

Let "not the foot of pride come against me," leading me to boast of any good work done by me; nor let me speak arrogantly, as did Peter of old, preferring myself to any other, or claiming equality with others. May I always act with Thy fear, humbly considering how frail I am by nature.

The fall of St. Peter and the flight of the Apostles, may they be to me a warning against sin, never a stumbling block in my way.

May their return to repentance give me a
sure hope of finding mercy after a fall; for,
who is there so holy that he does not at times
run into some kind of sin?

And when it happens, that I am forsaken by
friends and acquaintances, or despised, as an
alien and unprofitable, by those very dear to
me; then, as a special remedy, grant me to
remember Thy most grievous desertion and
rejection; and readily to give up all human
consolation, if so be I may, even in a small
degree, be worthily fashioned after Thy tribulations.

O most merciful Jesus! deal gently with me,
in that I have so often sinned against Thee, so
readily turned aside to the vanities of life; that
I have not diligently set my heart on that which
I so fully purposed.

Alas! how often do I look back, and see in
what trivial things my time is spent; and oh,
the anguish—Thy Passion so sadly forgotten!

Thou hast gone before me along the narrow
way, and I pass through with tearless eyes, as
if Thy sorrows in no way concerned me. Be
mindful of my poor dull heart, and pour into
me a loving recollection of Thy most bitter
Passion.

CHAPTER VII

ON THE BRINGING JESUS BEFORE ANNAS, AND ON THE SMITING HIM ON THE RIGHT CHEEK

I BLESS and thank Thee, O Lord Jesu Christ, Thou Guide of our life and Author of our salvation, for Thy first arraignment before Annas the High Priest; where, being questioned concerning many things, Thou wert roughly smitten on the cheek for Thy meek and truthful answer.

I praise and exalt Thee, O Christ, Thou glorious King, for that dishonor, and for the outrageous assault made on Thee by the hand of an audacious servant; when, to the answer of Thy mouth, he returned Thee a heavy blow on Thy face, saying:—"Answerest Thou the High Priest so?"

To whom Thou for Thy part, O most gracious Jesu, calm in mind and speech, didst not omit to give a gentle answer, thus saying:—"If I have spoken evil, bear witness of the evil; but if well, why smitest Thou Me?"

O most impious and vile slave, who daredst with guilty hands to strike the lovely face of Thy Creator! O adorable Jesus! how did the

ineffable virtue of Thy meekness display itself,
that Thou didst not at once indignantly resent
so insulting a blow; but rather with calm
reasoning didst correct the spirit of the striker?

Consider now, thou faithful servant of Christ,
and try thyself. Canst thou, for the love of
Jesus, bear a blow on thy cheek? Behold, if
thou canst not bear a harsh word without
anger, how couldest thou endure a blow?

Thou grievest over the unjust violence to thy
Lord, but more grievous far·is it, that thou
canst not, for the honor of Christ, suffer the
smallest injury.

Thou proposest what is noble—thy thoughts
are for what is excellent; yet art thou troubled
at the first utterance of the reviler; yea, thou
findest thyself weaker than thou didst suppose.

Flee then to Jesus, and only the more earnestly plead with Him for the virtue of patience.

O good Jesus, the strength and support of
the troubled soul, teach me to bear with a quiet
mind all reproaches, and reviling taunts. Let
me never resist indignantly complaints unjustly
brought against me, but vanquish them by a
gentle silence. If compelled to speak, may I
ever answer my adversaries with words that
soothe and win.

In the presence of all my opponents put into
my mouth a just and godly conversation; and,

while the hand of the wicked rageth against me, give me, O most benign Jesus, as an invincible shield, a firmness of purpose lowly and calm.

_____

CHAPTER VIII

ON THE THREE DENIALS OF CHRIST BY PETER, AND HIS BITTER WEEPING, WHEN JESUS LOOKED UPON HIM

I BLESS and thank Thee, O Lord Jesu Christ, Foreseer of all things to come, that Thou, by way of warning, didst foretell his fall to Thy most zealous disciple, Peter.

I glorify Thee for the sad dishonor that fell on Thee, through the denial of Thee thrice by Thy Apostle Peter. Dishonored indeed wast Thou, when he, charged by one of the weaker sex, denied all knowledge of Thee, saying :—" I know not the Man."

I praise and for ever magnify Thy Name for the gracious look Thou didst mercifully cast on the blessed Peter ; so that he, immediately on the second crowing of the cock, might perceive his guilt, and hasten from the midst of evildoers. He went apart that he might, with deep contrition of heart, pour forth tears of bitterness for the grievous sin of having denied Thee.

He had, however, by no means, like the most faithless Judas, fallen irreparably into the pit of despair. Thy unspeakable mercy yet continued. Trusting in the plenteousness of Thy pity and in the tender love so often experienced by him, he hastened, with bitter lamentations, to the saving remedy of penitence. And so he found the gate of infinite mercy open to him.

O the inestimable goodness of the Saviour! O the open inexhaustible fountain of divine compassion and overflowing grace! whence the sinner is wont to draw the fullest hope of pardon—the just, true, and abundant gifts of grace.

Would that I possessed a fountain of tears, that, with blessed Peter, I might worthily deplore my sins; and so, through the merits of my Saviour, be meet to receive pardon thereof, and the favor that once was mine.

Peter fell when, through the fear of death, he thrice denied the truth; but by me eternal truth is daily oft offended, for, with every light temptation, I swerve from the path of virtue.

When Peter fell suddenly, he rose again. I fall more quickly—more slowly do I rise. Rarely do I lament. Ill do I watch myself, and by me, alas! dangers are too lightly regarded.

Peter bitterly bewailed the occasion of his sin. Moved by his fall he fled, and sought

seclusion for his tears; bedewing with peniten-
tial prayers spots contracted through incautious
words.

O blessed tears! which by God's mercy so
soon blot out past sin. By them also favor
departed is restored.

Remember me, O Lord Jesus, and have compassion on me, a frail sinner, surrounded as I
am by so many evil affections. Let me not
sink under the burden of my sins, nor be
weighed down by remorse after committing so
much evil.

Help, therefore, O kind Shepherd, Thy poor
erring sheep; draw forth the lapsed soul from all
uncleanness; comfort the afflicted; strengthen
the faint-hearted; defend us from the adversary;
preserve us from the snares that encompass us;
and bring us, for whom Thou wast slain, to the
kingdom of heavenly felicity; of which Thou
art the Doorkeeper and Prince.

O good and most compassionate Jesus! with
deep yearning of soul I beseech Thee to look on
me with Thy most holy eyes, as Thou didst on
Peter, when he had denied Thee. Quickly pour
into me the grace of holy contrition, that I
may be cleansed from all that I have done
wilfully or negligently against Thee.

Hear the groanings of my heart; heal the
bruises of my wounded conscience; restore to

me the light of fresh grace; nor suffer the soul
of a penitent to perish, seeing that, for its redemption, Thou didst endure so many sorrows,
so many wrongs, and at last the bitter agony
of the Cross.

———————

CHAPTER IX

ON THE LEADING AWAY OF JESUS TO CAIAPHAS, THE HIGH PRIEST, AND HIS FALSE ACCUSATION

I BLESS and thank Thee, O Lord Jesu
Christ, Thou Priest of all Priests, and
High Priest forever, for being so contemptuously led away from the house of Annas to
Caiaphas, the High Priest; where the Scribes
and Elders had assembled to devise cruel counsel against Thee.

Alas! how cursed a joy was theirs, when
they beheld Thee bound and dragged before
them. Long had they desired to take Thee,
but in vain, for "Thine hour was not yet
come."

But "this is their hour and the power of
darkness," allowed them of God, that they may
complete their long-conceived hatred, and now
carry out openly their inveterate malice. All
this was for Thy glory and the salvation of the

faithful. Equally was it for the eternal punishment of unbelievers.

I praise and glorify Thee, Thou adorable Jesus, for Thy lowly bearing before the High Priest, with all the Elders of the people rudely gazing upon Thy lovely face. There Thou wast cruelly accused by witnesses most false, and by the High Priest ofttimes questioned; even strictly adjured to answer truthfully; yea, the very charge of blasphemy brought against Thee: until at last, condemned by all, with loud cries they pronounced Thee worthy of death.

I praise and honor Thee, O most noble Jesus, for every injury done Thee, every lie uttered against Thee; for Thy gentle demeanor and long-kept silence, while so many basely assailed Thee. No sign of complaint or murmuring didst Thou show, but stoodest an example of perfect meekness.

And now, devoted lover of Christ, mark with all seriousness what excellence of lowly patience shone forth in Jesus.

Behold what unworthy rebukes Jesus is compelled to bear, He whom the heavenly host adore. For a truthful answer He is charged with blasphemy.

Verily, all, who so speak concerning Christ, are themselves blasphemers and guilty of most heinous sin.

Yes, truly, in the madness of their hearts they work against Him all manner of wickedness, for they believe not Jesus to be the Son of God.

He, however, endures and is silent, and thus, while trodden under foot by the ungodly, the more does He conquer, the greater is His triumph.

Wherefore, O faithful soul, cease to complain of reproaches cast on thee, and yearn not to return unto thine adversaries evil for evil.

Bear and humble thyself under the weight of earthly tribulation; yearn not to prosper in this life, seeing that Christ gladly endured the world's contempt.

Blush, thou proud man, for thine honors and chief seats; for thy pomp and fine clothing; knowing, as thou dost, that Christ was poor indeed. Disgraceful is it to strive after man's favor and desire earthly pleasures, when Christ preferred the very opposite.

O most adorable Jesus! full of grace and ever gentle, grant me, a miserable sinner, the longed-for blessing of Thy propitiation; and teach me, by Thy lively example, not to dread the reproaches and terrors of the wicked, nor to be disturbed by false accusations; but even readily to seek pardon for their offences against me, bowing myself with all lowliness before

Thee and my superiors; so that I may be meet to receive gifts of grace more abundantly, and to return Thee more devout thanks for blessings received.

CHAPTER X

HOW JESUS WAS MOCKED, SPIT UPON, BLINDFOLDED, SMITTEN ON THE CHEEK AND BUFFETED

I BLESS and thank Thee, O Lord Jesu Christ, Thou Who art the honor and glory of Saints, for the very grievous contempt and unholy treatment shown Thee; when, after sentence of death had been pronounced, Thou wast so indecently treated and so insultingly mocked by heartless servants. Yea, with buffetings many and fierce did they smite Thee on Thy face and on Thy head.

Alas! that Thy most glorious face, on which Angels delight to gaze, should be shamefully defiled by the loathsome spitting of angry Jews, and struck with heavy blows from outspread hands.

Nor can we fail to believe, that straightway blood came forth abundantly, mingling with tears of lamentation; and that Thy lovely neck was bruised by the frequent blows of angry strikers.

Thy most bright eyes, which are ever over the righteous, were in mockery veiled after the manner of fools.

Thy venerable head, so far above all creatures, is violently smitten by the polluted hands of sinners, who with shouts of derision leap about Thee, saying:—"Prophecy unto us, O Christ, who is it that smote Thee?"

Who can hear of these Thy many injuries, O Lord, without great sighing and sorrowing of heart? Surely what Thou dost bear far exceeds the limit of human endurance; the weight of so many insults severely vexes the loving hearts of the holy.

Thou becamest an alien to Thy friends, deserted by Thine acquaintances, a scorn and derision to those that hated Thee without a cause, and winked with their eyes.

Alas! O Lord God, Thou joy of the Court of heaven, wherefore dost Thou, as if Thou wert one of the most simple of men, suffer Thyself to be thus mocked, spit upon, and buffeted by the ungodly?

O the raging Jews, all that night they spent in mocking and beating Thee! Glutting themselves with Thy sufferings, they rendered Thy face to all beholders almost beyond recognition.

There remained however in Thee an unwearied patience, and an incomparable beauty of soul, not to be discerned by Thine evil tormentors.

Nevertheless, having in perfect innocence suffered all these things out of love, Thou art become to Thine Elect much more beautiful and dearer far; according to the inner view of the mind, through which Thou, O Most High God, art perceived by them, most innocently suffering all these things out of Thy tender compassion.

With the vastness of this most daring contempt of Thee acutely before me, teach me, I beseech Thee, most patient Jesus, to consider carefully mine own vileness; and, having weighed my sins, to perceive how justly I have deserved to be despised and rejected of men.

Pity my imperfections, and strengthen my heart to bear the hard words of the world, even when my face blushes with shame for my unholy doings.

Thou didst in meekness bear many reproaches for me, a sinner despicable indeed; and that, because Thou wast so truly lowly. Nay, moreover, even bonds and blows were without a murmur endured by Thee.

O how unlike am I to Thee! how far am I from true humility! I, who for a slight offence or a thoughtless word, at once dislike a man; and in return for a reproof, well fitted to profit me and for which I should be thankful indeed, I, on the contrary, become impatient, grow out of heart, and so lose the blessing offered me.

I pray Thee, O Lord, pardon these my offences, and my frequent sins and levity. I have not kept my heart with a pure conscience; nor have I, as in duty bound, submitted myself with due reverence to Thee, and to every reasonable ordinance.

Give me a salutary penitence, with a fountain of tears. Grant me a love of discipline, that has Thy blows well in remembrance. When the world severely accuses me, bless me with the upholding palm of patience; and may I deem myself worthy of contempt.

May the cruel buffeting of Thy head lead me to bear patiently my bodily sufferings, and Thy scornful blindfolding restrain mine eyes from all vain curiosity.

Let the foul spitting upon Thy comely face keep down all carnal affections within me, and teach me not to heed outward glitter, but rather to honor the hidden graces of the soul.

Let the mockings practised on Thee drive away from me all light behavior and vain hilarity. Let the utter despisal of Thy dignity destroy in me all eager yearning for honor, and ever incline me to things which are lowly and little esteemed. Amen.

CHAPTER XI

ON THE BRINGING OF JESUS BOUND BEFORE PILATE THE GOVERNOR

I BLESS and give Thee thanks, O Lord Jesu Christ, Thou most righteous Judge of quick and dead, for being brought 'mid noise and clamor before Pilate the Governor.

When the morning was come, all the Chief Priests, being gathered together in one place at an early hour, and having taken their vile counsel to put Thee to death, they, by the hands of their officers, brought Thee bound with cords before one who was uncircumcised—a heathen Governor. Then they assailed Thy innocence with accusations most grievous, daring to call Him, whom the holy Prophets of old proclaimed with high praises the Saviour of the world, a malefactor and subverter of their nation.

O awful blasphemy of the Jews, to condemn the guiltless by false witnesses, to be ready to kill the Author of life, to seek the crucifixion of Christ their King, to desire one holy and just to be condemned to a death most shameful!

May all who persecute Thee be confounded and put to shame, for they are worthy of punishments heavier far!

I praise and glorify Thee, O adorable Jesus, for the perfect rectitude of Thy demeanor, and for the reverend bearing shown by Thee before the tribunal of Pilate, the Judge.

Where Thou, as a most meek lamb, didst stand bound with cords in the presence of Thine accusers; Thine head inclined, Thine eyes cast down to the ground, Thy countenance calm, Thy words few, Thy voice all so low and gentle, ready for reproach and prepared for stripes.

Behold now and consider, O devoted follower of Christ, how thy Lord and Saviour, the King and Judge of all men, suffered Himself to be dragged to judgment, submitting Himself humbly and of His own will to the powers of this world.

In this He has set before thee an example of most wholesome submission; that thou also, who art truly blameworthy for many faults, mayest learn to accuse thyself before God, and to show a fitting humility, when thou art charged with sin by thy fellows.

If thou desirest to escape the pains of hell, submit thyself humbly to the judgment of those set over thee, nor dare to resist the power ordained of God.

And, for the love of Jesus, when judged wrongfully endure it patiently, even though some heavy sentence be pronounced against thee.

Let not the wondrous patience of God, amidst so many false charges brought against Him, pass away unprofitably from thy heart.

Therefore, fall prostrate at the feet of Jesus, fast holden by bonds; plead with Him for pardon and grace, pray Him to forgive all thy negligences; that, in this thy day of mercy, He will correct thy excesses; rather than after a season condemn thee with reprobates for ever.

Be merciful, O good Jesus, be merciful to me, a sinner, for my " soul trusteth in Thee."

Breathe into me a good spirit, which may urge me to a more earnest progress; that I may heartily strive to humbly obey and submit myself to those who are over me in the Lord, and receive with patience their every order.

Grant that I may not fear man's judgment, and never be angry when accusations are brought against me. Rather let me desire to be exercised, accused, and disciplined, that the fear of presumption may be utterly trodden down, and my own will brought to nought. Thus, out of my self-abasement, may love of Thee every moment increase, and be forcibly drawn higher and higher heavenward.

CHAPTER XII

ON THE DERISION OF JESUS BY HEROD AND HIS SOLDIERS

I BLESS and thank Thee, O Lord Jesu Christ, Eternal Wisdom of the Father, Thou who art the Supreme Truth and the Infinite Power of God, for that shameful contempt and bitter mockery endured by Thee, when Thou wast despised and derided by Herod and his soldiers.

For, indeed, Herod had for a long time desired to see Thee, and, moved by curiosity, had hoped to behold some miracle done by Thee. But, when Thou madest no reply, nor wouldest without fitting cause work a miracle (surely it was the hour of suffering, not of miracle-working); then in his rage he ceased from all due reverence. Regarding Thee as simple, he haughtily despised Thee; and arraying Thee in a white robe, he mocked Thee and sent Thee back to Pilate.

I praise and honor Thee, O glorious Jesus, for these Thy wearying labors and cruel hurryings; when, with derisive clamor, Thou wast led to and fro through the lanes and streets of

Jerusalem, from place to place, from Judge to Judge, everywhere sorely accused, everywhere defamed; and, after much questioning and a long trial, wast demanded for death by crucifixion.

O what marvellous patience, at this special period, shone forth in Thee, and ceased not though tried by many mockings! The thought of this public contempt of Thee carries deep compunction to the hard heart, invites the angry to gentleness, and the devout soul to sorrow.

Behold Thou, the Most High God, art brought low as the meanest of Thy creatures. Thou, the Almighty One, art thrust aside as most helpless. Thou, the Allwise, art mocked as the most foolish. Thou, the most Innocent, art judged as one guilty of deadly sin.

Woe unto me, a miserable sinner! weighed down under a heavy burden of sin; who, according to the merit of my own doings, deserves eternal punishment; on whose behalf Thou, O gracious, holy, and just God, didst not disdain to be mocked and despised, that Thou mightest deliver me in my distress from the derision of devils, and from everlasting death.

I beseech Thee, therefore, O Jesus Almighty, whom no harshness could embitter, no contempt cast down, that Thou wouldest cut off from me everything outwardly vain and curious, and that I may learn to be content with lowly attire.

For disgraceful is it, that earth and ashes should seek show or delicacy in dress, when Thou, the King of Heaven, wast an object of contempt, arrayed in a white garment.

Set before the eyes of my mind Thy disgrace and derision, and teach me to follow Thee along the way of Thy reproach, yea, to rejoice when I am despised; never to put my trust in the sons of men, nor in the princes of this world, nor in the power of friends; but with my whole heart to despise all earthly things, and the lovers thereof.

Lead me with unshaken constancy to follow Thee, Lord Jesus, Author of my salvation; and to bear ever in memory the great and bitter taunts Thou didst endure for me, Thine unworthy servant.

CHAPTER XIII

OF THE WICKED CLAMOR OF THE JEWS, "CRUCIFY HIM! CRUCIFY HIM!"

I BLESS and give Thee thanks, O Lord Jesu Christ, Thou perpetual joy of the Saints, for the great and insolent tumult of the Jews in their rage against Thee, furiously crying out,

"Away with Him! away with Him! Crucify
Him! crucify Him!"

Alas, how violent the fierceness of the
wretched Jews! How inhuman the cruelty of
the Chief Priests and Pharisees! whom no fear
could keep from murdering Thee, no reason
hold back from shedding innocent blood!

The heathen Judge is moved to some compassion, but the Jews are hardened to fiercer
malignity. Pilate strives to excuse Thee, he
seeks some device for setting Thee free, he declares that he has found no cause of death in
Thee.

But the Jews, forgetting all their benefits,
oppose him with the reply, "If thou lettest this
man go, thou art not Cæsar's friend; for every
one who maketh himself a king, setteth himself
up against Cæsar."

Alas, how falsely do they invent these things
against Thy humility! For neither by word
nor deed hadst Thou sought worldly honors.
So far from that, when the multitude, who, by
a very signal miracle, had been fed with a few
loaves and fishes, determined to make Thee a
King, at once Thou didst retire to the solitude
of a mountain, there abiding alone in secret
prayer.

Nor were such evil doings enough; others
and worse were added thereto, that the Judge

might be moved to kill the God-man Christ:—
"We have a law (they cried), and by our law
He ought to die, because He made Himself the
Son of God."

The Governor hearing these things is afraid.
He inquires, "Whence art Thou?" and asks,
"What is truth?" No answer is given him,
because the Jews with wild importunity demand
sentence of death.

At length, yielding to their great wickedness,
and to preserve the favor of their leaders, the
base Ruler assents to their unholy cry.

O how bitter and offensive was it that the
words of malediction, "Crucify Him! Crucify
Him!"—the blessed Jesus—should be proclaimed throughout all Jerusalem!

Which of His lovers did not then grieve and
weep, who, perchance, heard the curses and
cries for crucifixion again and again uttered
against his most loving Lord Jesus?

O how mournful the voice, how most sad the
rumor that filled the ears of the most saintly
Virgin Mother; when the cruel sentence of the
people, and the tumultuous demand for the
Cross, were borne aloft from the mouths of the
multitude!

Moan, O devout servant of Jesus, and, from
the inmost recesses of thy breast, draw forth
the heavy groans of compunction.

Learn with what pangs the heart of the Mother of God is troubled, when her Blessed Son is called for, to hang on the hateful Cross.

He, who ever hears angelic songs sounding through the courts of heaven, "Holy, Holy, Holy," now hears Jews with their accursed tongues thundering out against Him in clamoring accents, "Away with Him! Away with Him! Crucify Him!"

Him, whom but a little before at the Feast of Palms children praised, singing glad songs of joy; now (how changed the scene!) their very parents with savage mind, call for His crucifixion, saying, "Not this man, but Barabbas."

Meditate seriously on this hour, thou lover of thy Lord's Passion. Against the worst rumors of the world close firmly the ears of thy heart; but open thine hearing widely to the dismal shouting for the crucifixion of Jesus.

Faithful soul, I say unto thee, that it will be more profitable thus to meditate, than to study the stars of heaven. If thou truly lovest Jesus, thou wilt not pass through this period without a heavy sigh of bitterness.

When, therefore, the world is against thee and assails thee with many unjust reproaches, be not broken in spirit by evil words, nor by the threatening of adversaries; but bear well in mind the most patient Jesus, and the revilings He endured for thee; and, with a deaf ear, suffer all foolish reports to pass by thee unheeded.

When also thy good works are accounted as evil, and the more part oppose themselves to thy witness for Christ, and are unwilling to take thy word, bear with it all meekly; because thou art not more innocent than Christ, against whom they insultingly cried, "Crucify Him! Crucify Him!"

Know, therefore, this beforehand; since in thy walk heavenward thou wilt have to suffer contradictions not a few, yet wilt thou have no praise whatever of God, unless, for His sake, thou shalt be tried in thy various movements in life.

Wherefore He hath said to His beloved friends, "Blessed are ye, when men shall hate you, and revile you, for the Son of Man's sake."

Follow then the innocent Jesus, rejected indeed on earth by wicked men, but chosen of God the Father, and crowned in heaven with glory and honor. Let not evil speaking, which is but for a moment, overcome thee, for whom "an eternal weight of glory" is prepared by God.

I now, therefore, beseech Thy boundless love, O gentle Lord Jesu Christ, that Thou wouldest inflame my heart with the grace of a large sympathy; and cause it to burn with so glowing a fire of Thy love, that I may rejoice to bear with a peaceful mind all revilings and wrongful charges; and never fear the terrors and annoyances of men; but desire with my whole heart to imitate Thee in the reproach of the Cross.

Arm me against the temptations of the flesh, and grant me with due discipline to crucify its evil affections; to bewail with tears of penitence the faults already committed by me; and never to yield deliberate consent to any evil assault against me.

Finally, in every spiritual conflict and distress of heart, by the power of Thy life-giving Cross, succor and defend me from the wiles of the enemy.

That which was prepared for Thy reproach, may it become my remedy; that even I, by the victory of Thy holy Cross, may devoutly bring back to Thee the grateful sacrifice of praise. Amen.

CHAPTER XIV

ON THE STRIPPING AND SCOURGING OF JESUS

I BLESS and give Thee thanks, O Lord Jesu Christ, Thou most gracious Protector of all who hope in Thee, for the shameful stripping of Thee in the presence of Thy deriders; when, at the cruel mandate of the impious Judge, the soldiers of the court spoiled Thee of Thy clothing, and presented Thee naked to be bound with hard cords, and scourged with the sharpest rods, as if a wicked corrupter and the vilest transgressor of the law.

And all this to gratify, forsooth, the angry minds of the Priests, who sought to devour Thy life, and bring Thee down with sorrow to the grave.

I extol and honor Thee with suppliant praise, especially for being fast bound to the hard pillar; that Thou mightest loose us from the bonds of our sins, and restore us to never-ending liberty in things celestial.

I praise and glorify Thee with continual thanks for Thy barbarous scourging, and for every hard blow and acute piercing of Thy most sacred and tender Body; whilst these cruel scourgers pitilessly struck, and deeply tore Thy spotless flesh, stripe after stripe; inflicting on every side bruise upon bruise; so that there was no sound part in Thee!

Innumerable fountains of Thy precious Blood, like unto crimson streams, poured forth abundantly at every stroke. And this, that Thou mightest wash us from the inveterate pollutions of our sins, and cleanse our souls from all their guilt by Thy most precious Blood.

Alas! alas! O Lord, how great the madness of these base Jews! What hearts of stone had the smiters, who feared not, unprovoked, to scourge Thee, the fairest of men. Yea, they stood as giants against Thee, and spared Thee not.

O Thou holy Elect Child, the Child of my Lord, why didst Thou have pity on me, worthy as I am of so much bitterness? Verily, I am nothing. I, even I, a man of perdition, was the cause of all this Thy sorrow and confusion. The greatness of my sins was woe to Thee. To remove them, it was necessary for the Son of God to suffer bitter torments indeed.

Therefore, O devout soul, redeemed by the purple Blood of Christ, and with the affection of His great compassion, have well in memory the scourging of thy Lord, and return to Him the obedience of a devoted gratitude.

O superlatively sweet Jesus, who for me, the basest of sinners, wast cruelly beaten, grant me with rent heart to gaze on the wale of each stroke; and from my inmost soul, with tender love, devoutly and passionately to kiss the same. From whence I feel the savor of life to flow to me, and the soothing balm of eternal salvation.

Inflame me with the ardor of Thy unmeasurable charity, whereby Thou hast proved Thy love for me; when, for Thy condemned servant, Thou didst vouchsafe most patiently to endure so many stripes.

Help my infirmity by Thy grace in the hour of heavy tribulation; lest, when severely oppressed by disquiet, I be cast down or greatly disturbed in mind.   Full well remembering Thy unjust scourging, may I be found submissive under every trial.

Make me a partaker of Thy sufferings, and move me to amendment of life by the discipline of sons; that, being in all lowliness chastened, I may, here on earth, the more acceptably serve Thee; and, when this life is over, triumph with Thee in greater glory; where the Saints, having all fear of evil removed, rejoice in the eternal victory of patience.

CHAPTER XV

ON THE STRIPPING, MOCKING, CROWNING, AND SMITING OF THE HEAD OF JESUS.

I BLESS and give Thee thanks, O Lord Jesu Christ, illustrious King of Saints and radiant Crown of eternal glory, for the many unheard-of scoffs and vexations, with which Thou wast at length exercised by base torturers, when brought by cruel soldiers into the Judgment-hall.

Where, the whole band being assembled, Thou wast shamefully stripped of Thine own garments; and, in place thereof, wast contemptuously clad in a purple robe, that Thou mightest clothe us, who are devoid of all virtue, with the cloak of Thy righteousness, and adorn us with the sweetness of Thy nature.

I praise and glorify Thee with the special devotion of my sympathizing heart, for Thy most grievous punishment—the crown of thorns —which, for us poor worms, Thou didst patiently bear on Thy sacred head.

For then Thy blessed head, sanctified above all Nazarites, was so crowded with thorns, and so sharply pierced, even to the tenderest parts thereof; that large streams of blood flowed on all sides about Thy neck, Thine ears, Thine eyes, and Thy cheeks; rendering that sweet face of Thine, on which the spitting of the Jews was yet scarcely dry, all bloody and disfigured.

O spectacle most sad, to behold the Son of God, in Whom no sin could be found, thus crowned with reproach and cruelty!

O most bitter rage of the soldiers, who shuddered not to pierce with so many thorns, so holy, so beautiful, so noble, and so venerable a head; but even dared to salute in derision, strike, and publicly mock the very King of Angels!

O most gentle Jesus, Thou King most loving, Crown of confessors, strength of warriors, the joy of potentates, the example of all Thy followers, how vilely art Thou treated in my behalf; how fiercely art Thou tortured; with how many worryings art Thou filled from without; with what unutterable sufferings art Thou overwhelmed from within! That Thou mightest snatch me from eternal confusion and the torments of hell, take out from my heart the thorns of vice, and crown me in the heavens with unceasing honor and glory.

I praise and glorify Thee for that derisive greeting, that false adoration shown Thee, when the ministers of cruelty, with bended knees, violently struck Thee. Scoffingly worshipping they scornfully called Thee a king, exclaiming with an impious shout, "Hail, King of the Jews!"

Alas, O mortal man, servant of sin, consider how great the anguish and contempt, to which the Only-Begotten Son of the Father is subjected for thee.

Open the ears of thy mind, and, at Pilate's cruel cry, "Behold the Man!" melt into holy sighs and tears. If there be in thee, therefore, any bowels of compassion, groan and weep in sympathy with the Creator of the universe.

I praise and bless Thee, O most noble Jesus, for that scornful mockery, when, to increase Thy confusion, in Thy right hand was placed a reed for a royal sceptre; as if Thou hadst been the rash usurper of kingly dignity.

I praise and exalt Thee for the severe blows on Thy sacred head, already wounded, received from merciless men and brutal torturers; blows repeatedly delivered from the loftily raised reed-staff. Foully also did they spit on Thee, and thrust out their venomous tongues at Thee.

Come forth now, ye daughters of Jerusalem, and behold King Solomon with the crown, with which His Mother (the Synagogue of the Jews) crowned Him on the day of His Passion.

Consider how great is He that goeth forth. With what deep affliction and reproach is He led out, at the command of Pilate, that to all may be made manifest His most piteous appearance. In good truth, sad is it to behold these things, very grievous are they to think on; devout love calls aloud for our compassion.

Behold the patient and meek Jesus goes forth from the Judgment-hall, wearing on His head the crown of thorns, and arrayed in a purple robe. Perchance the fury of a treacherous people might be a little moved to pity, seeing the Christ so terribly dishonored and afflicted.

But alas! alas! the malicious crowd rage the

more violently, and to the Governor's public
cry, "Behold the Man," exclaim with increased
fierceness, "Away with Him!   Away with Him!
Crucify Him!"

Hearing all this, and, with the words deep
in thy heart, tremble and wax pale, thou faithful lover of Jesus, at the vastness of His sorrow.

Beat thy breast, pour out thy tears, prostrate
thyself before the crowned Jesus, bearing the
outward appearance of a king, yet filled with
the confusion of the most despicable slave.

Who submitted Himself to the miseries of
these awful punishments, that He might restrain
in thee all yearning for worldly glory, and subdue in thee the plague of pride.

O man, formed of the dust of the ground, be
thou ashamed to follow the glory of the world,
when thou seest the noble head of thy Lord so
dishonored.

Far be it from thee, that, under a thorn-
crowned head, there be found an effeminate
member; seeing that He, of the highest majesty, bows Himself down to a state hard and
lowly indeed.

Be thou unwilling to seek the paths of an
easy life; take to thyself rather the fervor of a
severe discipline.

Be confounded, all ye sons of pride, who pant

after higher things; who raise aloft your heads that ye may seem more worthy. Alas! it is thus ye become only the more degraded.

Blush, in the presence of the scourged and thorn-crowned Jesus, to walk majestic in your splendor, ye who adorn yourselves with silks and precious stones; who array those bodies, that so soon will perish, with chains of gold and silver, your heads in pride all delicately attired; but ye consider not the work of your redemption, with what dire agonies it was accomplished.

Be comforted, be comforted, thou poor ulcer-stricken Lazarus, the despised of the world, whoever thou mayest be; for thou, in thy infirmities and contempt, bearest a closer resemblance to Jesus of Nazareth, than the rich man in his evil way, clothed though he be in purple and fine linen.

And thou, lowly brother, be not ashamed of thy coarse and patched garment; for to thy special glory is it, in the sight of God and His Angels, if, when poor in dress, thou art seen richly clad in holiness.

For, how utterly out of order is it for one, who professes to be a follower of Jesus, to yearn for cloth of fine texture, when to this world he should be dead; and in the use of all earthly things, ever embrace poverty.

The man of God, apart from the world, whose life it is to meditate often with sorrowing heart on the torturing coronation of Jesus, when he himself is afflicted, how true and sweet is his comfort.

As often, therefore, as thou feelest thyself perplexed, call to mind all the thorns borne by Jesus; and thou wilt bear thy trouble more meekly, whether thou hast been greatly annoyed by others, or severely visited by pains in the head; or (which for the most part is the more grievous), when thy good name has been torn by the many thorns of calumny.

Happier far for thee to suffer now with afflicted Jesus, and to bear a crown of thorns with crowned Jesus, by enduring many and varied grievances here on earth; than, having lived to thyself, to suffer hereafter the pains of hell, and (what will try most the lost) to be eternally severed and banished from the most delightful face of the Saviour Jesus, and from the sweet company of all the blessed.

O how joyful and devoid of all fear shall he stand in the presence of the eternal King, at the last and awful Judgment, who now is not ashamed to bear the reproach of his dishonor, and the pains of bodily suffering.

O how acceptable and dear to God is that soul, how fruitful will be found its meditations;

which is inwardly troubled for the sufferings of Jesus, is wounded to the heart for His wounds, and, out of sorrow for His Death, with a loving death dies with Him.

I sorrow over Thee, O good Jesus, patient and meek, so grievously scourged, shamefully mocked, and most cruelly crowned for me. O grant unto me, I pray Thee, the grace of a penetrative compunction, that I may be able to sorrow the more abundantly.

Wherefore, humbly prostrate before Thee, I adore Thy venerable Majesty, in Thy human nature so contemptuously degraded. With devout lips I earnestly plead, that Thou wouldest clearly imprint and ardently stamp upon my heart that miserable expression of Thy countenance; such as Thou wast seen to have in that hour when, as an abhorred leper, Thou wast thrust from among men, and 'mid confusion led forth, crowned with thorns—a spectacle unto the public.

May it enter—may that appearance most sad enter the recesses of my heart, and may I be so effectually pricked in my conscience and tortured, that everything worldly and selfish may perish from mine eyes, and all that is carnal and lustful utterly die away. May all that is bitter and vile become sweet and pleasant. May Thy sufferings subdue in me all evil affections, and Thy heaviest sorrows soften my daily troubles.

May this sacred impression of Thy crowning, seriously and deeply realized, comfort me greatly in adversity, and uphold me against the assaults of inconstant wanderings.

For the mind engaged with heavenly things, and given to contrition, is freed from noxious thoughts, and protected from the assailing darts of the enemy.

Free me, O Lord Jesu, of my every spot of selfishness, clothe me with real virtues, and grant me cheerfulness even when despised; that I may learn to endure calmly, when deprived of the necessaries of life; and never to be indignant should old garments be served me instead of new, or rougher dress in the place of that which ought to be better.

Let me not murmur against those who mock me, nor contend with those who upbraid me; but, in remembrance of Thy crown of thorns, may I, for my salvation's sake, calmly accept whatever pain and perplexity may befall me.

Prick at last the hardness of my heart, and with the sharpest thorn on Thy head pierce its very centre; that all in my blood that is hurtful, mingled with the evils of the flesh, may pour forth from the wound; and the great spur of Thy sacred love remain fixed therein, till I be fully purged from the thorns of vice, and the thistles of temptation, and so duly prepared for the seeds of virtue.

Thus may the ground of my heart, infected with the first curse, by the infusion of Thy sacred Blood, receive a new blessing.

And the end will be, that the rose of love will spring up in me, where once was the thorn of envy; the lily of chastity, in place of the nettle of lust; the violet of humility, instead of the briar of vanity; and the flowers of gentleness, where once flourished the brambles of asperity. Amen.

CHAPTER XVI

ON THE UNJUST CONDEMNATION OF JESUS TO THE DEATH OF THE CROSS

I BLESS and give Thee thanks, O Lord Jesu Christ, Author of life and Rule of justice, for Thine unjust condemnation to death, without any offence of Thine; whilst a man unworthy to live, a murderer and a rebel, was suffered to go free.

O judgment most perverse! O exchange most unhappy! For when among the people a mighty tumult was raging, and the Judge could in no way allay the fierceness of the Jews, he sat in judgment and passed the wicked sentence, that Barabbas the robber, who for a capital crime merited death, should be spared; and that Thou, pure from every offence, shouldest be given over to the Cross, there to be punished by a death most ignominious.

Alas! alas! such is the judgment of this world. How terribly is justice set at naught when the wicked have the dominion. Behold how the Righteous perisheth, and there is none to deliver Him.

O grievous indeed! The Man of Truth is made over to deceivers; the unjust scourge the holy; the innocent is given up instead of the guilty; a robber is preferred to Christ, and Barabbas in bonds is set at liberty instead of Jesus of Nazareth.

The lamb is exchanged for the wolf; the Saint for the criminal; the best for the worst; the deadly sinner escapes in the place of the true God. Darkness is preferred to light; vice to virtue; death to life; clay to gold; the shell to the pearl; the infamous to the honorable!

Who, hearing these things, does not sorrow? Who is not incensed against the Jews? Who does not condemn the Judge? Let that Judge wash his hands, let him excuse himself before men, let him say that he acted through fear of

Cæsar; that he was impelled by the importunity of the Jews; still is he in no way free from guilt, for he knew that "for envy they had delivered Him."

Better far would it have been for him to have lost the high place of honor, which is, at the best, but for a little moment, than to have condemned the innocent, whom he knew to be just. More to his profit had he lost the whole world, than to sin against God by murdering the Christ.

O how terrible will be the judgment of the wicked and unbelieving; when, at the last day, God the Judge, now judged unjustly, shall appear in the glory of His Majesty!

Then shall all the truly faithful be glad; who now so bitterly mourn over the cruel condemnation of Jesus Christ their Lord.

Then shall rejoice in safety all, who now bear with patience the trials of the world, the losses they sustain, and the contempt they receive.

O holy and sweet Jesus, Who wast unjustly judged by Pilate, the Governor, and condemned to the shame of the Cross! grant me humbly to undergo whatever sentence may be pronounced against me, never rashly to judge him who is òver me in the Lord, nor assail in anger mine accuser; but rather, following Thy example, may I strive after the like virtue of silence.

May I never deem it hard to be trodden under foot by one higher than I, but commit to Thee the scrutiny of every decree.

For "the servant is not greater than his Lord." If they have sentenced Thee falsely, Who art the Judge of all men and Thou, Who wert entirely guiltless, resistedst not the violence of Thine adversaries; how much more does it behove me, who in so many things do so often offend, to suffer patiently; readily submitting myself when under censure.

Help me, gracious Lord, readily to bear the yoke of subjection and the rod of correction, and in the hour of my every tribulation, let me have Thy sorrows well in remembrance.

CHAPTER XVII

ON JESUS CARRYING THE CROSS, AND BEING LED TO THE PLACE CALLED CALVARY

I BLESS and give Thee thanks, O Lord Jesu Christ, Thou true Vine, Thou Way of Life, and our Salvation, for bearing publicly the very grievous and ignominious Cross, which, for the redemption of the whole human family,

Thou didst condescend to take up and patiently to bear; that Thou mightest, on Thine own shoulders, carry back with Thee to the Courts of heaven, the lost sheep so long sought by Thee, and after so much labor found by Thee.

I praise and honor Thee, renowned Standard-bearer of the Christian Army, for Thy going forth sorrowful and in the midst of confusion; when, with the ponderous Cross of wood, cruelly laid upon Thee, Thou wast ignobly led without the beautiful city, in which Thou hadst before, by many miracles and discourses, so gloriously 'shone forth. But now the furiousness of the multitude is more bitterly raised against Thee, as against some associate of thieves—some leader of robbers, and Thou art declared worthy only to be hanged on the highest Cross, in the midst of the basest of men.

I praise and glorify Thee, O most excellent Jesus, for this trying and most oppressive march, this strange journeying about, which Thou didst undergo for us; for every step of Thy feet impressed on the earth, for the excessive weariness of Thy body, weakened by previous torturing; for the ascents and descents of a rough road, made so toilsome by the weight of Thy Cross; for the hurried driving and base dragging of Thee by Thine unfeeling attendants.

By them Thou wast ordered to advance, roughly wast Thou thrust forward, cruelly goaded on from behind, violently dragged on before; ofttimes hither and thither most cruelly worried. Thou didst make Thy way of sorrow, greatly pressed down and bent, compelled as Thou wast to bear an intolerable burden to the heights of Calvary.

Alas! alas! never hadst Thou such a journey —never so rugged a track—never didst Thou bear so painful a yoke.

I praise and highly exalt Thee for being utterly set at naught by the vilest of men, who led, dragged, and insulted Thee; for the many foul utterings they hurled at Thee; for the reproachful scandals against Thine innocence, falsely put forth by the way; for the insolent exultation of Thine adversaries, gloating over Thy cruel Death and shameful Crucifixion.

Amidst such miseries enclosing Thee on every side, Thou wentest forth like a meek lamb that is led to the slaughter; bent on man's salvation, pitying the blindness of the Jews, and deeply sighing over the malice of those in charge of Thee.

I praise and bless Thee for the heart's tender love shown towards Thee, for the plenteous tears of compassion poured forth by Thy friends, and for the devout attendance of the pitying women, who bitterly bewailed Thee. Modestly, with downcast looks, they followed Thee step by step for a season.

Turning to them with a gracious exhortation, Thou didst calm their mournful sobbing, thus saying: "Daughters of Jerusalem, weep not for me, but weep for your children. For if they do these things in a green tree, what shall be done in the dry?"

O how great was then the grief of all Thy dear ones! how especially great the lamentations of the holy women, looking after Thee with the deepest feeling of compassion, utterly unable to approach Thee—helpless to deliver Thee from death!

But, O, how inconceivable the grief which seized and agitated the inmost soul of Mary, Thy Mother; when she beheld her only, her dearly-loved Son bearing on His back the shame of the Cross, and hurried away to death!

O how readily would Thy Blessed Mother, the loving Mary, have borne for Thee the grievous scandal of the Cross; and, if it could have been permitted, how gladly would she have died in Thy stead, had she deemed it acceptable to Thee!

But that which in her earthly body she was neither able nor permitted to bear, she bore most completely in the depths of her soul. For she, who has loved most fervently, suffers most fully, is afflicted more severely, yea, and with Thee more truly bears the Cross.

For into the heart of no other did Thy unsearchable sorrow so penetrate, as into the loving soul of Thy dearly beloved Mother, Virgin of the purest charity.

Nor is it to be doubted that Mary Magdalene, Thy most fervent lover, now almost worn out by much and bitter weeping, would, impelled by affection, have in her turn with Thy Virgin Mother most readily seized Thy Cross, and have borne it in Thy stead.

And hence Thine inward grief was increased by various means, apart from that which oppressed Thee from without, viz., for the dispersion of Thy disciples, and the sorrow of Thy Mother; for the grave offence of many, and the distrust of those who despaired of Thy Resurrection. For, with the sole exception of the glorious Virgin, the faith of others wavered, or was to all appearance extinct.

O religious disciple of Christ, do thou also hasten to become a bearer of the mystical Cross; strive to follow the footsteps of Thy Redeemer, if thou wouldest secure joys eternal.

Dread not the short labor of penitence, nor desire the rigor of discipline to be relaxed; but consider little and light whatever the rule of the Church enjoins. Joyfully carry out whatever holy obedience demands.

If thou deemest it difficult to obey every direction, remember, that for thee Christ became obedient to more grievous commands, even to death on the most shameful Cross.

Keep, therefore, the strict rule of the early Church. Forsake not a path that leads to a kingdom. Avoid the softer track, which is wont to entice the idle to destruction.

Thou didst indeed take up thy Cross, when thou didst openly declare on the side of Christ. Thou didst take it up in good truth, when thou didst go apart from the world to devote thyself to Jesus.

In religion, to live nobly and righteously, is to imitate the Crucified One. Gladly dost thou bear thy Cross, if in thy station thou makest progress fervently.

If thou bearest it unwillingly and with murmuring, thou shalt not have glory with Jesus; thy punishment will be that of the godless robber. But if thou bearest all things readily and cheerfully; then, in a great degree, thou hast vanquished the evil one.

Fear not therefore the strictness of thy discipline, nor reckon on a life of many days. The love of Christ and the sweetness of a holy life will lighten the burden of thy labors.

For thou hast a Forerunner Who bore a harder life, a Leader providing the noblest example—Jesus the Son of God, the great Patron of the Cross, who in Himself has well proved the weight thereof.

Follow therefore the Saviour by the way of the Cross; never putting aside religion—never relaxing the purpose of a zealous disciple. Thus do and thou shalt be safe for ever.

For hadst thou wished to enjoy the delights of the world, or to occupy thyself with thine own business or pleasures, thou couldest certainly have remained in the full fling of this life. But now, having declared for Christ by entering on a life of holiness, hold firmly to the faith thou hast professed.

Pray Jesus with power to uphold thee; for He, who formerly moved thee to begin well, will also enable thee to bring thy work to a happy completion.

O most beloved Jesus, the Prince of the Kings of the earth, the Ruler of Angels, the glorious Standard-Bearer of all Christians, who, for the salvation and example of Thy servants, didst carry Thy Cross on Thine own shoulders, before the face of scoffing Jews; grant that I may follow Thee in this procession, albeit too slowly.

Forsake me not before the hour appointed for mine end, but lead my wandering soul from the body of sin to Calvary—the mount of myrrh and frankincense; where Thou didst suffer Crucifixion and Death for me; that there with Thee I may rest beneath the Cross, and thereby be protected.

Grant me earnestly to begin and carry on a new fervor, and not to follow the fickleness of the lukewarm; but with the eyes of my heart to gaze steadily on Thy Cross-bearing image, and so to escape the ever-changing curiosity of the unstable.

Be Thou a leader in the narrow way and companion in my progress, an upholder in my successes, a Comforter in adversity, and a fellow-laborer in all my efforts for the honor of Thy Name.

Help me to bear the burden and heat of the day, that I may be able to follow Christian discipline at all times, and in all holy observances.

Grant me also, in my greatest troubles and anxieties, to remember Thy oppressive weariness under the weight of the Cross; for the little I bear is scarcely worthy to be named, when I consider the trying weight of the Cross that was laid on Thee.

May I, therefore, willingly and cheerfully bear the burden of religion assumed and undertaken of my own free will; ever relying on Thy loving aid. Because, though for a short period, Thou permittedst me to be at seasons heavy laden, to increase in me the grace of humility; still dost Thou, in a fitting time and manner, succor me in Thy great mercy.

Teach me to keep down my own will, to be contented with little, and never be given to wandering. Let my hands be employed in godly labor, and my heart in meditating on Thy Holy Scriptures.

May all my members serve Thee, all my senses be under strict discipline; and, notwithstanding my many shortcomings, vouchsafe to number me among the true bearers of the Cross. Put far away from me all hurtful knowledge of worldly matters, and cleanse me from all that is impure.

May I have no pleasure in mere outward things, nor idly engage myself in foolish converse. Rather may my study be to learn my inner heart, and give myself to secret sorrowing; sending forth sighings many for my manifold negligences and excesses. May I cast from me all that hinders my progress in virtue.

May I follow the way of Thy contemplators, who know how to soar above all heights with minds calm and subdued. May I constantly have in memory Thy Cross so lovingly borne for me, and with a like step may I be moved to the love thereof, and so daily with meet obedience resign myself to Thy will.

Yes, may I bear the burden laid upon me, and never wantonly resist it, until I shall attain the place of longed for safety and peace.

CHAPTER XVIII

ON THE CRUCIFIXION OF JESUS, AND ON HIS HANGING HIGH AND LONG ON THE CROSS

I BLESS and give Thee thanks, O Lord Jesu Christ, Thou most benign Creator of man and Restorer of his corrupt nature, for the shameful denuding Thee before the Cross; where, in the sight of the whole multitude of spectators, and in the face of robbers roaring for their prey, Thou wast publicly stripped and ignominiously unclothed.

With all Thy garments cruelly torn from Thee and given for booty, there Thou stoodest blushing and trembling, girt only with a thin linen cloth, crowned with a wreath of thorns for a diadem; a reproach to all—an outcast mocked. In a word, nothing of worldly goods hadst Thou, but, like an exile and poor pilgrim, yea, the poorest of the poor, Thou wast destitute of everything, void of every human comfort.

For as the first Adam, when placed in Paradise, walked, before his fall, in naked liberty; so didst Thou in like manner ascend the Cross naked, to regain the lost home of peace, from which he for his sin was cast out and driven far, far away.

In order that man's innocency might be restored him, and he be clad in the garment of righteousness, and so made meet for Life eternal, Thou didst suffer Thy clothing to be taken from Thee, and Thyself to be filled with sorrows and perplexities—yea, at last, Thou didst pay the penalty of a most bitter death.

I praise and honor Thee, Thou most ardent lover of our salvation, for being rigidly stretched on the hard wood of the Cross, so roughly placed under Thee for Thy reception; for the sharp piercing of Thy hands and feet, and the driving in of the thick nails; the sound of which could be heard far and wide, and so move to tears the hard hearts of the spectators.

Alas! alas! so firmly wast Thou fastened to the Cross, that Thy veins suddenly bursting, broad streams of Thy precious Blood flowed forth from Thy hands and Thy feet.

So rigorously also wast Thou extended, that all Thy joints were loosened, and all Thy bones could be distinctly numbered.

And Thou didst allow Thy hands and Thy

feet to be thus pierced by the ungodly; so that, having Thy sacred hands nailed to the Cross, Thou mightest discharge the heavy debt of Adam, who put forth his guilty hands to the forbidden tree; and with Thy innocent Blood mightest wipe out the stain of long-standing guilt.

I praise and glorify Thee for being lifted up on high on the Cross, and for Thy long suspension thereon—on the tree so thoroughly despised; held by the Jews of those days accursed, but now honored by all Christians above all the trees of the forest.

On which, for our salvation, Thou didst hang some three hours or more; working out the great and wondrous mysteries of the Cross, to the whole world about to be so vast a blessing.

For, indeed, Thou wast exalted from the earth that Thou mightest draw up to Thee the loving hearts of the faithful; lest they should dally with earthly pleasures; that Thou mightest soften the loving spirits of the devout into compassion for Thee, and more ardently inflame them by the spectacle of the Cross.

Look up now, O faithful servant of Jesus, and with sad heart and mournful countenance behold thy God and thy Redeemer, hanging between the lofty arms of the Cross.

Lo, thy Beloved is naked, and presents Him-

self to be seen of thee. He stands with fixed
feet, and awaits thy approach. He longs for thy
free access; He spreads forth His most loving
arms; He shows His wide wounds; He bends
His head to kiss thee, ready to receive thee into
His favor, and at once forgive all thy sins.

Come then boldly to the Cross of Jesus, lovingly touch the hanging figure; ardently embrace, firmly hold and most devoutly kiss it.
There prostrate thyself; there lie and cleave
to the holy ground. Withdraw not from the
Cross, that at least thou mayest receive one
drop of the ebbing Blood of Christ; or hear
the words He utters therefrom; or be nigh unto
Him in His last agony.

May the earth, which received the dying
Saviour, in like manner receive thee; and
where Jesus has been buried, there also be thy
resting place. So that, being one with Him in
spirit, there may be also oneness in the burial
of the body.

Pay to Him all due lamentation; enter the
secret chambers of thy heart. Let the Crucified
One find thee a gracious and sorrowing disciple,
grateful, devout, and inwardly His; lovingly
drawn by His wounds, that all the world may be
crucified to Thee, and thou to the world; that
Christ alone be life to thee, and to die to Him
thy greatest gain.

Far be it from thee to glory, save in the Cross of thy Lord Jesus Christ. Far be it from thee to trust in thine own merits, because, on the Cross of Christ alone, depends thy salvation and redemption, and in Him thou shouldest most firmly place thy every hope.

Through Him also is given unto thee remission of sins; from Whom flows the rich stream of merits; with Whom are the rewards of the righteous, every man being recompensed according to his works.

Study, therefore, from the example of Christ Crucified, to cast aside the burden of earthly things; to withdraw thy heart from all that is hurtful to its inward liberty; to remove far from thee all the vain fancies of passion and the cares of the world; and to be exercised in pure and naked truth.

That thou mayest be able openly and simply to imitate the naked Jesus, by despising thyself and all transitory things; to become thyself a powerful and fitting ascender of the Cross; bearing, through the burning love of the suffering Redeemer, the insults and slanders of men.

Learn to rejoice when thou art set at nought and degraded. Grieve that it should happen to thee through the base doings of others; and pray the more, that all may be brought to a better mind.

Esteem thyself worthy of all contempt, and earnestly yearn for the salvation of those that oppose thee.

Put no great confidence in man. Few are faithful in the hour of trial, and firm friends are rare indeed.

Be not astonished thereat, nor let it grieve thee; for Christ was deserted by His friends; and of enemies had He a multitude. He, who was ever doing good, received in return the basest ingratitude.

Trust in thy crucified Guide and thine excellent Governor. Abide with Him on the Cross in the day of tribulation, and thou shalt obtain favor and victory over all that oppress thee.

With humility and devout penitence prepare a place for Him, and open a way for the grace of God; that thou mayest take a comforting delight in the pains and wounds of Jesus; and taste how sweet it is to suffer reproach, and be of no reputation for the sake of His holy Name.

Choose to retire within thyself, to cut off from thee all causes of distraction, to seek comfort in the Cross, to resist sensuality, to beware of that which stands between thee and Christ, not to break out hastily into idle words and deeds, to be silent in matters that concern thee not, and carefully to preserve all inward holiness.

For it ill becomes one, dedicated to the Passion, to be carried into wild laughter; and it is against the life of a follower of Christ, to walk his daily course without a serious bearing.

All these things are learnt in the Passion of the Crucified One, and blessed is he who has founded his daily doings thereon. For he shall advance spiritually far beyond others, his associates; and he shall eat of the fruits of the tree of Life, and rejoice in them for ever.

Look, O most holy Father, on the face of Thy Christ, hanging on the Cross for me. Moved by the glorious merits of Thine Only-begotten Son, pierced through with nails and smeared with purple blood, be merciful unto me, bound as I am with the many chains of my sins.

He was wounded to cleanse me from my sins. He will make satisfaction to Thee for all. For me He will make answer to Thee.

I present Him as my hostage; I choose Him as my advocate; I interpose Him as my mediator; I leave Him as the defender of my cause.

He will make good every loss. He, the blessed and sacred fruit of the Virgin's womb, will make full satisfaction for all offences committed.

Whom Thou, O most merciful Father, wilt hear with wondrous sweetness, and that readily, because of His very great love and singular reverence. And this for my eternal salvation, and that I may have hope and comfort upholding me in this life—and necessary also after death.

O good and holy Jesus, Son of God Elect, Who, at the mandate of Thy Father, didst deign to take the substance of our flesh without spot of sin, and to offer the same on the Altar of the Cross for the redemption of the world; have mercy on me Thy servant, pleading for pardon and grace.

For Thy great goodness' sake, and for the infinite merits of Thy Passion, remit unto me all my sins, recent or of old, whether wilfully or in ignorance committed against Thee.

For Thy merits exceed the wickedness of all men; and greater far is the plenteousness of Thy propitiation, than all my iniquities, however frequently perpetrated.

To Thee, therefore, under the protection of Thy Cross do I fly, putting my confidence in this Thy more abundant mercy; to Thee do I sigh from the very depths of my heart, seeking the perfect remedy of my salvation.

I reverence the standard of Thy holy Cross. I kiss the very path thereof; I implore comfort from Thy Passion.

Hear me in my misery, receive Thy fugitive, heal the contrite of heart, justify the sinner. I will not leave Thee nor depart from Thee, until I am received into Thy favor.

I beseech Thee, Lord Jesus, Thou Crucified One, cleanse my heart from all that is worldly; draw me upwards by Thy arms to the height of the Cross. I will follow Thee whithersoever Thou leadest.

Gladly with Thee am I poor and naked, in the world an exile and unknown; like unto Thee and near to Thee, raised above all that is earthly.

Transfix my flesh with a dread of Thee, lest I yield to lust. Pierce my hands lest I grow listless through idleness. Fasten my feet that I may remain steadfast with firmness of purpose, and bravely for Thee bear sorrows and labors.

Let Thy nails penetrate the very centre of my heart, and crucify me with a salutary wound; that, moved by the deepest contrition, I may be wholly dissolved into tears, and lose myself under the influence of love.

Quicken my grief, increase my devotion; let nothing be sweet to me, nothing firmly fixed in my heart, save Jesus Christ and Him crucified.

CHAPTER XIX.

ON THE WOUNDS OF JESUS, AND THE SHEDDING HIS PRECIOUS BLOOD.

I BLESS and give Thee thanks, O Lord Jesu Christ, author of our salvation, most gracious bestower of pardon, and most patient endurer of human depravity, for all the pains and every stripe and bloody wound bitterly inflicted on Thy most noble and tender Body—so that, from the sole of the foot to the crown of the head, there was no place free from pains and blows; everywhere a swelling lash, or a doleful wound, or warm purple blood flowing over Thy whole Body.

I laud and give Thee glory with my most devout and entire veneration, and with my inward mind prostrate before Thee, for that abundant effusion of Thy most precious Blood from Thy five sacred wounds, and from all the seams greater and lesser bleeding and dropping a life-giving stream; more precious than any balsam, for the effectual curing of our sins.

Ah! most meek Jesus, how terribly wast Thou racked and pierced by the cruel ministers of death—yea, to such a degree, that all Thy bodily strength exhausted—Thy very veins widely opened—not one small drop of blood remained within Thee. Whatever of the sacred stream Thou, living or dying, hadst hidden within, all went forth for the merciful benefit of our souls—the price of our salvation.

O the five precious wounds! special pledges of perfect love, full of heavenly sweetness; whence the sinner takes good courage, and so, though his conscience accuses him, he despairs not.

In these are the medicine of life, abundance of grace, fulness of pardon, boundless mercy, the gate of promised glory.

Whatever blemish I contract, whatever sins of the flesh I commit, in these five fountains I wash myself clean; I purify myself, and before God stand faultless.

I praise and honor Thee, O Christ, Thou only and beloved Bridegroom of Thy Holy Church, for Thine inestimable love, through which Thou didst vouchsafe to redeem my soul in the Blood of Thy Testament from the bond of original transgression, to cleanse it from all sin, to enrich and adorn it with the merits of Thy righteousness; that it might worthily be joined and united to Thee, made holy now through grace, and hereafter, in Thy bright kingdom, be with glory blessed.

Here observe diligently, O faithful soul, behold with how great and noble a price He has redeemed thee, Who of His own free goodness created thee after His own image and similitude!

For thou, who, of thine own perverse will, hast wickedly cast thyself away, wast not redeemed from the guilt of disobedience and the commission of many offences with corruptible things—silver and gold; but with the precious Blood of Jesus Christ, the Lamb Immaculate.

Who not only on the Cross poured out His Blood for thy cleansing, but has also in the Cup left the same for thee to drink; to receive it with faithful devotion in the Communion of the Sacrament; whereby the daily sins of the penitent are thoroughly cleansed and blotted out.

Alas! of how great punishment will he be thought worthy, who shall count the Blood of the Covenant of the Son of God an unholy thing, and shall not pay due thanks for the wounds of Christ Crucified.

Study then to show thy thankfulness to such a lover, to so bountiful a benefactor; if it only be by a short prayer, or a devout meditation, at some moment of the day, or in the night season.

Many of the faithful, inflamed by the fire of

His love, have with a holy eagerness shed their blood for Him.

More also, for the Cup of His Blood, have humbly offered the waters of a bitter contrition; by a fellowship with His sufferings through the trying paths of penitence.

Learn thou, also, from such examples to crucify thy flesh with the affections and lusts thereof, manfully to resist temptations, and to carry even unto death the yoke of a willing obedience; and if not called to a martyrdom of blood, to offer up on the altar of thine heart to Christ, the Redeemer, the sacrifice of a contrite spirit; to have well in mind the benefits that spring from the Cross; and in the deep wounds of Jesus, as in the clefts of a rock, to seek a place of refuge from the enemy and the avenger.

Succor me, O most gracious Jesus, in every necessity and hardship of the struggle. Stretch forth Thine hands over me, and with Thy right hand ever protect me.

Grant me devotion in my heart, truth in my mouth, virtue in my deeds. Purge me from all corruption and vice; heal my wounds by Thy precious Blood.

Let nothing impure remain in me; nothing defiled, nothing that can pollute; but may Thy sacred Blood, so abundantly shed, cleanse me from all that is hurtful, and sanctify me wholly;

that, at the coming of the last Judgment, my whole spirit and soul, for whose deliverance Thou didst endure so many grievous punishments, and expend the wealth of an inexhaustible treasury, may be presented unto Thee, my Creator, pure and holy.

CHAPTER XX

ON THE TENDER PLEADING OF JESUS FOR HIS ENEMIES.

I BLESS and give Thee thanks, O Lord Jesu Christ, Thou fountain of piety and sweetness, for Thy most perfect love and most devout supplication for Thine enemies, and for those who crucified Thee. With hands stretched out on the Cross, Thou didst earnestly plead for them, securing their pardon and tenderly excusing their transgressions, thus saying, "Father, forgive them, for they know not what they do."

O utterance full of tenderness and grace, fitted well to soften the hard heart of every sinner, and to bring him to repentance!

O most gentle Jesus, how willing art Thou to forgive, how ready to be appeased, how abundant in mercy!

How plenteous is Thy gentleness, O Lord, to all that love Thee! Thou, who didst show Thyself so gracious to Thy furious enemies. For, when hanging on the lofty Cross, Thou wast not moved with indignation against them that crucified Thee, to avenge Thyself of Thy tormentors.

Neither didst Thou pray that the earth might swallow up those workers of malice; or that fire, coming down from heaven, might consume the wicked doers; but didst shed over Thy most cruel enemies, as a refreshing dew, the sweetest words of love, "Father, forgive them."

In this appeared Thy super-eminent charity, together with Thine ineffable meekness; which could neither be subdued, nor cease from suppliant prayer.

They cried out, "Crucify! Crucify!" Thou, in response, sayest, "Father, forgive." They drive in the rough nails, and Thou excusest their infamous excesses, saying, "They know not what they do." How marvellous is Thy goodness, O Christ!

But, alas! for the frowardness of the obstinate people, who are not moved to compunction by words so full of compassion. Therefore didst Thou grieve more for their blind iniquity than for any injury done to Thee—the commission of such great wickedness pained Thee more than all the torture proceeding from the many wounds inflicted on Thee.

They did all the evil in their power. Thou, in return, didst render them all possible good. Therefore, was it most loving and generous of Thee to plead for men so vile; that they might be converted from impious ways, and confess that Thou, the very Son of God, wast come in the flesh.

And thus are fulfilled the memorable words of Isaiah, which he, as Prophet, most truly foretells of Thee: "And He bare the sins of many, and made intercession for the transgressors," that they should not perish.

Who now shall despair of pardon, seeing that they, who crucified the very Prince of pardon, found so great compassion?

Do not thou then, my soul, despair, though guilty of many offences. Although entangled in various passions and assailed with temptations, thou hast still, O wretched one, a hope of life. The bowels of mercy are open, and the Cross, the nails, the spear, and all the blood-stained wounds of Jesus, are witnesses thereto.

Enter, enter, the deep punctures of the Crucified Redeemer; kiss the marks of His stripes; lay hold of the tree of life with devoted arms; hold fast the most certain pledge of thy salvation—Jesus hanging on the Cross.

Adore Him with a devout mind, commit thyself to Him in all faith, to Him resign thyself wholly. For He, who was so gracious unto His adversaries, will be more favorable far to thee, weeping over thine iniquities.

Still, if thou wouldest be readily heard; if thou desirest to find favor in the sight of thy Redeemer, and to receive the fulness of His mercy; do thou also, with thy whole heart, freely forgive thy brother his trespasses.

Forgive him in his few things, that God may pardon thee in many; and pray for his salvation as earnestly as for thine own. So doing, thou shalt find favor; by imitating Jesus thou shalt become a son indeed of the Most High; for His command is, "Love thine enemies, pray for them that persecute thee."

Moreover, if, when suffering unjustly, thou learnest to forgive all injuries, and pourest forth an earnest prayer for thy debtors, then layest thou up for thyself great boldness in the day of thy departure.

This holy pleading for enemies has beatified the Apostles in glory, consecrated Martyrs, ennobled Confessors, adorned Virgins, made all the Saints conformable to Christ, rendering them meet for life eternal.

I pray Thee, most gracious Lord Jesus, who didst condescend, out of Thy tender compassion,

to plead for Thine enemies; that Thou wouldest, with like fervent love, entreat the Father
for me also; that He would vouchsafe me full
pardon of all my sins, and graciously absolve
me from the punishments in which they so
justly involve me.

Grant me a good and sure confidence in Thy
clemency, not to fall into despair on account of
the magnitude of mine offences; but in full faith
to remember, that Thou camest into this world
to save sinners—that it was Thy will to suffer,
to be crucified, to die for the ungodly.

May, therefore, Thy devout supplication,
poured forth on the Cross for Thine enemies,
avail to the salvation of my soul; and through
it grant me a lively hope of pardon, that what,
by my own merits I can by no means acquire,
I may be counted worthy to obtain, through
Thy most holy intercession.

Give me grace boldly and safely to take refuge under the shadow of Thy wings, and, by
the invincible standard of the holy Cross, keep
me, I pray Thee, from all fear of the old enemy.

Spread out widely over me, I beseech Thee,
the branches of Thine arms; that, fleeing to
Thy Cross, my poor sorrowful soul, whenever
summoned from this world, may neither fear
nor despair.

And do Thou, O tender and compassionate

Lord Jesus, receive me, a miserable sinner, calling to Thee; trusting nothing to my own doings, but to Thy exceeding great mercy.

CHAPTER XXI

ON THE STRIPPING OFF AND DIVIDING THE GARMENTS OF JESUS.

I BLESS and give Thee thanks, O Lord Jesu Christ, Creator of all things, and Giver of all good, for the violent plundering and insulting division of Thy garments; when, immediately after the cruel fastening to the Cross, Thou wast roughly robbed of Thy clothing; and even so reduced to the last farthing and disinherited, that Thou couldest not retain even a remnant to cover Thee.

Nor couldest Thou discern that a little linen was left Thee; in which Thou couldest, when dead, be swathed and decently buried.

For, if Thou wert not to be buried naked, it was necessary that fine linen should be bought at the charges of others, and out of charity presented to Thee, as to one poor and destitute.

O the too greedy coveting of the soldiers— soldiers, no, rather say an ignoble rabble!

O the shameless rapacity of the base guards!

who blushed not with sacrilegious greed to tear off the scanty property of Jesus; gratifying their insatiable avarice, by taking as booty the humble attire of the Crucified One.

For, dividing the garments among them into four parts, they assigned his share to each soldier—the seamless coat alone remaining untorn. For it they cast lots, because to cut it up would be to destroy its texture.

Alas, most wretched plunderers and cruel exactors, who had no pity on Jesus hanging on the Cross, poor and naked: they neither returned Him some small remnant, nor indeed did they leave the hem of His garment, as a comforting memorial to His sorrowing Mother.

No, none of these things did they, for, moved by the devil, and fearless of a Judgment to come, they carried out their awful sacrilege.

O my most dear Jesus, Thou neither sayest nor doest ought to resist these things, but endurest all in silence.

Surely in this loss of Thine, Thou showest clearly, how I should act when robbed of things necessary to me. For Thy will is, that I be more ready to endure worldly losses, than to demand debts legally due to me.

O that the Supreme Creator of Heaven, very God and very man, should be reduced to such straits! At His birth He had scarcely worthless clothes for a covering; now, when dying, He loses every garment.

Then a narrow manger bore the tender limbs of His infancy; now, stripped of everything, He has not, in the whole world He created, where for a little He can rest His head, save on the Cross.

For as poor and needy He came into this world, so also He wished to leave it naked and an outcast. When born He was wrapped tightly in swaddling clothes; dying He was pierced by nails and spear.

Meditation on so much misery surely invites compassion; the exhibition of so much endurance calls for imitation.

Be thou, therefore, only the more patient, when things necessary to thee are taken away; yea, even when things longed for are denied thee.

Learn to do with few things, and to be content with that which is of little worth; and thou shalt be free from murmuring, very peaceful in thy mind, and acceptable to Almighty God.

Honored, O Jesus, be Thy seamless coat-garment, never to be applied to any worldly use. Worthy is it to be set apart for the sacred service of God alone. For it was fitting to preserve it uninjured, on account of its singular reverence; and that it might commend, throughout the whole world, the unity of the Holy Catholic Church.

Which, though it be divided into regions, tongues, and dwellings; although distinguished by various orders and ranks of life, yet the whole body of the Church lives, and is governed and sustained, under one Head—one chief Shepherd; holding one Faith, one Baptism, and one God in perfect Trinity; having one Bridegroom, Jesus Christ, Who rules in heaven; and from Whom it cannot be rent asunder by any assaults of temptation.

Because Thou indeed, O Lord, hast given to the Bride, the Catholic Church, the word of truth, the light of knowledge, and the fervency of love, as an impregnable shield against all errors—to obtain thereby the never-fading crown of life eternal.

O Jesu, the poorest and the richest King of kings. O Lord, most poor in being robbed of Thy garments and deprived of Thy friends; O Lord, most rich in the fulness of gifts spiritual; grant me, Thy poor servant, out of the abundance of Thy powers, that I may at least be perfectly endued with one virtue—never to be naked and ashamed before Thee; like unto him who was found in the festive house without a wedding garment; and, for his neglect of order, was forthwith driven from the assembly of the Saints.

Let my heart be rent asunder with a salutary compunction, when I call to mind the division of Thy clothing into four parts. Then shall I be stirred, either by the fear of hell, or by the hope of future glory; by sorrow for past sins, or by love of the grace already received by me.

And, in token of Thy seamless coat, grant me also, for inward quiet's sake, to preserve the unity of brotherly love in the bond of peace; to put from me all occasion of quarrel; to avoid the noise and worry of the world; and to abstain from all idle wandering and foolish conversation.

May my desire be to spend a poor and hidden life with Thee; never to be over-anxious for earthly pleasures, nor to cling to any property of my own; since Thou wert utterly without this world's goods.

But the little which Thou seemedst to have for Thy simple use, even that Thou permittedst by the spoilers to be taken away and wasted; thereby affording to all who suffer wrongfully an example of patience, not to sorrow overmuch at the loss of their goods.

CHAPTER XXII

ON THE REVILINGS OF THE JEWS, AND THE
MIGHTY PERSEVERANCE OF JESUS ON THE
CROSS

I BLESS and give Thee thanks, O Lord Jesu
Christ, Thou glory and joy of the citizens
of heaven, for enduring, whilst hanging on the
Cross, all the reproaches and blasphemies tur-
bulently cast against Thee by the perfidious
Jews.

For all were opposed to Thee, from the greatest to the least; and, like unto mad dogs, they
ran together to rend in pieces Thine innocency.
Like dogs, they barked with their mouths;
with their teeth they gnashed, like lions; and
like serpents, they hissed with their tongues.

With their lips they cursed Thee; with their
faces they derided Thee; they clapped with
their hands, and leaped with their feet, and rejoiced in their hearts. In that they saw Thee
fastened to the Cross, they would not that Thou
shouldest die, without the vexation of these
cruel wrongs.

Then, they who passed by, like unto raving
and drunken men, filled with the gall of bitter

ness and the venom of envy, wagged their mad heads, crying, "Ah, Thou that destroyest the temple of God and buildest it again in three days, save Thyself."

The Chief Priests also with the Elders and Scribes, whose place it was to rule the people, and who ought to have restrained their evil doings, were of all the most grossly insulting.

For, with proud eye and neck erect they stood opposite the Cross, boldly staring Thee in the face; and, jesting one with another, vomited forth their vile blasphemies, "He saved others (they said), Himself He cannot save."

For the divinely-wrought miracles, and the benefits of healing, compassionately dispensed to others—wonders of which all knew them to be envious—these they strove to evilly interpret and to disparage.

Hence they urge a descent from the Cross, and falsely declare that they wish to believe— the very men who are proved so often to have opposed true believers.

For when greater miracles were wrought by Thee they devised malicious slanders against Thee, rather than give faith to them. They therefore neither thought of believing, nor of seeking salvation. Their sole object was to irritate Thee with malicious words.

At last, puffed up with daring insolence, they

cast forth impious words against Thy Godhead. Calling Thee contemptuously the Son of God, they said, "He trusted in God that He would deliver Him; let Him deliver Him now if He will have Him; for He said, 'I am the Son of God.'"

O most cruel and hard-hearted persecutors of the Son of God, does it not content you to have committed the awful crime of crucifixion? Must ye needs be guilty of the still greater offence, that of blaspheming and deriding the Son of God?

Alas! alas! what do ye? Why do ye sharpen your venomous tongues against one that is holy and innocent? Wherein hath Christ offended; or in what at any time injured you?

Has He not done all things well? He who made the deaf to hear, and the dumb to speak, did He not enlighten your whole country with many glorious signs and sweet doctrines? Yea, did He not even pray for His enemies?

What evil hath He merited for these things? Wherefore do ye render evil for good—hatred for love? Better far for you to weep for the expiation of so great a crime, than to laugh in the presence of the Crucified. But grievous indeed is it, ye heed not, neither do ye care!

There is certainly in hardened hearts neither compassion nor contrition, nor remembrance of benefits received; no, fiendish fury, making ready sharper taunts and insults, ever inclines to baser deeds. For, when they could no longer persecute Thee with swords and staves, they began to pursue Thee with the sharper weapons of their tongues.

And, in like manner also, the soldiers, executioners, of all their malice, puffed up with pride of place and ignorant of divine Law, corrupted by the favor and encouragement of their leaders, drawing nearer mocked Thee; and offering vinegar said, "If Thou be the King of the Jews, save Thyself."

O foolish soldiers! degenerate in deeds and morals! Who has taught you thus to soldier, that ye should fight against God?

It is not the part of noble men to persecute the godly, to despoil the poor, to leave the spoiled naked, to divide clothing, to mock the Crucified, to offer to the God-man Christ, when dying, vinegar to drink, which is so abhorrent to all men.

But still ye are not able to injure Christ; for wisdom conquers malice, and the patience of Jesus is not wearied out by your insults.

The thief also, placed on the left hand, and obstinate to the last in his iniquity, reviling, said, "If Thou art the Christ, save Thyself and us."

Alas wretched man! he falls into an abyss of evils; and he, who ought to have sought pardon for his unholy doings, impiously insulted Thee, from whom cometh all forgiveness. Wherefore the unhappy wretch died despairing, and perished most wickedly.

I praise and glorify Thee, O Blessed Jesus, for Thy invincible patience on the Cross Thou hadst assumed; from which no reproaches, no enticing promises would induce Thee to come down. No, not for one short moment wouldest Thou leave that, which Thou hadst ascended of Thine own free will.

For the place, which from love and pity Thou didst take, to remain and to die there, that Thou didst firmly hold unto the end; and thus, the work so salutarily begun, it was Thine own desire to finish, by an end worthy of all praise.

Thou, who didst teach others to persevere in a good work, didst Thyself on the Cross first make profession of obedience; establishing by Thine own example, that obedience should be steadily observed by all who follow Thee.

Draw near now to the tree of the Crucified, thou renouncer of the world, thou lover of the holy Cross, thou professed follower of Jesus.

Be firm and constant in thy holy purpose. To stand steadfast in the faith, to live under obedience, and to persevere in discipline, is the work of Christ, and the consummation of thy salvation.

Let no one, therefore, withdraw thee from thy condition as a child of God, from the path of perfection, from the study of devout conversation, from the vows professed by thee at holy Baptism.

Remember the words of the Apostle, that "Christ became obedient for us unto death—even the death of the Cross."

Whatever, therefore, the world may promise, however the flesh entice, and the devil sorely tempt; let friends dissuade, and they of this life scoff; turn not thou aside—pay no heed, utterly despise them all.

Stand firm in Christ, look upwards; lift up thine eyes to the Crucified, inviting thee more fully to His arms; promising thee for thy brief labor rewards that never fail.

"If (He says) thou shalt suffer with Me, thou shalt also reign with Me; if thou be dead with Me, then shalt thou also together with Me be glorified."

O Jesu Christ, Thou most devoted and most valiant Wrestler, Thou most ardent lover and consecrator of the holy Cross, grant me, having devoted myself to Thee, to serve Thee with an unceasing resolution; never, growing weary through labor, to relax from the fervor of my

endeavors; but always to press onward to the
things that are before; and, with a steadfast
mind, resist the temptations of the flesh and all
assaults of the soul.

May I exhibit all patience in adversity, not
fearing the revilings of man, nor caring for his
praises. Turning away the eyes of my mind
from things present, may I seek a complete
refuge in Thee, my only Saviour. May I not,
from anything dear or anything displeasing to
me, draw back from the embrace of Thy holy
Cross; but rather under its protection, as my
standard and my device, may I, in a spirit of
obedience, bring my life to a happy close.
Amen.

CHAPTER XXIII

ON THE WORDS SPOKEN TO THE THIEF ON THE CROSS

I BLESS and give Thee thanks, O Lord Jesu
Christ, Thou supreme and sole comfort of
sinners, for the infinite pity and superabundant
mercy, which Thou didst deign to show to one
hanging on a cross at Thy right hand—he who
was once a most wicked thief, but now at length
converted and deeply penitent.

For, no sooner did he acknowledge his guilt
and truly repent him of his misdeeds, than he

received, from the sure promise of Thy mouth, remission of all his sins, and entrance into Paradise.

For no repentance is too late or unavailing, where there is true contrition and entire conversion. O blessed and effectual penitence, by which the sinner is so soon deemed worthy, through Christ, to obtain the kingdom of heaven!

For this penitent thief, and now blessed Confessor, although he had long and grievously offended, still, when near his end and placed in the greatest straits, he came to a right mind. Earnestly sorrowing over his past misdoings, he humbly pleaded for pardon, and received abundant mercy.

For he acknowledged his own guilt, when he confessed himself justly condemned to death. He had a zeal indeed for justice, when he reproved his fellow-criminal close at hand for his wicked blasphemy. He showed a feeling of compassion, when he complained that Christ was crucified, though free from all crime— utterly without fault. He had a giant faith, who despaired not of the mercy of Christ, but prayed to be remembered in the Kingdom of God.

Therefore, abounding in these heavenly gifts, to Thee, O Lord Jesu, as to the tender Shepherd of souls, and true Priest, and most faithful Confessor, fully acquainted with the whole course of his life, he in full confidence says, " O Lord, remember me when Thou comest into Thy kingdom."

To whom Thou, O most gracious Jesu, didst give this most sweet and most consoling answer, " Verily I say unto thee, this day shalt thou be with Me in Paradise."

O truly gracious and most amiable promise, lovingly proceeding from the mouth of God; but in the ear of the contrite sinner how sweetly sounding in his time of conflict—in such an hour most powerfully comforting the anxious and trembling heart!

O how confidently can he now die, to whom it was given to hear such a promise! For he, whom the Lord Jesus has engaged to defend, in the evil day shall not be afraid.

That which was denied to the prayer of Peter was granted to the dying robber. Peter desired to linger in the mount of contemplation, but his wish was not granted. And, before the hour of the Passion, he would fain have followed Jesus in all His troubles; but it was said unto him, " Thou canst not follow Me now, but thou shalt follow Me afterwards."

Peter was called among the first to the apostleship, but the robber is admitted into the Kingdom before him.

O how wonderful are Thy works, O Lord; Thy thoughts are very deep! O how unsearchable are Thy judgments, how unspeakably gracious are the words of Thy mouth! "An unwise man doth not well consider, and a fool will not understand" these things.

O what a happy hour did that robber experience, who was in mercy permitted to suffer with Thee, to die with Thee, and with Thee to go into Thy Kingdom!

Concerning whom I find not any good thing he had ever before done in his life; but this I know full well, when his end was at hand, he, through Christ, forthwith purged all his past misdeeds by his humble confession.

Wherefore, the greatest mercy was it that so wicked a man obtained pardon, as soon as he had humbly poured forth his supplication to Thee, "Lord (he said), remember me when Thou comest into Thy Kingdom."

And Thou, O Lord, merciful and gracious, didst from Thy Cross at once hear the heart-stricken sinner; comforting his outpouring soul with the most loving answer, "Verily, I say unto thee, this day shalt thou be with Me in Paradise."

O how comforting and refreshing to me to weigh with careful thought the death of this robber, and Thy most loving reply to him!

Not that I may sin with the greater security, or defer my repentance the longer; but it teaches me that, should I be overtaken by any sudden infirmity, I need not despair, when I have before me the speedy conversion of so wicked a man; and behold him, by Thy pitiful favor, eternally saved and restored to Paradise.

For I should, indeed, be heavily oppressed because of my many sins, did I not know Thy mercies, O Lord—had I not heard of the examples of penitents lovingly received by Thee. For Thou hast said by the Prophet, "I would not the death of a sinner, but rather that he should be converted and live;" and also by Thine own mouth, that "God so loved the world, that He gave His Only-begotten Son, that whosoever believeth in Him should not perish, but have everlasting Life." And again, "I am not come to call the righteous, but sinners to repentance."

Thou didst at once forgive all the sins of Mary Magdalene, when at Thy feet she wept abundantly. Thou didst again receive Peter into Thy favor, seeing that he poured forth tears of bitterness, after having thrice denied Thee.

By the exercise of Thy mercy, Thou didst heal those that were taken with divers diseases; and, by a larger gift of grace, Thou didst set free those who were bound by very grievous sins. This, how manifest was it with the adulteress, whom Thou didst rescue from the hands of her accusers, that she should not be stoned to death.

O most benign Jesus! my merciful friend and my refuge, my defender, and my deliverer from the anger of mine enemies. Be Thou gracious unto me, and destroy not my soul with the ungodly, for the redemption of which Thou didst willingly endure the shame of the Cross.

Remember Thy holy word that Thou spakest to the thief; in which, also, Thou hast left to me a hope that cannot be moved. O Saviour of my life, when the hour of my death draweth nigh, say Thou to my soul, "To-day shalt thou be with Me in Paradise."

What more joyous to be heard, what more sweet to the dying man, than to be gladdened by such a response, "To-day shalt thou be with Me in Paradise?" Remember me, O Lord, in Thy Kingdom, and forsake me not in the awful moment of death.

When my strength faileth, and my voice is silent; when my eyes begin to wax dim, and my hearing is dull; then uphold me, O good Jesus, and send forth Thy holy Angels to encourage me in the conflict; that the rancorous enemy, craftily assailing at the last hour, may not prevail against me. That evil one, who even dared to seek something in Thee, which might be made his; but, finding nothing, he departed from Thee utterly confounded.

So let them be confounded who seek to make a prey of my soul; let them be turned backward and suddenly put to confusion. But let my soul be glad in Thee, O Lord, and be joyful in Thy salvation; meditating on Thy gracious speech, the second Thou didst utter on the Cross, "Verily, I say unto thee, to-day shalt thou be with Me in Paradise."

May this promise, which is sweeter to me because it was uttered by Thee on the Cross, be often in my mouth, but oftener in my heart!

For words, uttered by the mouth of my crucified Lord, possess a special sweetness, a fuller efficacy; therefore they should receive the most earnest consideration—the very closest meditation.

May I so live—may I so study to serve my Lord, that, in the hour of my departure from the body, I may be found in Christ, meet to hear from heaven those words most sweet, "This day shalt thou be with Me in Paradise."

O that Thou mayest say to Thy servant those equally cheering words, "Well done, thou good servant and faithful in a little, enter thou into the joy of thy Lord."

For then nothing will be more precious, nothing more delightful, than to have led a good life ; and served Thee, O Jesus, faithfully even unto death.

CHAPTER XXIV

ON THE REMARKABLE SUPERSCRIPTION OF THE NAME OF JESUS, PLACED OVER HIS HEAD

I BLESS and give Thee thanks, O Lord Jesu Christ, Prince of all power and King of the universe, for the distinguished Title of Thy sacred and blessed Name, openly set up over the crown of Thy head.

Which Title, in the three most widely-known languages of the world, viz., Hebrew, Greek, and Latin, was clearly written by Pilate the Judge, in form and words as follows :—" Jesus of Nazareth, the King of the Jews."

O truly distinguished Title, not devised of human skill, but rather by divine appointment ; foreseen and fore-ordained from all eternity !

Therefore Pilate neither could, nor ought he to write otherwise than inspired by Thee. Whence also, in the excellent writings of the Prophets, expressed in their own special terms, are found the words of this Title, with their mystic meaning.

What, therefore, the Sacred Scripture had long before predicted; what also common rumor had spread abroad in praise of Thy holy Name; this, the gentile Governor, under divine guidance, inscribed on a small board, to the perpetual memory of Christ Crucified, "Jesus of Nazareth, the King of the Jews."

When, therefore, many of the Jews had read this Title, the Chief Priests, burning with envy, could not endure that, by such an inscription, the glory of Thy Name should be proclaimed. With all their might they strove to degrade that glory; nay, with a still greater folly, they fain would destroy Thy life and Thy Name together.

Therefore was it they remonstrated with Pilate, the Judge, touching so distinguished a Title, saying, "Write not, The King of the Jews; but that He said, I am the King of the Jews." For the Jews were afraid that they themselves should be put to shame; that the base act of cruelty should be charged to them —that they had killed the very king of their own nation.

And that such charge might not be more widely spread abroad, they sought to have the Title changed; so that Jesus might not appear to have been crucified through their malice, but rather for the crime of seeking to be ruler— daring to call Himself king, whereas in the world no royal dignity had ever been assumed by Him.

O most wicked Jews! It is not as ye pretend, for ye are in every respect guilty. Ye are the chief murderers of the Son of God. Neither have ye any excuse; although, with much cunning, ye seek to cloak this most serious crime.

For, in the presence of Pilate, " ye denied the Holy One and the Just, and desired a murderer to be granted unto you." And now truly ye have come, that ye may mar the truth of the Title, and so yourselves appear faultless.

But Pilate was, in the death of our Lord, far more innocent than ye, and in writing the Superscription more truthful—yes, and in answering your appeal of envy more faithful when he said, " What I have written, I have written."

If you wish to read, read; but, if you are not satisfied, you will not for one moment turn me from a decision which I have once declared. " What I have written, I have written." I have not set forth this Title at your suggestion, neither will I change it through your remonstrance. As I have appointed, so shall it remain.

God inspired it, not man. Therefore I confirm it, and declare it true. Nor shall any one persuade me to have it falsified; but, to all languages and to all peoples, I proclaim His dignity, and charge that it be published, "Jesus of Nazareth, the King of the Jews."

O noble-minded governor! Thou hast well written, and rightly hast thou answered them. I commend thee, for having formed so beautiful and so sacred a Title concerning Jesus of Nazareth, and for having so boldly refuted the Jews.

But in this I commend thee not: that thou didst consent to the death of Christ; for, in so doing, thou didst commit a great crime indeed.

And now, O devout disciple of Christ, learn wisely to consider, thoughtfully to read over, and reverently to utter, the words of this sacred inscription. For reading this Title, "Jesus of Nazareth, the King of the Jews," availeth much, when fear of the enemy sets in. Yes, study prayerfully those words, and thou shalt find marked support in the hour of terror and perplexity.

For, having invoked the saving Name of Jesus, then the power of Christ and a firm faith in God will not suffer thee to be in jeopardy.

"Jesus of Nazareth, the King of the Jews." The sweetness of this most fitting Title no words can fully express, no mind can duly contemplate.

Only four words are there, yet they invite the whole world to venerate Christ's divine Name.

Come now, all ye princes of the world, all ye tribes and peoples, hear, and read, and say, "Hail, Jesus of Nazareth, King of the Jews, who suffered for the salvation of all men."

O Jesus of Nazareth, bright flower of the Virgin Mary, O glorious Son of David, the Only-begotten of the Most High Father, write Thy sweet and excellent Name firmly and beautifully on the table of my heart; together with the sacred and noble Title of Thy Passion, containing as it does the cause of Thy death; that I may diligently look thereon, and frequently read it, to the praise of Thy venerable Name.

May that Title be a cordial comfort to my heart in my day of distress, a very present help when temptations assail me.

May the evil spirit flee from me, may the lust of concupiscence die within me, and all the world be as bitterness to me, when I think or read of "Jesus of Nazareth, the King of the Jews."

For nothing is sweeter than Jesus, nothing more wholesome, nothing more efficacious. Nothing brighter than the Nazarene, nothing purer, nothing more holy. Nothing worthier than the King of the Jews, nothing mightier, nothing more exalted.

Therefore, no enemy can withstand me, no plague infect me, no calamity overwhelm me,

when humbly I call on Thee, O Jesus, or picture
Thee stretched on Thy Cross; or with my heart
and my lips dwell on this Title, "Jesus of Nazareth, the King of the Jews."

O Jesu, supremely amiable, Thou art my King
and my God, delightful and far above all praise.
Lovely in the manger, more lovely on the Cross,
most lovely on the throne of Thy kingdom.

For though Thou wast crucified through the
weakness of the flesh, yet Thou now livest by
the power of God, sitting at the right hand of
the Father, exalted above every creature for
ever.   Amen.

CHAPTER XXV.

ON THE COMPASSION OF THY SORROWING MOTHER, AND THE MUTUAL COMMENDING OF THE BLESSED VIRGIN MARY AND ST. JOHN

I BLESS and give Thee thanks, O Lord Jesu
Christ, Thou Comforter of all that mourn,
for the sorrowful look, with which Thou didst
tenderly regard Thy most beloved Mother, as she
stood by the Cross, worn out by heavy grief.

How great that sorrow was, Thou, the most
searching discerner of all her heart, alone knewest best; for Thou on earth hadst nothing
dearer than Thy Virgin Mother, and nothing

loved she more than Thee, O God, her Son; Whom she knew verily to be born of herself, yet Lord of all things—yea, her own Creator.

Therefore, seeing Thee, Whom she so tenderly loved, hanging on the Cross, lost to self she dwelt in Thee. As if taken entirely out of herself, she also was, as it were, suspended above, crucified in spirit to Thee; although, with body still on earth, she stood clinging to the Cross weeping.

I praise and glorify Thee for Thy exceeding great compassion, with which Thou didst then filially condole with Thy grief-worn Mother, who, in truth, regarded all Thy sufferings as her own. She bewailed Thy several wounds as if inflicted on herself. She endured new tortures as often as, with maternal eyes, she beheld the Blood flowing from Thy Body; or when she heard Thy voice speaking to herself from the Cross.

I praise and give Thee honor for the very tender address, with which, at the last, Thou didst in few words console Thy desolate Mother; commending her to Thy much-beloved disciple John, as to a most faithful supporter; associating a virgin with one of virgin purity, by the indissoluble bond of love, saying, "Woman, behold thy son." And then to the disciple, "Behold thy mother."

O happy union and pleasing commendation, formed and consecrated by virginal innocence! For in those words Thou didst show a feeling of holy care for the honor of Thy Mother, in affording her the solace of a chaste disciple. In a certain way, Thou didst substitute for Thyself another son; one suitable to her pure manners, and well fitted to provide her duly with the necessaries of life.

For thus it behoved Thy filial providence to do; that Thy holy Mother, the Blessed Virgin, might not want a faithful minister; lest she, who was at once to be deprived of Thy most delightful presence, might seem to be left lonely and helpless in the world, and a very stranger among the Jews.

This holy arrangement and most excellent commendation, made by thy Son, let it now, O Mary, thou loving Mother of God, be pleasing indeed to thee. Receive with grateful feelings this disciple, whom Thy Son Jesus has chosen for thee.

This is John the Apostle, elect, and beloved more than the other disciples. In manners agreeable; kind in word; bashful in countenance; modest in deportment; temperate in food; homely in apparel; fit to administer; ready to obey.

This is the most beloved disciple, related to

thee by family; of good report; pure in mind; chaste in body; acceptable to God; loved by all; in all things worthy of thy companionship, O Mother of God.

I know, indeed, that what has pleased thy Son has always been pleasing to thee, and does please thee; that what He has arranged to be done, that thou most desirest; for, in all His doings, He sought not His own will, but the glory of His Father.

And, therefore, it was, I doubt not, pleasing to thee that, when He was about to depart, He bequeathed John to thee, to occupy His place.

Receive now, holy John, the desirable treasure intrusted to thee. Receive the blessed Virgin, the revered Mother of Jesus, thy beloved aunt, sister of thy mother. Till now the Virgin Mary was called thy aunt by blood alliance; henceforth she shall, as by special grace committed to thy care, be called by a more sacred order, yea, by divine authority, thy mother.

And thou, also, who wast formerly, according to the flesh, called the son of Zebedee, brother of James the Great, and kinsman of the Lord our Saviour, and wast afterwards made a disciple of Jesus, shalt now be called by a new name, the adopted son of Mary, henceforth to minister to her with filial love.

Carry out, therefore, what Christ commanded; fulfil the order of holy commendation, and thou shalt be acceptable to all, the honored of the whole world.

The most blessed John did as Christ on the Cross charged him. For, "from that hour the disciple took her to his own home," where he watched over her, and diligently ministered to her. His life was devoted to her in all obedience, as if she were his own mother—most tenderly he loved her.

Rejoice and be glad, O blessed John, for the trust committed to thee. What Christ held most dear on earth, He, in full confidence, intrusted to thee. Greatly enriched He thee, when He bequeathed to thee the blessed Mary.

Christ gave to St. Peter the keys of the kingdom of heaven, but thee He verily constituted chamberlain of His own Mother.

It was said aforetime to St. Joseph by the Angel, "Fear not to take unto thee Mary, thy wife;" but now the Lord of Angels saith unto thee, "Behold thy mother."

This great privilege was the reward of thine abundant virtues, viz., utter contempt of the world; devotion to Jesus; sweetness of manner; spotless integrity; calmness of mind; liberty of soul; purity of conscience; probity of life.

Take, therefore, the Mother of Christ under

thy care, and an abundance of grace shall be thine. The Lord of Life shall open to thee divine mysteries, and teach thee the hidden life; thou shalt perceive things wonderful, and learn "the great things of God."

Dwelling with the Blessed Mary thou wilt be very chaste, and very pure; thou wilt increase in holiness, and in thy dedication to all that is godly.

Her very presence is purity, her discourse prudence, her actions heavenly, her reading Jesus, her meditation Christ, her contemplation God.

Stand now by the Cross, watch by the side of the Virgin, support her in thine arms when fainting, raise her when sinking, comfort her in her tears. Weep thou with her that weeps, mourn with her that mourns, go where she goes, stay where she stays, and abide where she dwells. Leave not Mary in her grief; hold on thy compassion to the end.

Then prepare thee for the due interment of thy dying Jesus. Accompany the Mother to the place of burial; bring her back to the city and conduct her to her house. Be thou unto her as a ministering Angel, though in this case comforting one more worthy far than thyself.

For Christ, we know, in His Agony was comforted by an Angel. He needed it not, yet His will was that an inferior should assist Him. He did not repel the messenger of consolation.

Now, therefore, I humbly beseech Thee, O Jesus, grant grace to me, a sinner, that I may be fervent in my love of Thee; and having well in my memory Thy new Commandment, that we love one another, may I be ever found a ready helper, to comfort and uphold the sorrowful and afflicted.

CHAPTER XXVI

ON THE LOUD CRY OF JESUS ON THE CROSS: ELI, ELI, LAMA SABACHTHANI

I BLESS and give Thee thanks, O Lord Jesu Christ, most loving Son of love Paternal, for Thy great and solitary abandonment on the Cross; when, in Thy dire need, Thou wast forsaken by God the Father, and all the heavenly host, and also by all creatures upon earth; as if Thou wert an alien and an outcast, no very Son of God, of no power, no strength. Thy sorrow-stricken Mother alone continued by Thee, with the disciple commended to her, and a few weak women; but that Mother, alas! could scarcely say a single word to Thee, so oppressed was she by anxiety and grief.

I praise and glorify Thee for that loud cry, when, in the presence of many hearers, Thou didst break forth into that mournful exclamation, saying, "My God! My God! why hast Thou forsaken Me?"

By which words, indeed, Thou didst distinctly declare the magnitude of Thy sufferings, and the withdrawal of all comfort; what Thou didst endure for the salvation of men; by whom, notwithstanding, Thou wast deemed of no reputation—yea, they dealt with Thee as the basest of malefactors, utterly unworthy to live.

Consider very diligently, O my soul, the present words of Jesus, uttered for thy special instruction.

Behold, wonderful to relate, how the Lord of the universe, Who has need of nothing, is reduced to such a state of misery, that He must pour forth His wants into His Father's ears; how He, who does all things with the Father, by the Father is forsaken; He, who upholds all things without being wearied, declares that He Himself is heavy laden.

How He, who is wont to console the sorrowful and weak, confesses Himself an exile and in distress; how He, the arbiter of all vows, the ever-ready listener to the cry of the poor, utters the words of lowly inquiry, saying, "My God! My God! why hast Thou forsaken Me?"

From the beginning of Christ's Passion until now, never was heard so lamentable a cry.

Acknowledge, therefore, Thine own voice, O Christ, pleading for me on Thy Cross, in Thy suffering flesh. For Thy state of desertion is my consolation; Thy complaint, my support; Thy weakness, my strength; Thy punishment, the satisfaction for all my sins and offences.

Thou art the heavenly Physician, Who, by a great exercise of tender compassion, didst immerse Thyself in innumerable sorrows and sufferings.

And, therefore, with the weak Thou art weak; with the sorrowful Thou lamentest; with the sinner Thou art sad; with the sufferer of violence Thou complainest; and, crying out in behalf of Thy weak ones, Thou pleadest earnestly for their protection.

Wherefore that cry is the voice of the flesh and of sentiment, not of murmuring or despair. The flesh indeed, which knew not the taint of any sin, feels the pain.

A body most innocent suffers the severest torture, while the soul enjoys the most perfect happiness; from the presence of Deity there is no diminution of pain, but a power of wonderful endurance is manifested, that the redemption of man may be accomplished.

What believer, hearing these things, will not

proffer sympathy? Who so hard as not to be deeply moved by the words of this cry? In good truth, the elements, generally so senseless, showed mighty signs of compassion.

From the sixth hour until the ninth the sun held back his rays of light from the earth, refusing to shine on the unworthy, shuddering at the injuries done to his Creator; grieving that the Author of Life should suffer humiliation and torture, and proclaiming that he himself could not behold His death.

Therefore, while the sun is mourning and the earth trembling with fear, do thou also, O rational man, take up the mourning, listen to the cry of Jesus, why He cries, and what His words.

Behold, in His every tribulation and strait the Lord Jesus passed through meek and patient; nothing proceeded out of His mouth but sweetness and pity.

To His Father above He directs His prayers; no other name than that of God does He mention; to His notice only does He bring His desolate condition. No solace does He seek from His Mother, no help does He ask from His friends.

Jesus, therefore, teaches thee how, when in great distress, thou shouldest imitate Him. Art thou weak in body? Is thy mind heavy laden

and weary? Art thou despised by others, and
hast thou lost the world's good word, through
poverty or any other unfitness? Be not sad
nor indignant, but forthwith let this be thy re-
course—make this thy place of refreshing; and
with Jesus despised on the Cross of men, and
for a while forsaken of the Father, take part in
His colloquy, meditating on the words He uttered, "My God! My God! why hast Thou
forsaken Me?"

Study, then, in thy weakness to show thyself
gentle; and murmur not, if sometimes thou art
neglected by thy servants, or rarely visited by
thy brethren.

Remember the exile Jesus on the Cross, and
cease to complain of some light trouble. Desire
His presence with thee. Seek from Him alone
thy comfort. He will soothe thee, however
desolate thou mayest be.

Hold of little worth the world's solace. Be
not over-taken-up with the love of friends; but
rather lift up thine eyes to thy crucified Redeemer, meditate on His sacred wounds. Stand
by His Cross, and hear Jesus, with a loud voice,
crying to the Father.

Therefore, laying aside all earthly matters,
lift up thy mind to the heavenly country. Hold
to God as thy Father, Jesus as thy Brother, the
Angels as thy friends, and all the Saints as thy

kinsfolk. Thou art of noble and high family, not in the descent of the flesh, but in the liberty of the Spirit.

Entrenched within such defences, thou mayest, with sure and certain hope, await the day of final visitation, trusting in the tender mercy of the most gracious Saviour.

I beseech Thee, high and adorable Father of Jesus Christ, my Lord, have respect to the prayer of Thy servant; which I this day, by the hand of Thy beloved Son, hanging on the Cross, humbly present to Thee.

Grant me pardon for all my past sins, and hold not far back from me the gift of heavenly grace. Suffer me not to be endangered by grievous temptations, nor to be disturbed by the sharp goadings of the passions.

Examine me, Lord, and prove me, as Thou knowest to be best for me. But keep my soul, and with the temptation make such a way to escape, that I may be able to bear it. What the crafty enemy hath prepared for the destruction of my soul, that turn Thou into the means of my salvation; and so produce in me a more abundant increase of grace.

By how much the more I am pressed down by troubles, and the less able to put any confidence in men, be Thou so much the more powerfully and nearly present with me. For

Thou, in my gravest necessity, remainest to me a most faithful Friend.

If I must be proved and deprived of all comfort for a season, then grant this to me, that I may suffer patiently, and faithfully commit my whole burden to Thee; and also, that I may have well down in my heart the remembrance of this, the desolate hour of Jesus, Thy dearly beloved and most acceptable Son; Who, when no friend was near to help, in His most trying season, was mindful of Thee alone.

CHAPTER XXVII

ON THE THIRST OF JESUS ON THE CROSS, AND ON HIS BITTER CUP

I BLESS and give Thee thanks, O Lord Jesu Christ, Thou fountain of living water and stream of healing wisdom, for Thy violent thirst upon the Cross. Then, Thy sacred and precious Blood being shed, and all the natural moistures, through the extreme tortures of the body, being exhausted, Thou wert corporally thirsty with an oppressively trying drought—but even more by far didst Thou thirst with the ardent desire for our salvation—yea, as a very pauper and mendicant didst Thou ask for drink, saying, "I thirst."

But to this small request no one took heed, no succor came; not even to offer a cup of cold water to Thee, the Creator of all waters.

Some, indeed, among the bystanders, on hearing this, instead of taking pity on Thee, became only the more cruel. For, in order to satisfy the deadly hatred of their envenomed hearts, they forthwith filled a sponge with vinegar mingled with gall, and offered to Thy sweet mouth the bitter draught—unfit for the very dogs to drink.

I praise and honor Thee for Thy most gracious endurance, in accepting and tasting this most acrid draught, which Thou didst, by way of punishment, take in expiation of the unlawful pleasure of our first parents. That as the tasting of the forbidden fruit was the cause of death, so the tasting by Thee of this bitter cup might become to us the medicine of salvation.

But woe to thee, thou godless Jew, a race stiff-necked and grievously wicked! How couldest thou be brought to such iniquity, as to release Barabbas and crucify Christ? How couldest thou be moved to such madness, as to offer vinegar when drink was asked?

Offer that to the High Priest or to the Ruler of the people, and see if either will drink it. What hath Christ done unto thee, or wherein hath Jesus of Nazareth troubled thee? Answer me, I pray thee.

Did not God rain down manna on thee from heaven, did He not bring forth water from the hard rock, that thou mightest have abundance to eat and to drink?

And lo! for the sweet manna thou dost offer Him wine mingled with myrrh; and for the many streams of water thou dost not indeed so much as hold out a single drop to the thirsting Christ.

Yet, surely, if Christ desired, He could turn all thy water into bitterness; and, when thy bread and water failed, thou wouldest soon perish through excessive drought—fit punishment for thy refusal to show compassion.

Moreover, if Christ had wished to have a pleasant draught, the holy Angels would most assuredly have cheerfully and speedily ministered to Him refreshing dew from heaven; sweeter far than earth could give; just as they formerly ministered unto Him, when thrice He had been tempted of the devil.

But He would not avenge Himself, or show any sign of His power. On the contrary, He exhibited the sign of patience and long suffering, that He might uphold all professors of poverty.

And do thou, therefore, O disciple of Jesus,

take from this bitter mixture a remedy against all excess of appetite. For, if thou desirest to feast with Christ in the Kingdom of His Father, let not your heart be set on costly dishes, or on cups of precious wine; eschew soft couches and all gay apparel. Know thou that such things are contrary to the very pure life of Jesus, and to His most sad Passion.

But, if thou hast gone to excess, either by eating too much, or by a too dainty use of delicacies, correct thy failing by daily exercises and nightly watchings; often meditating with sorrow on the bitter Cup of Christ.

O Jesus, Thou heavenly manna and most sweet nectar, Who, when in dire thirst on the Cross, wast offered vinegar and gall to drink, and couldest not obtain one drop of water to refresh Thyself withal; grant that, when seated at my daily repast, I may earnestly call to mind this Thy most bitter draught, and so not have my thoughts eagerly intent upon food for my body, but rather be earnestly occupied with holy meditation.

May I learn, in Thy fear, to take only what is needed for my support, and then devoutly to return thanks to Thee for the blessings bestowed. Let me not be dissatisfied with my diet, if little in quantity, or common in quality; yea, may I deem myself unworthy to feed on the alms of the poor; may I dread to be sustained at the cost of other men's labors.

Grant that I may hunger after the meat that perisheth not, but endureth unto everlasting life. May I thirst for the fountain of Life eternal, and from the banquet of the heavenly table at times obtain a crumb of living bread, together with if it be but a little draught of inward savor. Thus shall I experimentally taste how sweet is Thy Spirit, O Lord, freely poured out on the children of grace.

CHAPTER XXVIII

ON THE WORD OF CONSUMMATION PRONOUNCED BY THE MOUTH OF JESUS

O LORD JESU CHRIST, Revealer of mysteries and Fulfiller of the Law and the Prophets, I bless and give Thee thanks for Thy perfect accomplishment of the Father's will, in this brief and comforting cry, " It is finished "—words justly uttered by Thee, immediately after Thou hadst received the vinegar, as the closing of Thy whole life.

As if Thou hadst openly said :—" Now is fulfilled whatsoever the old Law foretold concerning Me; all that the sacrificial rites and the holy ceremonial worship prefigured. Now have truly come to pass the predictions of the holy Prophets, and the long hoped-for desires of the Fathers of old. Now is everything that pertaineth to the redemption of man fully completed.

" Whatsoever in the Holy Scriptures has been promised from heaven, all, in a necessary and becoming manner as regards place and time, has openly come to pass and been brought to a fitting end; and the few things that remain will, undoubtedly, in due season, be accomplished.

" I have fulfilled the commandment of My Father Who sent Me into the world; I have finished the work which He gave Me to do.

" I have already before healed the sick, and shown clearly the signs of My Godhead; and, as My Father has taught Me, so have I declared to the world. Never have I kept back any profitable doctrine from the ears of the faithful.

" For thirty-three years have I now sojourned upon earth, and held sweet converse with men. Often have I been wearied by journeys, grievously slandered by adversaries, betrayed by a disciple, deserted by friends, seized by enemies, beaten by officials, condemned by Judges, insulted by Chief Priests, and here, being innocent, hanged on the Cross.

"What more ought I to do that I have not done? What more ought I to suffer that I have not suffered? If there be ought wanting, either as to doing or suffering, that I am ready to supply before My Death; yea, by My Death every debt will I pay to the full. Therefore this day I declare all to be finished.

"Nor do I suffer the term of My life to be further prolonged, but, in My love, I lay down My life for My sheep. In the very hour, in which I know that the first man incurred everlasting death, by tasting the forbidden tree, I freely, for the offences of sinners, undergo the death of the flesh—a death I have not merited by any transgression of Mine.

"For the things concerning Me shall soon have an end. Henceforth I will not talk much in the world, because I shall not be long here, for I hasten to the Father. All labor shall now come to an end, sorrow and sighing shall now flee away, strife shall cease. There shall be no more trouble—yea, death itself shall also be destroyed.

"Nothing further remains to be done, save to commend My Spirit to My Father, and to leave My Body in the earth until the third day. Of this I feel assured, that loving men, mindful of former friendship, will take that Body away with them, and bury it in a new tomb.

" Therefore, to show the complete fulfilment of all righteousness according to the Law, and to secure the institution of the new Law, I make public, to all who hear Me, this last brief sentence, and say, It is finished."

O Lord Jesus Christ, Thou most illustrious and most faithful Master, as Thou sayest and testifiest, so in truth it is; in Thy words can no fault be found. For all that Thou utterest Thou confirmest by holy deeds, and showest Thy doings to be in accordance with the sure word of prophecy. Now, verily, is the time that Thou shouldest rest from all Thy work on earth.

And, indeed, Thou O Lord with the Father didst, in the beginning, create all things, and now, together with the Father, Thou hast re-created all things. In six days Thou didst complete the creation of the world; and now, in the sixth age of the world, Thou hast completed the redemption of man.

On the sixth day, Thou didst make man from the dust of the earth; and on the sixth day Thou didst redeem him with Thy Blood. On the sixth day Adam was tempted and deceived by Eve; on the sixth day Thou wast announced by an Angel and conceived in the Virgin. On the sixth day man sinned and lost Paradise; on the sixth day Thou didst suffer for our sins, and the thief by Thy mercy recovered Paradise.

Therefore, in order that new things may correspond with old, and the last acts with the first, Thy sixth cry on the cross was fittingly, "It is finished."

Go now, O Lord Jesus, whithersoever Thou wilt, and return to Thy Father in heaven, because Thou hast finished the great work of mercy on earth. Go before Thy servants, prepare for them the way to follow Thee quickly. Open the gate of the kingdom of heaven, which the rashness of our first parent had long closed.

Go, visit the holy Fathers in the place of departed Spirits. Give light to them that sit in darkness; break the power of the devil; loosen the bonds of the captives; help the weary; comfort the sorrowful; redeem those that are anxiously looking for Thee; lead forth Thy captives from their prison-house below.

And when Thou hast led them forth, and placed them with the Angels in the high mansions of heaven; then, O Lord, remember me in Thy kingdom; that Thou mayest lead me forth from this bond-house, from this earthly habitation of the flesh, from this my perilous state, from this world of uncertainty and misery.

Imitate then Christ in this sentence, thou

follower of Christ; cease not to labor so long as thou hast time and strength. What thou hast begun, finish; so that, when the end of thy life is near at hand, thou also mayest say with the loving Jesus, "It is finished."

Wherefore, walk in the way of true virtue, follow righteousness, strive against sin even unto death, that thou mayest lay hold on eternal Life, and be able to say, with the Apostle Paul, "I have fought a good fight, I have finished my course, I have kept the faith."

Thou wilt have but light labor, thou wilt after all suffer but for a short season; soon thine hour shall come; and then, having finished life in a little time, it will be as the completion of a long period.

O Jesu Christ, brightest and most perfect example of all virtues, and the endless reward of good works; Thou ruler of heaven and earth, guide me, that, in all I do, I may please Thee; purify and enlighten the thoughts of my heart.

Teach me, to the praise and glory of Thy blessed Name, to begin all my works humbly, to continue them diligently, and to end them happily.

Grant that I may not become lukewarm before the time appointed of the Father; but, looking for Life eternal, may I night and day labor in Thy holy vineyard, and earnestly strive in the school of heavenly doing, until my spirit shall pass from me.

Then, at the last, by Thy mercy, after many struggles and long laborings, I may be able, in the hour of my departure, joyfully to say with Thee, " It is finished."

Render to me, O good Jesus, reward for the labor, rest for the fatigue, gladness for the sorrow, a crown for the struggle, glory for the shame, blessedness for the misery I have in this world endured. For Thou art, and hast ever been, the final cause of all my works, in this place of my pilgrimage.

Be Thou my recompense in the Kingdom of Heaven ; for there is none that I desire like unto Thee for the reward of my labors, Who art the blessedness and glory of all Thy Saints.

CHAPTER XXIX

ON THE SOLEMN DEATH AND EXPIRING OF JESUS, AND HIS LAST WORDS FROM THE CROSS

I BLESS and give Thee thanks, O Lord Jesu Christ, Thou Life of the living, Thou Hope of the dying, and the Salvation of all that put their trust in Thee, for Thy departure from this world for a season, and Thy happy return to the Father, through the torture of a dreadful death, and for the notable martyrdom on the Cross.

I praise and glorify Thee for Thy pallid appearance, when surrendering Thyself to death, and for Thy blessed Agony in Thy last moments; for the complete loss of all Thy strength, and for the penal breaking of Thy loving heart. Thou art the Quickener of all spirits, yet Thou fearedst not to undergo the sentence of death, that Thou mightest open to us the way to Thy heavenly kingdom.

I praise and give Thee glory for sending on high a loud cry from the Cross, a cry far beyond the power and manner of men; for the sad divorce and bitter separation of Thy most noble soul from Thy most loving body;

For the most devout commendation of Thy Spirit into the hands of the Father; for the lowly bending of Thy sacred thorn-crowned head towards Thy breast, so worthy of honor —sign, indeed, of filial obedience steadily accomplished;

For Thy loving yielding up of Thy most holy Life for the salvation of the world, and for Thy last utterance in this mortal life; when Thou didst break forth into these words of pious supplication, and didst recite this most devout versicle: "Father, into Thy hands I commend My Spirit." Having so spoken, Thou didst forthwith give up the Ghost, and finish Thine earthly pilgrimage in a sweet sleep.

O how precious and victorious a death was that, which slew our death, and restored to us eternal Life!

May therefore Thy Death, O Christ, ever remain fixed in my memory; and in Thy blessed Death may I be mindful also of mine own; lest, when the end of my life, all so uncertain, shall come upon me, I be found trembling in despair.

This is the hour which, from Thy conception, Thou hadst ever before Thee; towards which Thou didst hasten as a traveller to his fatherland, as a wise workman to the end he had in view.

From the highest heavens, indeed, Thy going forth was into the world, from the world even to the grave; and from the grave to the throne supreme didst Thou retrace Thy steps.

Now, O my soul, sorrow deeply over the most bitter Death of thy most loving Lord God. Consider how Jesus died, and what the signs at His departure.

Behold how the just man dies, and no man layeth it to heart; no one reflects what and how great He was, save His poor Mother, who, with a few of His acquaintances, stood by the Cross weeping.

For, indeed, she sees her most beloved Son hanging before her, His Body naked and bleeding; she marks the pallor of death setting in; she watches Him in His Agony; she hears His dying cry.

Surely no marvel is it, if, on beholding such a sight, her heart was heavily oppressed; if she grew exceeding pale, and her very soul failed her touching her Saviour, now in her very presence crucified and dead.

And do thou, therefore, with Mary, draw near to the Cross, and with sorrow meditate on the Death of Jesus. Behold, the innocent Jesus dies; in nakedness He is exiled; never was man more miserable than He. No one more beloved of God, no one more despised of men, than Jesus of Nazareth, crucified by the Jews!

Mark the return rendered Him by the world, for all His glorious works and wonders. He is put to death as the vilest of robbers, He dies the poorest of all men. No bed of down is His, He lies on the rough wood of the Cross. No home, no roof has He: nought but the open field, a spot foul and despised. No private chamber, His is the public scaffold. No dying with His disciples around Him, He hangs between two thieves. No comfort of a Mother's arms has He, His sole embrace the arms of the lofty Cross.

Beneath Him He had not a morsel of straw, nor over Him one single covering of the lightest linen. No pillow was there for His head, in its stead a crown of sharp thorns. No shoes were on His feet, no protection on His hands, but in the place thereof were iron nails, piercing flesh and bones.

In His so great necessity, not even a single servant had He; His only neighbor an evil-doer —a base robber, who loaded Him with heavy reproaches. No comforter had He, for nearly all who once had sat at meat with Him, and they who had been His followers, He found deserters.

He could move neither hand nor foot, nor could He change His position, nor turn Himself from one side to another, and so find some little relief to His bodily suffering.

He stands firmly fixed, rigidly extended, intensely tortured, straitened on every side, neglected, helpless, unconsoled, as one dead at the very heart.

His tongue alone was left at liberty to speak, that He might pray for His enemies; and deliver to us, from the pulpit of the Cross, seven most salutary utterances against the seven deadly sins. But, verily, His very tongue was not free from trouble, for, when He thirsted, it was worried by gall and vinegar.

Thus, from the sole of the foot even to the crown of the head, Jesus is wholly sunk in the waters of affliction; and at the ninth hour, crying with a loud voice, gives up the ghost.

O what, and how great is He, Who, thus crying aloud, dies; at Whose departure heaven and earth mourn; from Whose presence death flees away!

At Whose voice the dead rise again; before Whose face the gates of death are broken; Whose presence the evil one cannot endure; Whose power none can resist; before Whom, they who are beneath tremble, they who are above adore.

Whom Angels serve, and to Whom Archangels are obedient; by Whose brightness the resting place of the Fathers is lit up, the whole body of the Saints is rejoiced, bonds are loosened, and many spoils of souls set free.

"Truly this was the Son of God," says the Centurion. For, when this blessed man saw that Jesus so cried out and gave up the ghost, he perceived that the God Invisible dwelt in the human nature; and forthwith confessed that He, who was mocked of the Jews and crucified, was truly the Son of God.

O, ye Jews, your hearts are as adamant, for

ye are neither softened by the punishment of the sufferer, nor converted by the unheard-of wonders at His Death.

Hearken then ye deaf, mark well ye blind, who ask that a sign be shown you from heaven.

Behold, signs are wrought in heaven above and on the earth beneath; the elements of this world are Christ's ministers, and in the hour of His departure all things are moved with compassion; while ye, wretched creatures, laugh Him to scorn.

For the sun, refusing to look down on His Death, at midday becomes dark; and the earth quakes with fear, unwilling to bear quietly the injury done to God.

The rocks are mightily torn asunder, and with loud noises mourn for their Creator. The veil of the temple is rent; that, by the taking away of the old veil, the sacred mysteries of Christ may be made manifest. For He is our true Sacrifice, that taketh away the sins of the world. He is the spotless Lamb of God, offered on the Cross at the Paschal season.

He is the true Priest consecrated by God, Who offered up Himself a Sacrifice to the Father, for a sweet-smelling savor. He is the High Priest, who, once every year, enters alone into the Holy of Holies, that He may plead, not only for the Jewish nation, but for the salvation of all who believe in Him.

This He truly did by dying once for the human race in the end of the world. The graves also were opened, that the future Resurrection of Christ with many Saints might be shown near at hand.

How many who had come together to the sight, on beholding these miracles, severely conscience-stricken, smote upon their breasts and returned.

Return thou also, O my soul, into thine inner self, and mourn with them that mourn; weep thou with them that weep for Christ, lest thou be found harder than the rocks, and more faithless than the Jews.

Blessed are the tears poured forth for the love of Christ crucified; for it is godly and sweet indeed to weep for so sweet a Lord.

This is the great comfort to a loving soul, deeply to grieve in compassion for the Beloved.

Jesus Himself often wept over the miseries of man, and, when tears failed, out of His abundant compassion, He poured forth His Blood.

Since then for thee the Lord Jesus Christ died on the Cross; let, therefore, this world henceforth be wholly dead to thee.

Learn, in the death of Jesus, to bear in mind thine own death, and strive earnestly to pre-

pare thyself for it. For thou knowest not at
what time the Lord cometh ; thou knowest not
when thy Maker will take thee away.

Ever be on the watch, and pray that thou
mayest find a peaceful hour. So act and so
speak, as if this very day were thy last.

Learn before death to die, that, when death
does come to thee, it be not thy terror, but the
gate of life. Christ is dead and the Prophets
are dead, and thou wilt quickly follow in the
way of the Fathers.

Still there is a great hope, a very great comfort in the words of Jesus, when He says, "He
that believeth in Me, though he were dead, yet
shall he live."

And again, "He that heareth My word, and
believeth on Him that sent Me, hath everlasting
Life."

Therefore, make Jesus thy Friend whilst thou
livest ; that, when thou diest, thou mayest find
Him propitious.

Cast from thee whatsoever hinders thee from
the love of Jesus, whatsoever keepeth thee back
from the Kingdom of Heaven.

Beware of everything that can defile the purity of conscience ; forsake whatever may take
away peace of mind.

Keep thyself apart from the world, alone
with God, intimate with Christ.

Walk with Jesus in the liberty of the Spirit. Take no care for the things of this life.

Make ready for Him the house of thy mind, show Him a large upper room furnished; that with His disciples He may keep the mystic Passover with thee before thou diest.

And when thou beginnest to wax feeble, and perceivest the time of thy call from this world to be at hand, then send forth thy humble prayers to Jesus, and say with Mary and Martha, "Lord! behold! he whom Thou lovest is sick."

For the gracious and merciful Jesus, Who wept at the grave of Lazarus and raised him from the dead, is able to take care of thee under every trial; and, when thou art dead to this world, to raise thee up again at the last day.

Think then earnestly and specially on the Lord's Supper, how the lowly Jesus washed the feet of the disciples; and, before His decease, gave to them the comforting mystery of His sacred Body.

And do thou, therefore, humbly ask the Lord Jesus to wash thee from the pollution of all thy sins; and that, by the spiritual food of His most precious Body and Blood thou mayest be surely strengthened before thy departure.

When this thou hast taken, occupy thyself in

thanksgiving, and devoutly meditate on the sweet words of His command.

And then, with eyes raised heavenward, desire, from the depths of thy soul, union with Christ.

After this, turn thee to the Passion of Christ, and draw therefrom the very essence of comfort.

Enter, also, with Jesus and His disciples, into the garden by the Mount of Olives; that is, go apart from thy friends, that thou mayest be more thoroughly alone with God in secret, and pray to thy heavenly Father for a happy ending of thine earthly sojourn.

Bend thy knees with Jesus, fall on thy face to the earth, and, resigning thyself into the hands of God, say these most perfect words of Christ: "Father, not my will, but Thine be done." For He knows perfectly whether to live or die is best for thee.

And also ask the brethren who come to thee, and all the faithful, to watch with thee in prayer, lest the wiles of the enemy disquiet thee.

In any time of distress flee to Jesus, and follow Him as He bears His Cross, even to Mount Calvary. There firmly stand; there desire to end thy life, and there draw thy last breath.

Place the Passion and Death of Jesus between

thee and the Judgment to come, and look steadfastly on the Crucified.

Against the terrors of the devil call on the name of Jesus, and lift up the standard of the Holy Cross.

If he lay to your charge past misdeeds and many sins, do thou display the infinite merits of Christ.

Remember, also, the seven utterances of Jesus, which He spake on the Cross for thy instruction.

For, no sooner had He ascended the Cross, than He prayed for His enemies, and pardoned those that sinned against Him; that thou in thine heart shouldest forgive all thy debtors, and again plead thyself for forgiveness.

Secondly, to the penitent thief He promised the joys of Paradise, that thou mightest not despair on account of the greatness of thine offences; but mightest also with confidence ask Him, to remember thee in the Kingdom of Heaven.

Thirdly, He commended His most blessed Mother, the Virgin, to St. John; that, when thou art in the agony of death, thou shouldest earnestly commend thyself to the prayers of all that are near and dear to thee—yea, of all the faithful in Christ.

Fourthly, Jesus showed Himself deserted

during His punishments; that, when thou art weighed down with sorrows, thou shouldest not be impatient, if thou art not immediately relieved, but in all things submit thyself to the ordinance of God.

Fifthly, He saith "I thirst," that thou shouldest ardently thirst after God, the Living Fountain; and shouldest desire to die and be with Christ. For this is far better than to sojourn longer in the world, and be still involved in sundry perils.

Sixthly, He uttered the word of consummation, "It is finished!" that, when thou perceivest the end of thy days to be at hand, thou shouldest praise God for every good work done in thee; and shouldest pray that, whatever thou hast failed to do, it may, by the mercy of Christ, be looked on as finished.

Seventhly, He, with a strong cry, delivered His soul into the hands of the Father; that thou also, when about to leave this world, shouldest not fail to read and frequently repeat the words of blessed commendation of Himself; than which, in thy last moments, thou wilt find nothing more sweet to be remembered.

O most loving Jesus, Brightness of the Father's glory, and Sun of righteousness, who didst deign for me, Thine unworthy servant, to suffer the vilest form of sorrow; and on Calvary didst, for the Redemption of the world, deliver up Thy soul, and commend it to Thy Father in prayer, grant that I may bear about continually in my breast a sorrow and a love for Thy most bitter Death.

May I, by mortifying all my evil affections, daily exercise myself in dying with Thee; so that, when the end of my life approaches, I may by Thy merits be deemed worthy to breathe in the light of Thy mercies, and to enter peacefully with Thee into the joys of Paradise.

Be Thou with me when I am dying; support me in the conflict; come to me longing for Thee. Defend me from the enemy, rescue me from misery, comfort me in my mourning, strengthen me when trembling, revive me when drooping, receive me at my death.

May Thy last words on the Cross be my last words in this life; and, when I can no longer speak, hear my last craving: "Father, into Thy hands I commend my spirit; for Thou hast redeemed me, O Lord, Thou God of truth. Amen."

CHAPTER XXX

ON THE VICTORIOUS DEATH OF JESUS OUR RE· DEEMER

O LORD JESU CHRIST, Thou spotless mirror of the Divine Majesty, I bless and give
Thee thanks for Thy miserable and pallid appearance, caused by death's assault on Thee;
when, on Thy Soul leaving the Body, certain
signs of mortality appeared in Thee.

Alas! alas! O Jesu, Thou of all the fairest!
The beauty of Thy most pleasant countenance
has perished, through the foulness of those
who spat upon Thee with unclean lips; and, in
the struggle of death, the flower of Thy most
acceptable youth has faded.

Oh! most gracious God! all these things
came upon Thee for the cleansing of my sins.
Thou didst freely submit to be disfigured in
body, that I might be pure in soul; and that I
might be delivered from everlasting death,
Thou didst, for a season, taste a most cruel
Death.

O Death, what hast thou done? Wherefore
wast thou not afraid to lay thine hand on the
Lord's Anointed? What right hadst thou over

Him ?　Or what fault couldest thou find in the Son of God ?

Thou hast fallen upon Him, thou hast slain Him; but thou hast not assaulted Him without injury to thyself.　For, in destroying life thou hast destroyed thyself; and having been pierced through with the hook of Christ's Divinity, thou hast lost the sovereignty of thy cruel dominion; and, through Christ's soul descending to the realms below, thou hast been compelled to give up all the Elect that died in Adam, so long held captive by the prince of darkness.

For so had it been foretold by the Prophet of old : "O death, I will be thy death; O grave, I will be thy destruction."　Whence also in the Church, with loud voices, is fitly sung : "Life dies upon the tree, the grave is deprived of its sting."　Therefore, in Thy death, O Christ, the hope of life is restored to me; and, the prince of death being vanquished, a crown of joy is granted me.

Truly great and manifold favors flowed from Thee, when, for our life, Thou didst die on the Cross.

For original guilt is blotted out, our own iniquity is forgiven, pardon is extended, punishment is softened, vengeance is stayed, every debt is paid; to none who weep is mercy denied, for inexhaustible is the merit of Thy Passion. Truly Thou hast not died in vain!

For whom then hath He died? Since the Angels needed it not, for they remained steadfast in the truth. The devil never can rise again, for straightway after his fall he became hardened.

For man, therefore, hast Thou died; who, being beguiled by the devil, became ruined and subject to death. And fitting was it Thy love should raise up him, whom the malice of an alien had cast down.

O vast compassion! O ineffable depth of Divine counsel! O adorable and ever to be remembered mystery, by which man, through the Cross, obtains salvation; through the offence, comes to the kingdom; through suffering, enters into glory; and through death, is brought back to Life eternal!

Thy most sacred Passion, therefore, O Lord, is a medicine for all wounds. Thy Cross is the ruin of all enemies, and the renowned defence of the faithful. Thy Death is death to all vices, and the source of all virtues.

I will, therefore, rejoice in the benefit and fruit of Thy Passion. I will take comfort from my redemption. Yet will I grieve, as I behold Thy love, and for Thy most bitter Death.

For it is an act of piety to rejoice with Thee, because Thou hast overcome death; equally pious is it to sorrow with Thee, since Thou hast been a man of sorrows indeed for me.

Come now, O faithful soul, behold the sad and pallid form of the Crucified Saviour. Study every member of the dead Jesus, and, in the abundance of Thy compassion, let thine eyes run down with tears: for, when thou gazest upon Jesus hanging on the Cross, profitably art thou occupied; very holy is the exercise in which thou art engaged.

As a cluster of camphor in the vineyards of Engaddi, so is the image of the Crucified in the heart of a just man. If, therefore, thou hast an eye of pity, if thou hast within thee any human kindness, look upwards, and gaze in meditation on the Crucified God, dead on the Cross for thee.

Behold the Cross, on which hangs thy salvation, the redemption of the godly, the scorn of the infidel; His head, covered with thorns, is bent low towards His sacred breast; nor is there now any sign of life in Him.

The eyes of Him, from Whom no secret can be hid, now see nothing. The ears of Him, Who knoweth all things before they come to pass, now hear nothing. He, Who gives to flowers their sweet odor, now cannot smell. He,

Who giveth life and food to all things living, can now no longer taste.

He, Who opens the mouth of the dumb, moves not His lips. He, Who teacheth man knowledge, utters not a word. The tongue, which always spoke fitly, now lies firmly fixed. The face, once brighter than the sun, is now veiled by a deadly pallor. The cheeks, comely as the turtle-dove's, have lost the perfection of beauty.

The hands, which stretched forth the heavens, are pierced with sharp nails. The knees, so often bent in prayer, hang senseless and naked. The legs, which like pillars of marble bore the weight of the whole body, are devoid of strength and vigor. The feet, often wearied with preaching the gospel, are, as if in the pillory fixed, iron-bound to the wood of the Cross.

All His members seem full of pain, covered with wounds, besmeared with blood. Yet, that the Holy Scriptures might be fulfilled, His bones were not broken, as were the bones of the malefactors. For He is the true Lamb prefigured in the Law, whose bones are commanded to be kept whole.

Such is my Beloved, and this is my Friend, ye daughters of Jerusalem. And this is the end of the Death of Him, for which, were I to offer ten thousand lives, it would be no worthy repayment of His love.

O most sweet Jesus, Redeemer of my soul, would that I could die on the Cross with Thee! May there be for me a like happy season with Thee on my departure from the body!

Grant me, I beseech Thee with all my heart, so to live in this frail body, and so to direct all my doings and my desires according to Thy good pleasure, that I may be able to finish my course in a state of grace; and, after sundry perils and temptations, to obtain through Thee, O Christ, the prize of everlasting blessedness.

CHAPTER XXXI

ON THE CRUEL PIERCING OF THE HOLY SIDE OF JESUS CHRIST

O LORD JESU CHRIST, Thou never-failing Fountain of love and grace, I bless and give Thee thanks for the cruel piercing of Thy most sacred side, after Thy life had departed.

For then, O Holiest of the Holy, Thou wast so violently smitten and pierced in the right side by one of the soldiers, that the point of the iron, penetrating inwardly, reached Thy tender heart. From the wide wound came forth a most saving fountain of water and blood, that, sprinkled therewith, the whole world might be saved.

O sacred and wondrous flow of the precious Blood of Christ, pouring forth, for the redemption of man, from His right side, while He was sleeping on the Cross!

O bright and grateful flow of blessed water, issuing from the inmost parts of the Saviour, to cleanse us from all our sins!

Moses, the servant of the Lord, struck of old the rock in the wilderness, so that the waters gushed out abundantly; and the people and their cattle drank from that stream with joy, and all murmuring ceased.

But Longinus, a soldier strong and rough, spear in hand, with great force struck the rock, when he opened the right side of Jesus, and forthwith there came out blood and water. From thence our chaste Mother, the Church, has drawn the Sacraments of salvation.

For, as Eve is called the Mother of all living, and was formed of the rib of Adam, her husband; so also the Holy Church Militant is called the Mother of all the faithful, and is formed anew out of the side of Christ, her Spouse.

O great and precious wound of my Lord! to be tenderly loved above all wounds, deeply pierced and widely opened, that all the faithful may enter; marvellous in its flowing, abundantly blessed; last formed, but chief in note.

Whosoever drinketh from the sacred and divine fountain of this wound, or once taketh a draught of love therefrom, he shall forget all his evils, he shall be no longer inflamed by the heat of worldly and carnal desires; but shall ardently burn with the unspeakable love of things eternal, and be filled with the sweetness of the Holy Spirit—yea, it shall be in him a well of living water, springing up into everlasting Life.

Enter, O my soul, enter into the right side of thy crucified Lord. Enter, by this renowned wound, into the most loving heart of Jesus, out of love transpierced; that, in the cleft of the rock, thou mayest find a resting place from the tempest of the world.

Draw near, O man, to this heart, all so deep, hidden, and secret; to the heart of God, Who openeth His door to thee. Come in, thou blessed of the Lord, wherefore standest thou without? The vein of life is open to thee—the way of salvation—the heavenly ark, from whence flow sweet spices abundantly.

Behold a place of refuge from the face of thine enemy, the tempter—a place of propitiation from the wrath of the judgment to come.

This is the ever-flowing fountain of unction and grace, which never ceases to provide pardon for sinners, who seek to draw near with a hearty repentance.

This is the source of the sacred river, going forth from the midst of Paradise, to water the face of the earth: to quench the thirst of the parched mind, to wash away sins, to keep under all carnal desires, and stay the ragings of anger. Take thou, therefore, the cup of love from this fountain of the Saviour.

Draw from the side of Jesus the sweet solaces of life; that thou mayest now live, not in thyself, but in Him Who was wounded for thee.

Give thy heart to Him, Who opened His heart to thee. Enter, by the door of the hallowed wound, into the inward recesses of the Redeemer.

He bids thee enter, and pleads with thee to abide with Him. His desire is that thou shouldest have one heart with Him. "My son (He says), give Me thine heart." Nothing more does God require of thee; if thou givest this, thou presentest an offering most acceptable to Him.

Give it therefore to Jesus, not to another; give it to Christ, not to the world. Yea, give thine heart to eternal wisdom, not to a vain philosophy.

For this, therefore, it was, He caused His

side to be opened so widely, and to be so deeply
pierced; that a way of approach to the heart
of thy Beloved might be clear to thee; that
thou mightest be able to penetrate the secret
places of the Son of God, and to be joined to
Him in true union of heart; that thou mightest direct all thy affections towards Him; and,
with singleness of heart, do all thy works to
His honor; that thy whole study may be to
please Him alone, and to cling to Him with a
pure mind and with all thy strength.

For, where wilt thou be able to rest more
securely, dwell more safely, and sleep more
sweetly, than in the wounds of Jesus Christ,
Who was crucified for thee?

Where wilt thou possibly find greater wisdom, and receive a better guidance of life, than
in the depths of Christ, Who suffered for thee;
from under Whose breast pours forth for thee
a fountain of living water?

Where, when lukewarm, wilt thou be so effectually restored to the glow of love; where
so quickly rescued from all turmoil; where so
perfectly brought to inward recollection; as in
the heart of Jesus, which, out of love of thee,
received the piercing spear?

Nothing so inflames, draws, and penetrates
the heart of man, as the love of the Crucified
Redeemer. Hence, indeed, a Saint of old (Ig-

natius) was wont to say, "My love was crucified." To whom I affectionately reply, "My
love too was wounded and pierced, that to me
may be given a ready entrance to His loving
heart."

Hasten then with all becoming eagerness, apply thyself to the sacred side of Jesus, that thou
mayest be sprinkled with His Blood and Water.

And, as far as can be, draw out thine own
heart, and place it near the heart of Jesus; that
He may guard, rule, and have possession of it;
that it may be no more hurried hither and
thither, and so defiled.

Lay open thine heart to Him; commit thyself boldly to Him; before Him place thine
every wish and fear; be of one heart and one
soul in God; ever to think and feel with Him
in all things, according to His highest good
pleasure.

Then, in great peace, thou shalt not be easily
disturbed, nor oppressively grieved; when thou
hast given thine heart entirely to Jesus, to keep
it and dwell therein for ever.

O Jesu most pure, the Creator of all things
secret, and Who dwellest in the hearts of them
that love Thee! O Thou that art to all the
contemplative a Cross-formed spectacle! O divine Treasury of all gifts and graces! O Christ,
our King, Redeemer of the faithful! Who didst

cause Thy most sacred side to be opened by the sharp point of a dreadful spear; open to me, I pray Thee, the gate of Thy compassion.

Suffer me to enter, by the great and open door of Thy side, the secret recesses of Thy most loving heart; that my heart may be united to Thee by the inseparable bond of love, and vehemently inflamed thereby; so that Thou mayest dwell in me, and I in Thee; and that I may remain one with Thee for ever.

Wound my heart with the arrow of Thy love. Let Thy spear, as it were a soldier's weapon, pass through my flesh, and penetrate my inner self.

So that, from this salutary wounding, my soul may obtain perfect health—admitting no lover save Thee, seeking for no consolation beyond Thee.

May my heart be accessible and open to Thee alone; alien to the world, closed to Satan, and strengthened on all sides, by the standard of the Cross, against every trial that may beset it.

CHAPTER XXXII

ON THE TAKING DOWN OF CHRIST FROM THE CROSS

I BLESS and give Thee thanks, O Lord Jesu
Christ, Thou strength divine, for Thy humble descent at eventide from the lofty Cross; on
which, for our Salvation, Thou didst hang until the setting of the sun; and from which
Thou wast ordered to be taken down, according to the regulation of the old Law; and because of the approaching day of the Paschal
Feast, to be kept on the holy Sabbath.

I praise and glorify Thee for the ready service so lovingly rendered Thee by Thy familiar
friends, when those pious men, Joseph of Ari-
mathæa, and Nicodemus, a Doctor of the Law,
coming with their servants to the Cross,
mounted ladders raised aloft; the one ascending on Thy right hand, the other on Thy
left; while a third was occupied loosing Thy
feet.

With all honor and reverence they extracted
from Thy sacred hands and feet three precious
nails, more valuable far than shining gold.
Then, with the assistance of powerful compan-

ions, reverently embracing Thy most noble Body, they modestly and carefully lowered it to the ground.

Blessed men of mercy are ye, who paid this loving attention to the Lord your God, that ye might duly deliver Him over for burial! For the fidelity which ye formerly manifested to your Friend, when He was alive, ye afterwards took care to exhibit, with even greater devotion, when He was dead.

Therefore from God, to whom ye proved yourselves so faithful on earth, ye shall in heaven receive a special reward. He, for Whom ye have now prepared a place of burial on earth, will doubtless, in return, prepare for you a happier mansion in heaven; just as He promised His disciples, the night before His Crucifixion.

O that I also, the least of the servants of God, had been allowed to attend the burial of my Lord; there to have rendered some service however small! How readily would I have held the ladder to the Cross, or have stretched forth the workman's pincers to extract the nails, or even have aided those who lowered the sacred Body!

O what a privilege for me, had I stood near enough to receive into my bosom, for a sweet memorial of His Passion, one of the nails of my Lord, as it fell from above; that, as oft as

I gazed thereon, I might forthwith be moved to tears!

I laud and glorify Thee for that enviable embrace, when Thou wast received and embraced within the hands and arms of Thy most sorrowful Mother; yea, when, out of compassionate devotion, Thou wast delivered to her by Thy faithful ones, and placed in the Virgin's lap.

O what precious tears then flowed from her most pure eyes, what warm drops ran down those cheeks all-chaste, and from the maternal face quickly bedewed Thy dead Body.

O what pure lips Thy pure Mother then impressed upon Thy lifeless limbs; how sorrowfully and how ceaselessly did she look on the all-holy wound-marks!

O with what clinging arms did she embrace the blessed fruit of her womb; that fruit which she saw offered up on the Altar of the Cross, for the salvation of the world!

Who, however devoted, could conceive the cutting misery of such anguish? Who declare the abundance of those tears?

Draw nearer then now, O my soul, and devoutly kiss the blood-marked wounds of Jesus. For, when He was hanging nailed on the Cross, no way of approaching Him was open, because of the pressing crowd and the loftiness of the

Cross; but now He is found in the bosom of His weeping Mother, lying there wounded and dead.

Draw near, therefore, however great a sinner; thou, whom the fear of eternal condemnation greatly alarms; because for thee the Lamb has been slain, for thee hath been offered a Sacrifice, which hath taken away the sins of the whole world.

So gracious and merciful is the Lord Jesus, that no one can go away empty, no one disconsolate; provided in penitence he heartily seeks for pardon.

O how sweet are those words to me, a sinner; sweeter than honey and the honeycomb to my heart. For whatever I read that Jesus suffered in the flesh, all, I perceive, was done for me.

May I, here on earth, with bended knees humbly adore Christ my Redeemer; until called away to give Him glory for ever in the Heaven of Heavens.

CHAPTER XXXIII

ON THE REVEREND BURIAL OF JESUS CHRIST

O LORD JESU CHRIST, Thou savor of life and brightness of eternal light, I bless and give Thee thanks for Thine anointment with the

sweetest composition of precious spices. For,
although it was not necessary for Thee to keep
away corruption, still was it, as a mark of the
devotion of Thy friends, very acceptable to
Thee. And further, it was to be lawfully applied to Thee in full accord with Jewish custom,
as we read concerning certain Patriarchs and
Kings, who received like burial.

I praise and honor Thee for the careful wrap-
ping of Thy sacred Body in a clean linen cloth,
and for the decent infolding of Thy blessed
head in a pure white napkin; which was afterwards found lying by itself in the Holy Sepulchre.

I praise and glorify Thee for Thy mournful
conveyance to the place of burial, for the solemn
laying Thee down, and for Thy lowly extension
within the new tomb, hewn out of the rock,
given to Thee by Joseph, an honorable Counsellor. There, as the hour was getting late,
with much weeping Thou wast honorably
buried, and firmly closed in under a large stone
rolled unto the door of the sepulchre.

Rejoice, O venerable Joseph, in an office of
such great piety, and in so sublime a labor of
love for Christ. I thank thee heartily, and
most highly commend thy noble bearing, in
that thou didst this—a matter most worthy of
all honor.

Because, not only didst thou ask of Pilate permission to bury Jesus, but didst also open to Him thine own sepulchre; which thou hadst prepared for thyself, to be thine own resting-place after death.

O how highly has God esteemed thee, that He should choose to be buried in thy grave, above all other places in the world! He, indeed, in Whose power are all the regions of the earth, and whatever is contained within the circuit of the heavens.

I tell thee, most illustrious of men, that, henceforth as long as the world shall stand, and the number of the faithful flourish, ye shall be honored before God and men. For this venerable Sepulchre shall be more glorious and renowned than all other sepulchres, whether of Saints or Kings; and, above all others, shall be told of with the highest praise in every region of the earth.

Many pilgrims will come from the far off corners of the world to visit this holy spot, and will worship in this place, where the Body of the Lord found rest.

Here Jesus was buried; here the Crucified One was laid; here the women bewailed Him; here soldiers guarded Him.

Here Christ rose again the third day; here Jesus was seen by Mary Magdalene; here an

Angel of the Lord appeared from heaven; here the guards of the Sepulchre were affrighted and became as dead.

Do thou, therefore, also abide here awhile, near unto the Sepulchre, and with the women lament for the Lord Jesus, who was buried for thee. For it behoves thee deeply to grieve for Him, from Whom thou longest to receive the gift of unceasing joy.

Consider how sorely the loving friends of Christ then sorrowed, and especially the holy women, when they beheld Jesus taken from them, and shut up in the Sepulchre.

For the love of Whom they had despised all things, and followed Him over a wide region round about; to Whom they had so often and so devotedly ministered of their substance. So much indeed did they love Him, that they could scarcely be separated from Him, even for a little moment.

With Him they ever yearned to live and hold sweet converse, and through Him they believed they were to be for ever blessed. Assuredly, the more intense their love, the more bitter was their lamentation.

But, above all, they chiefly sorrowed because the hope of a Resurrection seemed taken from them; and their faith, in a manner, was buried with Jesus in the tomb.

No consolation, therefore, seemed to be left to His heart-broken followers, save to mourn over the departed, or to go and prepare sweet spices; for, if they could not raise the dead, they could at least, by a most effectual anointing, preserve His Body from corruption.

But, O ye holy and devout women, ye that love Christ with unceasing affection, do not, I pray you, give way to over much sorrow; do not inwardly despair.

Remember the words of Jesus, foretold you by Himself, and wait a little season :—For after three days He will surely rise again.

Then ye shall behold, in great splendor and joyfulness of heart, Him, Whom now ye bewail, entombed in weakness and sadness.

Then to all His friends, who now so heavily mourn over Christ's death and burial, there will come a new joy. Your anointing then will be found in no way necessary, for, when He rises, He shall appear in the highest glory.

He will be clothed in the robe of immortality, nor shall death ever again have dominion over Him.

Learn thou, in the burial of Jesus, to meditate profitably on the dissolution of thine own body. What thou hast received from the earth must needs be committed to the earth, "for dust thou art, and unto dust shalt thou return."

Whence then this boasting, thou that art so soon to decay, and to be buried in the ground? What dost thou long for in the world, seeing thou art so soon to be driven from it, and to be trodden under foot of men?

When thou seest the sepulchres of the dead, remember thou art soon to join them. There, surely, is the appointed home of all living.

There the rich and the poor will lie stretched on one bed, common to all; contented with a small spot of earth.

There the noble is not distinguished from the vulgar, nor is the meek any longer trampled on by one mightier than he. There money profits not the greedy, nor clever villainy the crafty. There the delicate shall be food for worms, and the once gaily attired shall become an offensive odor. There the haughtiness of men shall be bowed down, and the praise of the lofty ones shall vanish.

Behold how the whole race of man passeth away; and all flesh, corrupted by sin, returns to that from whence it came.

Wherefore, labor now so to live and to mortify the deeds of the flesh by the spirit, that, when thy flesh moulders in the dust, thy soul may be meet, through Christ, to rest in peaceful repose.

For, if now, in the day of preparation, thou

livest in labor and sorrow, thou shalt have a holy Sabbath of quiet; and then, in due season, a joyous Passover at the Resurrection of the Just.

By how much the more strictly, therefore, thou now livest in the world, so much the more peaceably thou shalt rest in the grave. By how much the more tightly thou now clingest to the Cross, so much the more boldly shalt thou come to Christ. By how much the more bitterly thou deplorest thy sins, so much the less shalt thou fear to stand in the presence of Jesus, thy Redeemer.

Lament, lament in this thy day of grace, while the door of mercy is open, whilst thy repentance is acceptable to Him with whom is plenteous redemption.

Sorrow also over the miserable state of the world, and the sad ingratitude of man: that so few are found true imitators of Christ crucified; that so many wax cold and fall from their spiritual fervor.

Let it therefore be thy daily exercise to meditate on Jesus Christ, and Him Crucified. Ever set Jesus before thee—from the Cross of Jesus draw not back; but, living and dying, with Jesus enter into the grave, that, when Christ, who is thy life, shall appear, thou mayest with Him rise again in glory. Amen.

PART III

ON THE RESURRECTION OF CHRIST AND HIS SEVERAL APPEARANCES

CHAPTER I

ON THE MOST VICTORIOUS TRIUMPH OF OUR
LORD JESUS CHRIST ON THE CROSS OVER
DEATH; AND ON HIS MOST JOYFUL RESUR-
RECTION FROM THE SEPULCHRE

O LORD JESU CHRIST, I bless and give
Thee thanks, Thou Saviour of the world,
for Thy most victorious triumph over death on
the Cross; and for Thy glorious and joyful
Resurrection from the grave; in which Thou
hadst lain three days and nights, verily dead
for us. With much weeping wast Thou buried,
hidden wast Thou from human eyes, shut in by
a great stone; so that, by Thy friends and disciples, Thou couldest neither be touched nor seen.

Where also Thou wast guarded by faithless
soldiers in strong armor clad; lest, rising again
from the dead, Thou mightest escape out of
their charge; or that, perchance, Thy disciples
might privily take Thee away, and, craftily
carrying Thee elsewhere, might worship Thee
as God; telling to the people, "Jesus, who was
crucified, has risen from the dead."

But sin was surely its own betrayer; and all the subtlety of the devil, all the power of Pilate, all the perversity of the people, all the craftiness of the Priests, all the learning of the Scribes, all the counsel of the Pharisees and Elders, who strove to cast out Thy holy Name from the mouths of men—were brought to nought.

For, assuredly, there is no counsel against the Lord, neither does earthly power prevail against the Most High; nor does the carnal mind profit against the wisdom of God, nor can crafty plotting deceive the God who knoweth all things.

For Thou, who hast founded the earth on its bases, and placed to the sea its bounds, and hast created all things in due weight, number, and measure, knewest also the time and hour of Thy Resurrection; as Thou hadst known the time of Thy Birth and the hour of Thy Death.

Therefore, when midnight was past and the dawn of day near, Thou, O most gracious Jesus, didst with a glorious Body, in the greatest joy and ineffable brightness, rise again from the closed Sepulchre, alive and glad; in like manner as, at Thy nativity, Thou camest forth from the virgin womb of Thy most blessed Mother.

And this most sacred Feast of Thy Resurrection, brighter than the sun, yea brighter far than all the Festivals of the year, the Church hat ordained to be solemnly kept by all the Faithful throughout the world, and that by an ordinance for ever. With one heart and one voice is it to be kept, in hymns and psalms and oft-repeated hallelujahs; and so, in happy commemoration and thanksgiving, recalled to mind most worthily.

For at the break of day, while Angels were looking down and rejoicing with Thee in Thy noble triumph over death and the spoiling of the grave, Thou, Christ, O King, didst mercifully set open to us the gate of Eternity, as Thou hadst foretold to Thy disciples; and, whilst they were yet in their ignorance, Thou didst joyfully put on the robe of Thy glorious Body.

Then all the powers of darkness grieved and groaned at the brightness of Thy countenance, as seen in our human nature.

Great fear also fell upon the soldiers, while with force of arms they were guarding the Sepulchre; for, when the earth shook and they beheld the strange vision of Angels, they forthwith became like unto dead men.

For the Angel of the Lord descended from heaven, shining in snowlike whiteness, and rolled back the great stone from the Sepulchre; and so made ready a straight and secure way for the holy women, who were coming with precious spices to again anoint Jesus. Now they could safely draw near, and see that the tomb was empty, and that Jesus was not there, but had risen.

O Lord Jesu Christ, Most Mighty, King of kings, Prince of heaven and earth, Thou bountiful Creator of all things, I bless and highly exalt Thee for Thy stern overthrow of hell, and the strong binding of proud Lucifer, who was cast into the lake of burning fire.

I praise and glorify Thee for the great subjugation of the wickedness and power of Satan, as exercised by him against the human race; so that evil spirits can no longer prevail against us at their will, as once they were wont to do before Thine Incarnation and Thy Passion.

On whose head were recompensed, with a righteous judgment, all the scandal and plotting of the Jews, intended Thee by Thy death on the Cross between two thieves.

And now, behold Thou hast risen again and vanquished the Kingdom of Hell. Thou hast, by the Standard of the Holy Cross, dashed in pieces the powers of darkness; and under the feet of Thy humble servants, whom Thou hast chosen out of the world, hast Thou trodden their pride to destruction.

For now, all Christians, high and low, rejoice that they are signed with the sign of the Holy Cross, and, to the honor of Thy Name, bear it boldly on their foreheads against the terrors of the old serpent, and the insult of every infidel —Jew and Gentile; who yet hate the Name of Jesus Christ, the Son of God, Who, for the salvation of the world, was crucified.

I praise and honor Thee, O benign Jesus, for the loving visit to the Saints of the Old Testament in their resting place below; and for the liberation of all faithful souls at rest in the bosom of Abraham.

They, who were long ardently awaiting Thy coming on Thy descent into hell, and devoutly crying out to Thee with voices mingled with tears, now sing (as in procession in this our day is sung):—

"Thou hast come, O desired One, for Whom we have been waiting in darkness, that Thou mightest this night lead forth the captives from their prison-house."

Rejoice now therefore, especially thou, O Adam, our primordial father, nature's progenitor of the human race, with Eve thy noble wife, formed from thy side in Paradise. Because from thy race comes the Christ, who was born of a Virgin, and was sacrificed upon the Cross, to deliver thee and all thy fellow-captive

children, who have died in His faith, and in the
hope of heavenly grace. Thy delivery has been
from the holding of the grave, from the house
of bondage, from the shadow of death, from
the den of lions, and from the terror of most
wicked spirits; to restore thee and all thy holy
offspring with joyful sounds of sweetest songs,
to a Paradise of delight and eternal happiness.

And thou, O holy Patriarch Abraham, father
of many nations, rejoice together with faithful
Sarah thy wife, for the Incarnation of Christ,
promised thee of old, and in the present Festival completed;—that Christ, whose day thou
so long expectedst and so desiredst to see.

For, as thou firmly believedst, so now, verily,
thou deservest with joyful face to behold Christ,
born of thy seed, the bestower of a heavenly
Kingdom.

And do thou, most venerable father Isaac,
rejoice with the whole Church, for the bright
vision of Christ, and His descent into hell; the
Christ, of Whom, before thy death, thou didst
prophesy; and, in blessing thy son Jacob, thou
didst beautifully prenote and commend the
Anointed One as blessed above all Saints, saying, "See, the smell of my son is as the smell
of a field, which the Lord hath blessed. Cursed
be every one that curseth thee, and blessed be
every one that blesseth thee."

Wherefore, also, I, hearing and reading these things, give thanks to Thee, my God, and I bless Thy Name, O most sweet Jesu Christ, above all the names of Saints; that I may, with Thine Elect, be blessed now and forever, and may abound in all heavenly virtues, and be made happy with Thy holy Angels.

And, do thou, O Jacob, most renowned wrestler, rejoice in this day, and that especially for the joyful presence and celestial glory of Jesus Christ; of Whom thou in days of old, when blessing thy sons, didst, with faithful prayer, thus prophesy: "I shall wait for Thy Salvation, O Lord."

O truly sweet words to the ear! Full of peace to the pious! O salutary utterance! in which is latently signified the Name of Jesus, the Messiah, by Patriarchs and Prophets so long desired, so patiently waited for, and at last presented to sight.

"For there is none other name under heaven given among men, whereby we must be saved, than the Name of Jesus," sweetest of all names for ever and ever—blessed above all for all ages.

Jesus Himself, indeed, promised in the Law, the Salvation of God, born of a Virgin, and tortured on the Cross, rose again the third day; having fulfilled all things, which the holy Patriarchs and Prophets spake concerning Him.

Speak, therefore, now O holy Jacob—speak openly in the joy of thy heart. Tell of Christ appearing in the glory of His Father, before the Angels of God, " I behold now my Lord face to face, and my soul is made safe." What more dost thou desire? What greater happiness couldest thou have?

If thou hadst such great joy when thou sawest the Angel of God, how much more oughtest thou now to glory, in that thou art permitted to see the Lord of Angels. If thy spirit revived when thou heardest, "Joseph thy son is yet alive; and has rule over all the land of Egypt," how much more wilt thou rejoice over the Resurrection of Christ from the grave, never to die again, but to reign for ever over all things in heaven and on earth.

O all ye holy Patriarchs and Prophets, O kings and leaders of the people, O old men and young, O virgins and faithful widows, O Priests and Levites, Doctors and Scribes, O spirits and souls of just men, O ye that are holy and humble at heart, this day rejoice and be glad in Jesus Christ our Saviour!

Praise and extol Him for ever, because He came to visit you, and to rejoice the hearts of all who were waiting for the redemption of His people Israel.

And now, O most loving Lord Jesu Christ,

Thou true salvation of my soul, and my entire hope in this frail life, from my youth up unto mine old age; yea, at this present day and hour, forsake me not, I beseech Thee, when I am poor and weak, 'mid tribulations and temptations in various ways assailing me.

Comfort me, my God, in every trouble of my heart, by the merits of Thy most sacred Passion; and by the vehement grief and the plenteous tears, which Thou, out of compassion for me, didst pour forth on the Cross.

Make me also partaker of the gladness of all Thy beloved Saints—the Patriarchs, Prophets and Apostles, who rejoice with Thee in the Kingdom of Heaven.

Remember, O Lord, Thy holy Word which Thou spakest: "For many will come from the East and the West, and shall sit down with Abraham, Isaac, and Jacob in the kingdom of heaven."

Grant, therefore, I beseech Thee, O Lord, that I may be admitted to this holy fellowship and celestial feast in the Kingdom of Heaven; O Thou, who, on this day, didst rise from the grave in Thy glorious Body, and didst steadfastly promise the joys of eternal Life with the Angels above to all who love Thee; Who livest and reignest with the Father and the Holy Ghost, ever one God, world without end. Amen.

CHAPTER II

ON THE DEVOUT VISITING OF THE HOLY SEP-ULCHRE OF THE LORD JESU CHRIST

O LORD JESU CHRIST, the Comforter of all that are sad and sorrowing, I bless and thank Thee for that devout visit of the holy women, who very early in the morning, at the rising of the sun, came to Thy Sepulchre, there to see clearly all that had been done on that most solemn night, a night blessed indeed above all nights.

I praise and highly honor that sacred fervor of the saintly women—the noble ladies, seeking again to anoint Thy most holy Body; because, so early in the morning, while it was yet dark and the rest of the world deep in sleep, they hastily arose and went together to the Sepulchre (all so quietly and privately), carrying the spices they had prepared for Thine anointment.

O what great sorrow sprang up in their hearts, what tears came to their eyes, when, on their way, they passed by Calvary, and beheld the Cross, marked the traces of Thy Passion, and thought of all Thy wounds!

O what anguish oppressed them and forced

tears from their eyes, when they beheld the Sepulchre, and said among themselves, "Who shall roll away the stone for us from the door of the Sepulchre?"

For they knew full well, that they could not, by their own strength, remove so great a stone from the tomb.

Fear therefore urged them to go back, but love pressed them onward, regardless of the soldier-guard. "O, if Peter and John were here, we might then indeed hope that gladly they would aid us!"

It is better, O good women, that the Apostles should be in their homes, away unseen, and meanwhile pray for you; that God would protect you and fulfil your desire; far better than that they should come here into bodily peril, and the soldiers slay them.

For thence would arise a greater sorrow, and heavily oppress you: if, after our Lord's Crucifixion, His disciples also should be put to death.

What then will ye do, and whither will ye go? Hold together, I entreat you, and pray. Fear not, but in safety advance. Trust in the Lord, for help will soon be with you from heaven, and a comforting reply from the Angel, who knows what has come to pass concerning the buried Lord.

God sees your heart; who ye are and whence

ye are; whom ye seek, and what ye bear in your hands beneath your cloaks.

For a sweet savor from your spices ascends before God 'mid the heavenly hosts; and the holy Angels rejoice in the sweetness of your devout prayers, and the glowing love ye have for Jesus, now made manifest by your pious act.

Love truly overcometh all things and feareth no one. Love resteth not until it gains sight of the beloved.

Therefore make ye haste, go forward and be silent. Observe the Sepulchre diligently; and, if it be open, enter without fear.

If ye fear to enter, wait awhile and pray. Look heavenwards, knock at the door with mourning and weeping, until the Angel of the Lord descend from heaven, and say unto you, "Be not affrighted, for I know that ye seek Jesus which was crucified. Come and see the place where the Lord was laid. He is not here (as ye see) for He is risen as He said unto you." If ye now keep His words well in remembrance, no doubt ought ye to have of His Resurrection.

The love of Jesus during His Passion saddened you; the love of Him in His Resurrection will give you joy. Wait a little while and ye will assuredly see Him.

No longer seek Him lying in the grave, but

as living with Angels in Heaven. He is not in Bethany supping with Martha, but sitting at the right hand of the Father in the highest glory. He is not in a small boat sailing with Peter, but ruling over all the heavenly Hosts. He is not preaching on the mountain, but holding sway over every creature in heaven and earth.

Remember how He said, that it behoved the Son of Man to be crucified, and that He should be raised again from the dead the third day. Now, therefore, go ye hence comforted and strengthened by the Angel.

Go quickly, and bear the good news to His friends; and tell to His sorrowing disciples the glad tidings of great joy; lest they despair, because they all forsook Jesus and fled. Recall them now to the hope of pardon.

But to Peter, who denied Him thrice, and, in sorrow for his deed, ceases not to weep most bitterly, especially say, that there must be no distrust; bid him rather cast himself on the great and wonted loving-kindness of Jesus, which has been so often shown him; for this very day he shall assuredly see Jesus, and great shall be his joy.

Tell him, moreover, all that ye have heard and seen, that this very night our Lord Jesus Christ is risen indeed.

O Saint Peter, cease now to weep! Rise quickly and come. Run with St. John, enter with safety the Sepulchre, and see the linen clothes and the napkin of Jesus lying there.

Believe the words of the Angels, saying, that Jesus is risen and liveth; that He will go into Galilee, and there appear to His disciples.

O sweet response from the mouth of the Angel, well fitted to comfort the hearts of the afflicted, and to give hope of pardon to sinners.

They may take comfort from the example of Peter and many other Saints; who, having fallen, rose again, and became, in their service of God, stronger than ever.

Blessed be God, who forsakes not the troubled in heart, and saves such as are of a humble spirit, and strengthens in faith those that seek none but Him, and yearn not for any other.

O, holy women, who hear so much that is good concerning Jesus, should He meet you by the way and say, "Hail, Sisters," hold Him firmly by the feet, and let Him not go until He bless you.

Adore Him with knees bent on the earth, and salute Him tenderly with loving words.

I praise and honor Thee, O most gracious Jesu, for Thy great kindness and tender consolation, and for Thy words of joyful salutation, with which Thou didst greet the holy and devout women, when they met Thee; suffering them to embrace Thy most sacred feet, so lately nailed to the Cross—feet that were brighter than the sun, whiter than snow, more beautiful than the carbuncle, more precious than gold, more fragrant than all balm and perfume.

O glorious Jesus! I most earnestly thank Thee for sending Thy holy Angel from heaven to roll away the stone from the Sepulchre. That he might frighten away the impious guards from the sacred place, where Thou wast quietly at rest, like some strong lion in his den.

That he might make for the men and women a free access to the Tomb; that he might comfort all that mourned for Thee, dead and buried; that he might strengthen in the faith the feeble-minded, who doubted Thy Resurrection; that he might rejoice with Thee in every good thing, because of Thy prosperous return from the grave, and the happy opening of the gate of Heaven.

For so great a grief had seized their minds when they saw Thee crucified, that they lost all faith and hope in Thy future Resurrection; which Thou by Thine own mouth hadst so often foretold to them.

Whence from mortal man no comfort could they have obtained unless in the morning they had paid a visit to Thy tomb, and there heard from an Angel that Thou hadst verily risen; and had seen Thee palpably before their eyes, and, as full proof of the truth, held with their hands Thy glorious feet.

These things being done, after lovingly greeting and consoling them, Thou didst charge them with the duty of declaring the glad tidings; an office worthy of all acceptation and honor: and then Thou didst very tenderly uphold and strengthen them by Thy gracious exhortation, saying, " Be not afraid, go tell My brethren that they go into Galilee, there shall they see Me."

O how pleasant are those words to the ear, how sweet to be studied, how precious for meditation, how fitted to keep down all worldly fables !

O how bright the eyes that have seen the Lord, how pure the hands that have touched Jesus, how sacred the lips that have pressed on Him a kiss !

How swift have their feet become to walk, how eager to run; how ready their hearts to obey; how rejoiced their mouths to declare to the disciples that the Lord is risen !

Great as was the multitude of sorrows on the day of Preparation, when was seen the shameful Cross with Jesus thereon; greater far were the joys of the Passover, when His glorious Resurrection was proclaimed.

The reproaches of the Jews are turned into the great rejoicing of the Apostles; and the offence of the Cross into the remedy of eternal salvation.

The tears of the Saints are changed into the songs of Angels; and the stripes of the scourgers and the nails into remission of our sins.

O most sweet Jesu Christ, move my heart also to love Thy holy and blessed Name, which is far above all Saints in heaven and earth; that, every morning, at break of day, with Mary Magdalene and her companions, I may remember and seek Thee in the sepulchre of my heart. May I die entirely to this world, and devoutly cleave to Thee in the silence and secrecy of prayer.

Take from me all hardness of heart, all bodily sloth, and all drowsiness of mine eyes.

Pour into me the grace of penitence, increase in me the joy of devotion, to the glory of Thy holy Name; a Name worthy indeed to be celebrated in this holy solemnity.

Accept the first fruits of my lips for a sacrifice of perpetual praise, and may Thy holy Angels, who guarded Thy holy Sepulchre with so great reverence and respect, faithfully guard me, day and night, from all dangers ghostly and bodily.

And do Thou, O Lord, stand by me, especially

in the hour of prayer; lest I begin to wander by looking about me, and put vain fancies of things earthly where that which is heavenly should be; so neglecting Thee in Thy holy place.

Where it behoves me in every way, with great reverence and attention, to stand in the presence of Thy glory as a suppliant pleader, drawn in soul heavenward. Then shall I, forgetting for Thy sake all worldly things, be, as far as possible, wholly united to Thee with a pure heart.

For what are all things here below but vanity of vanities? Truly, in comparison with heavenly joys, every earthly pleasure is as nothing before Thee.

Grant me, therefore, O my God, Thou that art the beauty and glory of Angels, that I may ponder every word and the full sense of the Psalms, and other songs and hymns, which are sung and said in the church; as far as, in my frail condition, I am able to receive and understand them. May this continue until I come to Thee, the true Light, lightening my darkness, and causing all the citizens of the heavenly Jerusalem to rejoice.

Accept also, on this sacred day of the great Festival, in the place of the ointments of sweet savor, pressed out of frankincense and myrrh, the frequent and bitter secret sighings of my mouth; uttered for all my sins and negligences, committed by me in thought, word, and deed. So that now, as a new man, born again in the Spirit, and clothed in white, I may, with humble confession of my sins, be deemed in Christ meet to appear among Thy devout ones, pure and joyful.

Henceforth I offer to Thee, instead of the precious ointments of balsam and honey, all the holy desires of my heart, and the sacred exercises of the Faithful, together with the song of Angels and the rejoicing of all the heavenly host, in praise of the Blessed Trinity, and in honor of Thy joyful Resurrection. Amen.

CHAPTER III

ON THE APPEARANCE OF JESUS TO MARY MAGDALENE IN THE FORM OF A GARDENER

O LORD JESU CHRIST, Maker of all things and Discerner of the secrets of the heart, I bless and give Thee thanks for Thy friendly appearance to the blessed Mary Magdalene, Thy most fervently devoted follower, as she stood weeping near to the Sepulchre.

To her Thou didst deign to shew Thyself in

the form of a gardener, talking familiarly with
her, and, of Thy special favor to her, revealing
many secrets of Thy Divinity and mysteries of
Thy Humanity.

Thou didst first inform her, before all others,
of Thy glorious Resurrection; and, after her
mournful complaints and wearisome searchings,
Thou didst abundantly gladden her.

I praise and highly exalt Thee for Thy kind
visitation and sweet address to Mary Magdalene, all so desolate, inquiring of her:—"Why
weepest Thou?"   "Whom seekest Thou?"

O sweet Jesus, and most gracious Master!
Who knowest all things before they come to
pass, why askest Thou concerning things of
which Thou hadst perfect knowledge?

Thou knowest that she seeks nothing, desires
nothing, but Thee only, Whom above all things
she truly loves.   She grieves and weeps because
she found Thee not in the Sepulchre; for she
has lost her dearest friend on earth.

As oft as she thinks of Thee, or hears Thee
spoken of, or sees Thy Tomb, or pictures Thy
Cross—indeed anything pertaining to Thee—
forthwith her heart is moved within her, and
she weeps.   Love knows no rest unless it finds
what it seeks, has what it loves, and secures
that which it desires.

If, to-day in Thy presence she weeps on this

so great a Festival, be not Thou angry, O Lord; it is her love that works upon her; her entire devotion to Thee, which allows her neither to sleep nor to take rest.

That it was which constrained her to rise ere it was day, that she might anoint Thee. And now, because she finds Thee not, she weeps and sorrows sadly for Thee.

Just as the love burns within her, so is her desire inflamed to seek Thee. If she could fly as an Angel, she would assuredly wing her way over hills and mountains, and beyond the stars of the firmament, in search of Thee; even above the Cherubim and Seraphim would she soar, to find Thee in Thy Kingdom, seated on the loftiest throne of Thy Father.

This was not granted to her on that day, nor is it given to all to be caught up with Paul to the third Heaven; but only to those, for whom it is prepared of Thy Father, at the fitting season fore-ordained of God.

O gentle Jesus! Thou Comforter of sorrowing souls, have compassion on Mary in her tears; succor the mournful; speak to her that loves Thee; speak, if but one word, and her sorrow will be healed.

Speak but Thy Name, O Lord, let Thy voice sound in her ears, and straightway her spirit will revive. Show Thy face, O Jesu of a comely countenance, and her soul will in Thee most sweetly rejoice. Call her by her own name, and forthwith she will stay her weeping.

Why, I pray Thee, O Lord, dost Thou hide Thy face from one that loves Thee; so earnestly does she seek Thee, and so bitterly does she weep for Thee?

Why takest Thou the form of another? Why feignest Thou to be the gardener, when Thou art her loved Lord and Master? Her Lord in ruling her, her Master in teaching her.

Say then, "I am Jesus Whom thou seekest, be still and weep not; in place of tears let there be peace." But, O kind Jesus! in this what good designest Thou? for what cause deferrest Thou the desire of her soul?

I know Thy plan. It is because Thou doest and disposest all things with a wisdom that foreseeth. Thou deceivest no man, neither art Thou deceived; for Thou art a just God, in all Thy ways true and righteous.

And therefore didst Thou hide from the weeping Mary the brightness of Thy countenance, that she might not know Thee; that so Thou mightest the more stir up towards Thee the desire of her heart, and prove the strength of her patience; and, further, that Thou mightest, by afflicting and delaying, more thoroughly cleanse her; and bring her, after long sorrowing and many tears, to greater joy.

By this also Thou hast shown to the devout, for their much comfort in the hour of tribulation, an example of the patience and penitence of St. Mary. Who, though greatly beloved by Thee, and adorned with many gifts, was yet in this life often afflicted, grieved, oppressed, and for a time desolate. All this was for the increase of her own holy service, and for the profit of other Christians, but never was she wholly deserted or despised.

O how wisely and how tenderly dost Thou, O Lord, deal with Thy loved ones; whether by trials or by comfortings, until Thou bringest them to Thyself, and into the eternal rest of a heavenly Paradise!

And needful is it, that in various ways they should be proved by temptations, and, like gold, be purged in the fire of tribulation.

That therefore they may be made meet for the Kingdom of God, and fitted to enjoy the heavenly vision, they should consider whatever comes from Thy hand as a blessing, and an earnest of the Life eternal; that Life, which Thou hast promised to every devout soul that continues to weep and to pray, as did Mary Magdalene before Thee this day.

O God of Israel, how good art Thou to those

that are of a right spirit, who seek Thee in
truth and lowliness, with sorrow and weeping,
as Mary Magdalene sought and found Thee !

For whatever is laboriously looked for and
with difficulty found, the more valued is it when
secured, and the more carefully watched over.

After a long fast, bread tastes the sweeter;
after a bitter draught, water is more pleasant
to the drinker.

After night, the more cheering is day unto
the eyes ; and after cold, the more delightful is
a fire.

After sorrows, the harp has a more charming
sound ; and after heavy labors, the sweeter are
rest and sleep.

After fierce wars, peace to the sufferers is
only the more welcome. The stars shine
brighter, as the mist clears away ; birds sing
more cheerfully, when the sun is rising.

So, on the coming of Christ with grace, the
troubled soul is renewed like the eagle. These
things are sufficiently manifest in the beloved
Mary Magdalene ; who, after long weeping,
was abundantly comforted by the Lord Jesus
—"O how plentiful is Thy goodness, O Lord,
which Thou hast laid up for them that fear
Thee ! "

Verily, " Thou art a God that hidest Thyself,"
as says Esaias ; and " besides Thee there is

none other like unto Thee," Who knowest so wisely how to order all things for them that love Thee.

O good Jesus, eternal Wisdom of the Father, how humbly and lovingly didst Thou live among men, teaching them all things useful and salutary; to despise earthly things, to love heavenly things, and to endure tribulation!

O the sweet converse of Mary with Jesus, the Saviour of the world, with the King of Angels, with the Lord of Lords, with the Prince of the heavenly citizens, with the Ruler of all Saints!

Verily, O Lord, if Mary had perfectly known Thee, she would never have supposed Thee to be a gardener; nor would she have said to Thee, "Sir, if Thou have borne Him hence tell me."

O Mary! how durst thou so speak to Him, the greatness of whose power thou knewest not? Whence hast thou such great courage that thou boldly sayest, "I will take Him away?" How durst thou presume that, unaided, thou couldest carry such and so great a man?

Tell me where wilt thou bear Him? Who gave thee authority to take away that which thou didst not lay down? Thou knowest not what thou sayest.

Call first thy companions and prove what thou sayest, whether, with united efforts, ye are able to carry Him whom ye seek. Perchance, not having found the sacred Body of Christ, so wearied are ye by journeying, so greatly weakened by fasting and weeping yesterday and to-day, ye have not the strength.

O Mary! if thou art alone, and all others have drawn back, what wilt thou do? Wheresoever thy Beloved may be, ask this gardener to help thee seek and carry Him, whom thou lovest and fain wouldest find; that dear One, for Whom thou weepest and so often sighest.

No one can help or comfort thee better than this gardener. No one knows better, if he be willing to say, where thy Lord is carried or hidden. My belief is that, out of His great compassion, He hath come here to thee to show thee where He Himself, whom thou seekest, is now; and who has by night taken Him away from the Sepulchre.

O how great the desire of this holy woman, ever seeking, ever lamenting! Speak forthwith, I beseech Thee, O Lord, if it be but one little word, by which Thy dove, hearing Thy voice, may recognize Thee; and, rejoicing at the sight of her Spouse, may cease to mourn.

She seeks Thee, she longs for Thee. Angels suffice her not, nor any created beings; neither is she content with any human solace whatsoever. Speak, Lord, for Thy servant, Thy devout visitor, longs to hear Thy voice.

Say to her "Mary," as Thou wast wont to say so often to Thy beloved hostess. This is her name. By none does she more gladly hear it uttered than by Thee, her only hope. That is her sole desire, for Thou art her all in all.

O Mary, know Jesus, by Whom thou art known. Love Him by Whom thou art first loved. Answer, beloved, to thy beloved Master, the gardener of thy heart.

O Lord, my Master, I give Thee thanks because Thou hast appeared unto me. Behold now I have Him whom I have sought. Now see I Him for Whom I have wept. Far better is my lot than I dared to expect.

Happy day and blessed hour! on which thou, O Mary, after the mission and consolation of the Angel, wast permitted to see the Lord of Angels, and to hear His gracious words, saying unto thee, "Go to my brethren, and say unto them, I ascend unto My Father and your Father, and to My God, and your God."

Mary, therefore, did as Jesus commanded her. Without delay and without a murmur she immediately went, joyfully declaring to the disciples the glad tidings, "Lo, after much sorrow and weeping, I have seen my Lord."

O how grateful and acceptable were those tears, poured forth from a pure heart, moved by perfect love, sweeter far than the alabaster box of precious spices ready for anointing!

Now, therefore, O most merciful Jesu Christ, Who did deign to visit and comfort the devout Máry Magdalene, in her day of heavy sorrow, I beseech Thee by Thy tender compassion to show Thy mercy in like manner to me; when my soul is weary and sorrowful, oppressed by labor of body and grief of heart, through some evil passion acting against me; or the secret withdrawal of the sweetness of Thy grace, because of some fault of mine, better known to Thee than to me; or, it may be, through an evil conscience oppressing me with thoughts of the Judgment to come; terrifying me on account of my daily negligence and lukewarmness, so many duties neglected, so many vain cares allowed to intrude.

O Lord, I beseech Thee, in the day of my tribulation, withdraw not Thine hand from me, lest I lose all hope of the pardon of my sins; but, rather, in the abundance of Thy loving-kindness, open to me the bosom of Thy tender mercies; which are from everlasting, and will endure for ever upon all, who with their whole heart seek Thee and desire to love Thee.

And, of Thy wonted tenderness, restore to me the grace of Thy comfort, for which above all things I yearn; and, after the death of my body, show to me the saving joy of Thy countenance. Amen.

CHAPTER IV

ON THE EXEMPLARY GRACES AND PRIVILEGES OF THE BLESSED MARY MAGDALENE

I BLESS and give Thee thanks, O Lord Jesu Christ, Thou heavenly Physician, Who, for the healing of our souls, didst come into this world to save sinners, and through repentance lovingly to restore them to Thy kingdom above.

Thou, who didst deign to be born of Mary a virgin, didst not disdain to be touched, washed, wiped, anointed, and kissed by Mary, a sinner, coming a weeping penitent to Thee.

O gentle Jesus, Son of the living God, merciful Saviour of the world, many and great privileges didst Thou, in this life, compassionately bestow on the blessed Mary Magdalene.

For, when she had cast aside all the vanities of the world, and become entirely converted to Thee, Thou didst in pity accept her penitence, fully pardon all her sins, and absolve the sad mourner from all punishment.

Thou didst breathe into her heart great con-

trition, and, lest she should despair, Thou didst
in her grief pour upon her the comfort of Thy
grace, inflame her soul with the fire of the Comforter, and inwardly renew her with the sweetness of Thy love.

Thou didst bid her go in peace with good
courage; Thou didst warn her not to return to
her former sins; and didst urge her to continue
steadily in holy conversation, and in sweet
prayer.

Never didst Thou speak a severe word to her,
nor reproach her with the least sin; never didst
Thou reveal to any one the evil she had committed; nay, Thou didst rather excuse her, and
set forth the good she had done, as an example
for a holy life.

When invited to the house of Simon the
leper, Thou wast more pleased with the tears
of Mary, than Thou wast gratified with the
hospitality of the Pharisee.

When she would touch Thee, Thou wast not
indignant; when she would anoint Thee, Thou
didst not spurn her.

Thou presentedst Thy feet to her, Thou didst
incline Thine head, Thou didst not refuse her
kisses.

With Thy mouth Thou didst bless her, with
Thy hand Thou didst sanctify her, with Thy
touch Thou didst cleanse her, and with one

short sentence Thou didst heal the sufferer, saying, "Thy faith hath saved thee, go in peace."

O sweet utterance, coming from the mouth of God, full of grace and compassion, ever to be gratefully remembered.

Thou wast wont to visit the house of Mary and Martha, Thy hospitable friends, in Bethany, their village. There, being joyfully received, Thou didst lodge and find rest.

There Thou didst eat and drink whatever was placed before Thee and Thy disciples, food fitted for the poor and needy, who have but a few farthings in the world. No confusion was there, no noise, no foolish jesting, no light laughter, no vain word was heard.

There, with great reverence and due order, Thou didst sit at the table as the lowly Master. As a poor man Thou didst eat together with the poor.

There Thou wast Reader of the Refection and Doctor of Divinity, and in place of wine, Thou didst pledge Thy beloved friends with the words of eternal Life.

There Thou didst in Thy wisdom instruct Martha, who was ministering to Thee; and didst graciously excuse Mary, who was sweetly at leisure, listening diligently to the words of Thy mouth. Thou didst, when her sister

complained of her indolence, meetly commend
Mary's life of deep contemplation.

And when Judas, the traitor, murmured concerning the ointment poured out on Thee, Thou
didst justly defend Mary. She was herself
modestly silent, but Thou didst, on her behalf,
forthwith reply to the objections, setting forth
her good deeds—not one word didst Thou say
of her failings.

When Mary wept over her brother Lazarus,
lying dead in the grave, Thou didst weep with
her. So deeply didst Thou mourn with Thy
afflicted friends, that many said, "Behold!
how He loved him."

O how high was the character and upright
the bearing of this said Lazarus; whom Jesus
loved when he was alive, raised again when he
was dead, and supped with when life had been
restored!

O gracious Jesus, Author and Rewarder of
all good, Thou didst not forget the faithful services, so often rendered Thee in the house of
Mary and Martha. Small benefits Thou didst
repay by great; for bodily aid Thou gavest
spiritual blessings; for that which is passing
away, Thou didst bestow that which is eternal.

What shall I say more? No one can easily
tell forth or comprehend all Thy mercies vouch-
safed unto men; neither can any one suffi-

ciently discern the signs and miracles which Thou didst in Galilee, in Nazareth, in Bethany, in Jerusalem, in Judæa, and in all the region of the Holy Land—wondrous acts, wrought before Thy disciples and all the people, in testimony of the truth; that, from Thy words and all Thy deeds marvellous and divine, they might believe in Thee. For, verily, Thou art Christ, the Son of God, Who came into this world for the salvation of men.

O how sublime in the heavens! how lowly on earth! how holy and humble to men when Thou didst heal them! how severe and awful to devils when cast out by Thee!

O how merciful to penitents! how severe to evildoers! how compassionate to the afflicted! how generous to the needy! how comforting to those who mourn!

Who, under all circumstances, is so faithful a friend, who so powerful a helper in every trouble, as Thou, our God?

O how great the joy which Thou didst cause to these sisters, when Thou didst cry aloud, "Lazarus, come forth!" And immediately, in obedience to Thee, the Lord of life and death, he, who had been dead, came forth.

Then didst Thou say to Thy disciples, as to Thine appointed ministers of souls, "Loose him, and let him go."

O that Thou, O Lord, wouldest also vouchsafe to absolve me from all the bonds of my
sins, that I may die in peace, and joyfully come
to Thee; with the holy Angels, and with Mary
and Martha, to praise Thee, and to be free from
all sin for ever.   Amen.

CHAPTER V

ON THE GREAT COMPUNCTION OF MARY MAGDA-
LENE IN THE PASSION OF THE LORD

ETERNAL praise and glory be to Thee, O
most loving Jesus Christ, for the very
great sanctity of Mary Magdalene, and her devout lamentation at Thy sacred and bitter Passion.   It did not suffice her to attend on Thee
only in Thy lifetime—to follow Thee through
towns and villages, that she might see the signs
and miracles which, worthy of all praise and hon-
or, were wrought by Thy divine power; but she
also constantly and sorrowfully followed Thee in
Thy Passion, even to Thy death upon the Cross.

She was with the holy Mary, Thy Mother,
and with many other devout and holy women,
who grieved for Thee and most bitterly wept
on the way, because of Thine innocent Death,
and Thy most grievous Crucifixion.

Therefore, as long as she could see Thee, she followed the Cross, weeping, moaning, sorrowing, watching Thy footsteps, wringing her hands, beating her breast, and wiping her eyes, while floods of tears poured down her cheeks.

For she perceived that nothing more loving could she do, no better help could she offer, than inwardly to grieve, all day and night bitterly to weep, unceasingly to meditate on Thy sufferings.

Because she deemed Thine every wound her own, and, by how much the more she loved Thee, by so much the more vehemently did she sorrow and weep.

And, when she saw Thee naked and nailed to the Cross, she stood thereby with Thy Mother, as near as she dared approach; and, though inwardly oppressed by grief unbounded, nothing in the world would induce her to leave it; until Thy Death most faithfully did she cleave to Thee and to Thy Mother.

But when she saw Thee die on the Cross with a loud cry, her soul, oppressed by overwhelming grief, sank within her. Her mouth refused all nourishment. Sleep vanished from her eyes. Tears were her sole comfort, and bitter, indeed, seemed it to continue in this world without Thee.

Unless, therefore, she had fully submitted

herself to Thy will, she could, after Thy departure, hardly have remained with patience in the
flesh. Her frequent lamentations showed, that,
without Thy presence, this life had no pleasure
whatever for her.

But, O Mary, bear up yet, for a little season,
in this hour of heavy necessity. For the love
of thy Beloved hanging on the Cross, bear up
with the Mother of Jesus and her kindred.
Forsake her not; quit not the side of the heart-
rent Virgin Mother of Jesus, as though thou
couldest no longer endure such sad mourning,
and hear such cries of bitter lamentation.

Sorrow with the sorrowing, and weep with
them that weep; that thou mayest rejoice with
the joyful, in the glory of the Resurrection.

O good and loving Jesus, Mary acted as
Thou didst suggest. In accordance with Thy
prediction and order, she reserved the ointment
that remained to anoint Thy Body for burial.

She did not forget Thy words, neither did she
sell it as Judas advised. She carefully kept it
in alabaster, bought yet more, and so made
preparation for Thee.

Truly in the hour of need, a friend is proved.
It is the act of kindness that manifests true
love.

Therefore, this holy faithful Mary, as she
loved Thee in life, so, at Thy Death and Burial,

she shows it by her deeds; for deep was her lamentation and devoted her care.

Nothing necessary for the due burial of Thy holy Body did she omit. She swathed, anointed, covered, and bound it, and sewed together the linen clothes; and, as a fitting ornament, reverently placed the napkin about Thy sacred Head.

Meanwhile, she wept without ceasing; finding her comfort in being permitted to wait on Thee, to attend Thy Mother with other devoted followers, and to see that all things about Thee were done decently and in order.

Therefore, when Thy holy Body was buried, and closed in firmly by a stone duly sealed, there arose fresh sorrowing and wailing; as though henceforth Mary would not in this world see again One, with Whom she had once enjoyed so close an alliance of spiritual life and joy.

Nor yet, when the tomb was closed, was she able forthwith to leave the place, in which lay hidden the treasure of the world.

With many other devout women she sat till sunset weeping, until tears utterly failed them; and loving lamentations abundantly poured they forth from their inward hearts, as it is written of them, "The women, sitting before the Sepulchre, wept and sorrowed for their Lord."

Would that I had such a sorrow, O Jesus Christ, my Lord, in meditating on Thy sacred Passion, as that endured by the devout Mary Magdalene, on the day of the Preparation; when she beheld Thy Crucifixion, Death, and Burial; and saw Thee, by nearly all, despised, mocked, and reproached.

But, thanks to Thee, O most patient Jesu, this false rumor concerning Thee continued not long; for, after three days, Thou didst overcome and confound Thine enemies, by rising again freed from the dead.

Truly, O Lord, Thy word was fulfilled, which, in the presence of Thy disciples, Thou didst foretell of Mary Magdalene, in praise of her good work wrought on Thee, "Verily I say unto you, wheresoever this Gospel shall be preached throughout the whole world, there also shall this, which she hath done, be told for a memorial of her."

Verily, Thy whole house is filled with the odor of the ointment, *i.e.*, the universal Church of the Faithful, widely spread throughout the world, is clearly imbued with apostolic doctrines, and made steadfast in divine truth.

For by Apostles and Evangelists is the fame of her great sanctity set forth, and therefore by Preachers and Doctors is it openly proclaimed. Moreover, by all the Clergy, and by laity of both sexes, is her glorious festival yearly honored and celebrated in holy Church, with marked devotion. There is joy that her happy soul hath passed from this world to Thee, the Lord Jesus Christ, to dwell with Thee for ever in Thy eternal habitations.

CHAPTER VI

ON THE APPEARANCE OF CHRIST TO ST. PETER
IN SECRET, AND ON ST. PETER'S RUNNING
WITH ST. JOHN

O LORD JESU CHRIST, Thou Chief
Shepherd of Thy Holy Church, and our faithful High Priest Godward, I bless and give Thee thanks for Thy great love and unspeakable pity, which Thou didst, in divers ways, show to Thy blessed Apostle Peter; for the divine converse which Thou didst hold with him; and for the secret visions which Thou didst so often manifest unto him.

Nor didst Thou, after his thrice denying Thee, cast him away from Thy love; but, out of Thy tender compassion, Thou didst forthwith bring back his heart to bitter weeping, and didst mercifully and fully pardon his every offence against Thee—yea, Thou didst of Thy clemency, after his heavy fall, lovingly restore him to his wonted high and honorable rank.

O Fountain of mercy and never failing stream of heavenly gifts, cleansing the penitent, and all who weep over their past sins! O most tender bestower of pardon and giver of celestial grace! O sweet Lord Jesu Christ, beloved by all Thy Saints and friends, the Elect from everlasting; Thou who ceasest not to do good, but pourest forth blessings on all that flee to Thee for succor, and with hearty repentance humbly seek Thy forgiveness!

I praise and specially honor Thee for Thy great goodness, in that this day Thou didst in some secret place, better known to Thee than to me, verily appear to Thy beloved Apostle St. Peter, for his special comfort, at that time so greatly needed by him.

For he who had offended the most, the most stood in need of consolation and support; and no better Comforter, no mightier helper can there be, than Thou, Jesus our Creator and Redeemer.

Therefore, O blessed Jesu Christ, the discerner and restorer of all that are in tribulation, and have fallen into sin, I render Thee thanks for Thy timely succor of Peter, Thine erring sheep: lest, oppressed by excessive grief, he should despair of pardon; or, not having found Thy sacred Body in the Sepulchre, he should doubt Thy Resurrection.

As a loving and wise Physician of afflicted souls, Thou didst send Thy holy Angel to encourage Peter, and restore him to the hope of pardon. Thy messenger, tenderly speaking to the women, directed them thus to say to Peter, "Go quickly, and tell His disciples and Peter, that Jesus is risen."

O good and holy Angel, lest Peter should despair on account of his thrice denying Christ, how well and rightly didst thou especially call him by his familiar name, given him first by his Lord, when summoned to the dignity and office of an Apostle!

For hearing himself named by the Angel, and kindly greeted by the holy women, he became more cheerful in mind. With confidence renewed, and forgetting all labor and sorrow, swiftly he ran with John to the place of burial.

But when he saw all things so done by the Lord as had been declared to him by the women, and also by the holy Angel, who deceives not, but is a witness of the truth, and a faithful herald of the Resurrection accomplished, there at once revived in him a hope of life—a firm assurance of eternal salvation.

Therefore, inwardly full of wonder and greatly rejoicing in the Lord, Peter longed also to see Jesus, that He would appear unto him, as at first He appeared to Mary Magdalene.

"Let her be first among women, sufficient for me to be second or third among men, or the last among His Apostles and Disciples. Yet, be it unto me as to Himself seemeth meet and right, according to His good pleasure, for the salvation of my soul.

"I ardently desire to see my Lord, that I may be perfectly reconciled to Him, and comforted by the words of His mouth. 'Let Thy tender mercies come unto me, O Lord, that I may live,' and let me never again rely on my own strength.

"Remember, I beseech Thee, all Thy loving-kindness, and the holy supplication which Thou didst make to the Father for me, and, also, Thy prayer on the Cross for sinners.

"Come, O gentle Jesus, tarry not. Thou art my hope, and the alone salvation of my soul. Show Thyself to me, and I shall be safe— greater will be my joy, in that I saw Thee on this holy day of the Passover."

And so it came to pass; Jesus assented to the pious desires of His beloved Apostle Peter. For the tender and compassionate Saviour was soon present with one, who so zealously sought for Him.

And, therefore, He received the weeping

penitent back to His bosom, graciously blotting out all the offences against Himself, so cowardly committed in the night season.

Jesus, moreover, further instructing the Apostle, influenced him, the more fully, to a bold confession, and a perpetual love of His holy Name.

O boundless love of Christ, full of celestial sweetness, to be celebrated with all praise, and told forth for ever to all the faithful, lest any fallen one should despair of pardon; or having been made whole, should rashly presume on grace poured down on him abundantly from heaven.

O vast example of compassion, this day openly shown by the Lord to St. Peter! Whereat Angels rejoice, Archangels are glad, the lost take hope, and the slothful are aroused; yea, all faithful people unite with one heart to praise God for the mercy of the Lord, and especially for His tenderness towards the blessed Peter, now fully confirmed in the faith of Christ.

O how gracious and friendly a colloquy Jesus then had with Peter, when he received the kiss of peace. How joyous and calm, in the meanwhile, was the heart of the Apostle, when he gazed on and heard the comforting words of the risen Christ, his most loving Master.

And now, O benign Jesus, remember me a poor unworthy sinner, in the time of my trouble and desolation. After my sad exile in this world render to me, when about to depart from the body, a ready help; and grant me safe guardianship to the Courts of Heaven.

Open to me, by Thy Passion and Death, the gate of Paradise; promised to all penitents, until time shall be no more. Guard me from the snares of the ancient adversary, and rescue me, Thy pleading servant, from the punishment and darkness of hell.

For to Thee have been given all the kingdoms of the world, and the keys of Heaven are Thine to open to those that knock at the gate of Life; to all, who, at the last, heartily repent them of their sins, and turn to God with faith unfeigned. Amen.

CHAPTER VII

A PRAYER TO OBTAIN FROM GOD THE GRACE OF TEARS

TURN thou, O my soul, to the Lord thy God, with all thy heart, with weeping and mourning; pray for the remission of all thy sins, and for pardon, in that thou hast, from the day of thy birth to this very hour, a season granted thee by God, left undone so many good works, and neglected so many opportunities.

For lowly prayer and contrition of heart, tears and sighs for thy daily shortcomings, and for all who are afflicted, tempted, and oppressed, are well pleasing to God.

Holy and blessed is it to pray to God for oneself, and for one's neighbor; for, in this world, none are without sin—none without danger.

In this our exile we have grief and many a sorrow; in hell is a fire, that is never quenched, and punishment that ceaseth not. True peace and rest eternal are found in heaven alone.

Therefore, O Lord God, for all my past misdoings, in every circumstance and failing that has befallen me, with heart, word, and deed, to Thee I pray, and will pray continually.

Receive my lamentations, offered with a pure purpose, and full desire of immediate amendment. Suffer me, in this my pilgrimage, by an entire resignation of myself, and giving up all that is of this world, to secure now Thy favor and the pardon of all my sins, through the merits and mediation of Thy Son, our Lord and Saviour, Jesus Christ.

O that I may follow the example of Thy Saints, shunning all idle talking on worldly matters—all fellowship with ribaldry and levity !

Jesus prayed on the mountain, watched during the night season, ofttimes wept, never vainly laughed, nor uttered a light word.

When accused before the Governor, He was silent; when He spake, it was with gentleness; and in answering, even the wicked, He was ever kind.

Mary the Mother of Jesus also prayed often, wept most bitterly at His Passion, sorrowed grievously, endured patiently. Outwardly she was bashful, inwardly calm and quiet.

Mary Magdalene wept bitterly, bewailing her sins; most lovingly she wept, in thankfulness for mercies; very abundantly, in compassion for the sufferings of Jesus; most fervently, in contemplating the joys of Heaven.

St. Peter also wept, with deep sorrow at heart, when thrice in the night he heard the crowing of the cock, and remembered how he had denied Christ his Master. For, through the sudden answer, proceeding from his frailty, arose a long lamentation of his crime, and a deep compassion for the misery of his Brethren.

St. Paul also wept bitterly for his former error, when he persecuted the holy Church; and also for the excesses and falls of others, who, touching ordinances and usages, were unfaithful. His desire was to bring all to the true faith, and contrition for their sins—to win them to the fervor of a holy life and conversation, and a steady walk in the footsteps of Christ.

St. John, the Apostle, also wept bitterly at the Passion of Christ. He was ever close to the Cross with Mary the Mother of Jesus, condoling and upholding her. He wept also for the errors of many, and through the ardor of his charity towards the lukewarm. He wept also for a certain youth, who was given up to the pleasures of the world. Through many tears that sinner was restored and cleansed.

Our holy Father, Augustine, wept very bitterly for his past worldliness, as he humbly confesses in his writings. An example to all converted to God, that, to increase their humility, they should with sorrow meditate on the sins they have confessed; and so, by God's help, never repeat them. For all past misdoings daily should they mourn, weep, and pray.

The same holy and devout Father poured forth his weeping, when hymns, and psalms, and divine songs were echoing through the house of God. The more readily he turned his mind from things earthly, the more ardently was he drawn upwards to things heavenly.

For his manner of life was to lament over

the adversity of others, and to rejoice in their salvation—to soothe the afflicted with the honey of charity, and ever to help the needy.

There are also very many other examples of holy men and devout women, who have received special grace from God, for the pouring forth of sacred tears.

CHAPTER VIII

ON THE ADVANTAGE AND GRACE OF HOLY TEARS

HOLY and devout tears repress the violence of the flesh, quench the fires of discord, cleanse the vicious appetite, take away the pride of the eyes, shun vain speaking, seek privacy, love silence, secure the fruits of prayer.

They drive away idleness, that enemy of the soul, destroy falsehood, jesting, and laughter. They calmly consider the hour of death, the terror of judgment, and the pains of hell.

They break the snares of the devil, overcome the world's tumult, and lead the mourner to the kingdom of Heaven. They blot out past transgressions and recover lost blessings.

They teach us to shun dangers, to be much in retirement, to read holy books, to write well, and to pray often. They preserve the penitent in grace, and gladden the devout with the hope of eternal glory.

O that I could more frequently experience this grace of tears, guard it more carefully; when lost, regain it by penitence, and so seeking speedily find it.

He, who desires to have and hold this gift, should look closely into his evil ways, heartily thank God for His blessings, and bend before Him in profound lowliness.

This is a task hard and grievous, yet most useful to the doer thereof, and in the end comforting indeed to the dying.

Blessed, therefore, are they who, sorrowing for their sins, ofttimes mourn; for, in due time being comforted, they shall rejoice with the Angels for ever.

CHAPTER IX

ON THE TEARS OF JESUS OVER LAZARUS

O GRACIOUS and sacred tears of my Lord Jesu Christ, shed in compassion so lovingly and abundantly at the death and raising of Lazarus, with Mary and Martha, and their friends, and mourning Jews; succor my withered heart, soften the hardness of my breast, and especially at the place and time of prayer and meditation; that I may deeply lament me of my sins; and in thought, word, and deed be cleansed from all my iniquities, whether secretly or openly committed, for heavily do they oppress me.

For day and night, morning and evening, do I grieve over my sins, O Lord, as often as I call them to mind, and Thy loving-kindness; which Thou hast so pitifully and so frequently bestowed on me and all mankind.   Amen.

ON THE TEARS OF JESUS OVER JERUSALEM

O loving and holy tears of my Lord Jesus Christ, copiously shed from streaming eyes, out of tender compassion for the overthrow and destruction of Jerusalem—that faithless city. Unavailing possibly to infidels, yet to me, and to all believers, and to the devout, very acceptable are they, and truly lovely.

I, therefore, a man slothful and full of misery, humbly pray Thee:—Let those tears fall upon me abundantly, and cleanse thoroughly the face of my soul, defiled by the many evils of my whole life, from all the foulness of sin: that, made pure within, I may be deemed worthy, with the holy Angels, to behold in Heaven the glorious face of the Father.

O may I, when the sorrows of this life are

over, be counted meet to receive abundant
mercy at the hands of the just Judge, my Lord
Jesus Christ; and, through His sacred Passion
and Death, may also, after the general Resurrection of the dead, be admitted, with the Elect,
into the heavenly Jerusalem.   Amen.

O blessed Jesus! let Thy tears wash not only
my feet, which I have so often polluted when
carrying into action my evil thoughts and impure affections, but both my feet and my head
—that is, my evil words and works; thus shall
I have remission of all my sins, that I have day
by day committed.

O most loving Saviour! uphold my soul in the
last hour of my life, and come in the multitude
of Thy loving-kindnesses, and defend me from
the terrors of the enemy, and the pains of hell.

And do Thou, O heavenly Father, remember
the most precious Blood and Death of Thine
innocent Son, Jesu Christ; who, for me a sinner, endured the Cross and was pierced by the
cruel spear.   Remember, I pray Thee, the tears
that He shed, and have mercy upon me in my
last moments, when I breathe out my soul to
Thee.

As often as I think of the tears of Christ,
and reflect on the weeping and sorrowing of
the Saints of old, well may I be inwardly confounded and greatly ashamed before God.   I

proclaim myself worthy of many stripes and reproofs, and am at my wits' end. For I am a leprous sinner, and lament not; wounded, and grieve not; full of sores, and groan not; polluted, and wash not; poisoned, and I seek no remedy; weak and helpless, and I look not to the great Physician for timely aid.

Woe is me! that I am not so quickly moved to tears by the words and doings of Jesus, as I am stirred to laughter by the tales of men.

Daily do I sin, and every moment, in some way, I am an offender. What I propose doing, that I neglect, yet can I be merry.

Woe is me! that I do not with Mary Magdalene cast myself down at the feet of Jesus, and with a broken heart weep, that I may with her find pardon.

O blessed Jesus! remember me in this my hour of trial, and plead for me, so long as I dwell in this frail body and in so many things offend.

Woe is me! that I weep not with St. Peter in the choir or in some secret place, when I hear the cock in public crow aloud. The very birds of the field should move me to rise early from my bed, and seek pardon for the negligences and offences, that night and day I have committed.

Woe is me! that, with blessed Paul, I do not

ever lament and weep over my many wick-
ednesses, wilfully or ignorantly done by me.
Surely I ought ever duly to grieve over them
and sigh and pray; and, when troubles and
adversities assail me, patiently and piously
should I bear them.

Woe is me! that I have not the purity of
St. John the Apostle, and that I care not to
secure it. I grieve not so much over my own
uncleanness, as he sorrowed and wept over the
sins of others.

O holy and blessed Saviour! with an humble
voice and penitent spirit I beseech Thee, stand
by me in this troublesome life, and through the
perils of death; that, in the conflict, the cruel
enemy may not prevail against me. Having
no trust in myself may I be strong in faith,
with a full confidence in the Passion of Christ
my Redeemer.

O gracious Jesu! Would that I were able
to collect into a fountain all Thy tears, warmed
by the fire of Thy Holy Spirit, and to bathe my
soul therein; to wash away all the spots of my
past and daily sins, earnestly deploring and
bewailing them; and so to cleanse, purify, and
refresh it: that therein, as in the Baptismal
Font and in the waters of Jordan, I might be
born again, restored, and created anew.

Being then purely washed and purged from

all my sins, may I now, while here on earth, find compassion and mercy; and at my death may I with Thy Saints obtain eternal glory, through Thee, O Jesu Christ, who with the Father and the Holy Ghost, livest and reignest, ever one God, world without end.   Amen.

CHAPTER X

ON THE APPEARANCE OF CHRIST, UNDER THE FORM OF A STRANGER, TO TWO DISCIPLES GOING TO EMMAUS

O LORD JESU CHRIST, the Way, the Truth, and the Life, our Salvation and Redemption, I bless and thank Thee, that Thou didst graciously appear as a stranger to two of Thy disciples, as they were walking on their way. Garbed wast Thou as a traveller unknown to them.   This Thou didst, that Thou mightest bring back erring sheep to the heavenly Jerusalem, and, by Thy loving visit, instruct them fully.

O friendly act indeed, that Thou didst draw near and go with them on their journey, for sadly did Thy Passion depress them. They talked together not of wars and the vanities of this world, but of Thy good deeds, Thy holy words, and Thy miracles.

But, as they were still doubtful of Thy Resurrection that had already taken place, and in no way satisfied with the story of others and the vision of the Angels, they remained sorrow-stricken, until the truth should be more clearly made known to them.

And who could better teach them, better clear away their doubts, than Thou, O Jesu, good Master, the Way, the Truth, and the Life; by openly showing Thyself to them, and giving them a well-known token in the Breaking of Bread?

And so it came to pass. For presently, on drawing near and going with them, Thou didst inquire of them the cause of so much sadness —what it was that grieved them; as if Thou wert a stranger, and knew nothing thereof, saying:—"What communications are these which ye have one with another, as ye walk and are sad?"

I praise Thee, therefore, and highly glorify Thy sweet Name, for Thy friendly converse with these two disciples; who, on their way, were very sad at heart, and perplexed by all that had happened in Thy Passion and sentence to Death.

Thou didst, by proofs and examples relating to Thyself, taken from Holy Scripture as set forth in the Psalms, the Law, and the Prophets, greatly comfort and most seasonably instruct them.

I laud and heartily thank Thee, O most worthy Jesu, for the various passages then brought forward, expounded, and clearly explained by Thee; which before were obscure, concealed beneath sundry figures, and by few indeed understood.

I bless Thee, O Holy of Holies, the most Holy Jesu Christ, Teacher of teachers, and Master of all laws and decrees, who aforetime didst open the mouths of the Prophets, that now Thou Thyself deignedst to make known, to the little ones and the unlearned, the hidden things of the Scriptures—inviting them to believe Thee in Thy every word and deed.

O how were their faces filled with joy whilst Thou wast speaking! As Thou didst draw aside the veil from the Divine records, with what love were their cold hearts inflamed, for among lawgivers and interpreters of mysteries there is none like unto Thee.

O how didst Thou lighten their journey, how joyful the moments, how pleasant the day, even unto its close, when Thou didst enter their house, and they set meat before Thee!

O how earnestly did they invite Thee to sup with them, for fain would they have learnt more and more from Thee, all the night through! And why? Because never on earth did man speak so excellently as spake this Stranger.

"No Prophet, King, Priest, or Levite; no one of the sons and disciples of the Prophets, who wrought wonders and taught the precious things of heaven, no Saint, yea, not all the Angelic Host can, in teaching, be compared to Thee, O Stranger.

"And, therefore, we pray Thee, O Lord, abide with us. It is late; extend not Thy journey, for it is toward evening and the day is far spent. Speak yet more unto us, for we are not weary or drowsy; gladly do we listen to Thee, we verily long to do according to Thy will.

"For Thy words are sweeter to us than honey and the honey-comb; more precious are they than gold and silver; all things that the world so longs for are, in comparison of them, of little worth."

O that I had then been present, and gone secretly with Jesus by His side; or had been behind Him, carefully attending to all the words of my Lord and Saviour Christ, and had diligently hidden in my heart all that I had heard; so that I might after often have meditated thereon! Then should I have had help to go on heavenward, avoiding all vain converse with men likely to harm me.

But what I am not permitted to enjoy in the body with Thee, O Lord, grant that I may spiritually pursue the same either in retirement, at my meals, in my time for recreation, or in my hours of labor; that, whether alone or with my companions, I may have Thee ever before mine eyes as truly present and discerning all things, walking with me in the way, and breathing into me a life of holiness. Who livest and reignest with the Father and the Holy Ghost now and for ever. Amen.

CHAPTER XI

ON THE RECOGNITION OF CHRIST IN THE BREAKING OF BREAD

O LORD JESU CHRIST, Thou Bread of Life, sweet Guest of my soul, and Heavenly Giver of grace, I bless and thank Thee for Thy marvellous condescension, and for sharing the friendly feast, with Thy two disciples in their dwelling.

Very affectionately they invited Thee to enter their home; with prayers they besought Thee; they, verily, with their hands drew and constrained Thee, unwilling without Thee to enter, sit down, and eat.

Therefore, O meek and gracious Lord, yielding to their pressing entreaties, Thou didst enter with them to sup and hold sweet converse concerning the food of souls, prepared by Angels in the heavenly mansion.

And, when seated at table with them, not yet fully known by them, Thou didst, in Thy usual manner, take into Thy holy hands bread from the table; and raising Thy right hand, Thou didst bless the bread with Thy sacred mouth, as Thou wast wont to do in the presence of Thy disciples, when they sat at meat with Thee.

And then, first breaking off a part and eating, Thou didst, with outstretched arm, joyfully give a portion to them, as to beloved friends.

And straightway their eyes were opened, Thy divine power being known of them in Breaking of Bread, lovingly dispensed to them with new gladness as a mark of Thy friendship.

O how joyful the supper, when bread, blessed by the hand of the Lord, had been tasted and eaten! How blessed indeed, the eyes which perceived the Lord in the Breaking of Bread, blessed by the mouth of God!

But alas! how brief the stay, when the season was so delightful, and the supper so sweet. "And He vanished out of their sight."

" O the change of the right hand of the most

High God," here a little, there a little! For
under heaven there is nothing durable; only
with the Saints in heaven is there true and
eternal joy.

"Whither goest Thou then, O Lord? Why
dost Thou retire so quickly, and leave these
Thy disciples desolate?" "Do not marvel, fret
not. I know what I have done; I know well
what I am about to do. I have yet other sheep
to visit, to comfort, and strengthen in the faith.
They are waiting for Me and greatly do they
long to see Me.

"I go therefore to them according to My
promise; that they may see Me and rejoice;
and in no wise doubt concerning My words.

"I will show them My wounds; that, having
seen those well-known marks, they may firmly
believe Me, and not vainly cleave to human
reasonings, nor gainsay My power. For all
things are possible to Me, the very elements
obey My behest."

O sweet Jesus! I laud and give Thee glory
for all Thy deeds, and gracious words, and ap-
pearances, to Thy disciples, scattered in divers
places. Thou wast unwilling to leave them
comfortless, for ofttimes they sorrowed and
wept for Thee.

For they ever loved Thee tenderly; their delight was in seeing Thy face, in talking with

Thee, in walking with Thee, in sailing with Thee, in lodging with Thee, in eating and drinking with Thee, in watching and praying with Thee, in lying down with Thee, in rising up with Thee, and in readily obeying the words of Thy mouth.

And when Thou didst pass through the corn fields on the Sabbath day, they, fasting and with feet all bare, cheerfully followed Thee. And, being pressed by hunger, they plucked a few ears of corn, as was lawfully allowed them.

Fain would I now meditate on, and carefully examine these things; which are to my shame and grief, but to the praise and honor of Thee, O good Jesus, and of Thy disciples.

Whom Thou didst exhort, as stated by St. Mark, to take a little rest, when they were weary through the toil and wear of their long journey.

For, as a hen gathereth her chickens under her wings to shelter them from the cold and rain, and heat; and to protect them from pounce of kite or bite of dog; so didst Thou gather together Thy little ones, the humble in heart, who, while despised by the world, are beloved of Thee, saying to them: "Come ye apart to a desert place, where the vanities of life shall not be seen by you, nor any distracting cry heard by you. There rest awhile in holy meditation, banishing from you all earthly follies."

And now, O most loving Jesus, Thou Visitor of the sick and Comforter of poor strangers driven from the joys of Paradise, visit me also in the day of my trouble and disquietude; whether I am sitting idly in my chamber, or singing in the choir with an arid heart, or, when at meals, rashly indulging in savory food; and by the sacred words of Thy mouth, addressed to me as it were from heaven (sweeter far than any bodily pleasure), restore me, I pray Thee, speedily to spiritual delights.

Open to me a clear understanding in the dark places of Holy Scripture, and, in the plain and devout teaching thereof, inflame my heart with the fire of love, as Thou didst with those two disciples, who were holily moved by Thy appearance and Thy discourse. Refreshed on the way by the Word of God and with meat, they thankfully said: "Did not our hearts burn within us while He talked with us by the way, and opened to us the Scriptures?"

These words are most sweet and holy. With devout hearts and joyful voices they are said and sung in the choir, chiefly at Eastertide and Festivals of certain of the Saints, by Clerks and Priests, and by a great company of the Faithful in all lands, to the praise and glory of God

O most holy Jesu! I pray Thee, during my pilgrimage here below, pardon my negligences, for still am I ofttimes vexed by my passions, from within and from without. Let me not be overcome by my ghostly enemies, nor deprived of the everlasting joys promised to Thy servants in heaven. Those joys ought greatly to encourage me to fight manfully against the sinful inclinations and yearnings of my heart. With devout prayers and pious meditations on the Life and Passion of Christ, daily ought I to call to mind some particular one, at least, of Thy so many wounds and sorrows, O Lord Jesu, Who wast crucified for me. Thy wounds are the medicine of my soul. Thy sacred words are a golden shield against the fiery darts of the enemy.

May Thy divine protection, with the grace of Thy Holy Spirit, be with me at all times, and in all places! Amen.

CHAPTER XII

ON THE APPEARANCE OF CHRIST TO THE DISCIPLES IN JERUSALEM, WHEN IT WAS LATE, AND THE DOORS WERE SHUT

O LORD JESU CHRIST, true Peace of the godly, Hope of the just, Joy of devout souls gathered together in one body, Com-

forter of the penitent, and Visitor of those who
are apart from the world, I bless and give Thee
thanks, for Thy glorious and marvellous appearance to Thine Apostles, assembled, when
it was now late, in an upper room.

No one opened, no one knocked; the doors
and windows were all securely shut, for protection of the house, and for fear of the Jews.

This was done, that Thy appearance and entrance might be seen, as truly and certainly the
work alone of Divine power; not of human
might and craftiness, nor by the artful wiles of
the devil.

For Thou art the true God. Thou deceivest
not, but hatest and punishest deceivers. Thou
art Omnipotent; therefore, whatever Thou
willest, at once it cometh to pass.

But the simple and devout, such as were the
Apostles and other disciples, assembled at that
hour in the inner chamber, them Thou didst
visit, enlighten, comfort, and lovingly salute,
saying: "Peace be unto you—It is I, be not
afraid."

I praise and honor Thee, for so sweetly and
gently greeting them after their so great tribulation; and I rejoice in Thee for so cheering a
vision, after their grievous trouble and terror.

For greatly needed they to have Thee again
present with them, to comfort, strengthen, and

uphold them. They had fallen into difficulties and trials so great, that never before, we may believe, had they experienced the like.

They had fled as a flock of sheep, when the shepherd had been seized and slain. Scattered hither and thither, they mourned and were afraid; and at length, when evening was come, they with difficulty gathered together in one place, and found rest for a season.

O most gracious Jesus! I praise and exalt Thy sweet Name above all in heaven and earth, because this day Thou didst vouchsafe to come to Thy Apostles, who in their terror had fled, disappointed and sorrowful; distrustful, and doubting Thy words, which Thou hadst aforetime so often spoken unto them.

But now Thou hast made them inexpressibly happy, by addressing them as their Friend, and that with Thine own mouth.

Forthwith Thou didst openly show to them the manifest marks of Thy Passion, in Thy hands, Thy feet, and Thy sacred side. Thou didst remove all their fear and distrust, when Thou didst eat before them honeycomb and a piece of broiled fish; and with Thy glorious hand didst give them of the same, that they might eat with Thee and rejoice.

During refreshment of the body, Thou didst place before them portions of Holy Scripture.

Thou didst remove doubts, make clear that which was dark, enlighten their understanding, and kindle their affections. Whatever was necessary and good for them, that Thou didst teach and reveal unto them.

Moreover, when Thou hadst pronounced peace to them with the heavenly benediction, having seen their Lord, they rejoiced with exceeding great joy. As formerly with the Wise Men, when they saw the Star in the heaven, all fear and doubt at once passed from them.

And now, to strengthen them against all unbelieving foes, and to blot out their transgressions, Thou didst breathe into them the grace of the Holy Spirit, saying:—

"Receive ye the Holy Ghost" (the greatest of gifts to those, who, for My Name's sake, have left all things of this world); "Whosesoever sins ye remit, they are remitted unto them; and whose-soever sins ye retain, they are retained."

O how truly great the grace, given to the Apostles by the inspiration of the Holy Ghost, from the breathing of Christ, after He, through the Glory of the Father, had risen from the dead! So that, not only they themselves were safe and absolved from all their sins, but were also invested with full power to absolve others, to reject the unworthy, and to bind the guilty.

O how glorious the day, how peaceful that evening hour, when Christ came to the Apostles with such great glory and gladness, filling with heavenly blessings those, who remain apart from the world under the discipline of God!

O Thomas! thou holy and beloved Apostle! would that thou hadst now been here, and hadst remained with thy fellow Apostles, when Jesus came and said, "Peace be unto you." But perhaps some necessity compelled thy absence.

Would that thou hadst returned in good time, and, with the others, hadst heard and seen all the words and doings of Jesus. How well would it have been for thee to have been present, and believed.

But who has known Thy mind, O Lord, or who has been Thy counsellor, that Thou shouldest then come suddenly, when Thomas was away, and that, possibly, but for a little moment?

Why, good Jesus, didst Thou thus? Why not wait awhile till Thomas returned? Wherefore, O loving Jesus! didst Thou not say "Where is Thomas?" he who so fervently called on his fellow disciples, "Let us also go, that we may die with Him."

O holy God! why didst not Thou send for him, that he might come quickly and see Thee?

Had I been present, how gladly would I, with Thy approval, have gone out and brought him to Thee.

Did not Samuel, the Prophet, send and call David, who was feeding the sheep; that he might come, and, in the presence of his brethren, be anointed King.

But now, O Lord, who, by Thy wisdom, hast made the heavens and the earth, I know full well and believe, that, with a true and right judgment, Thou didst allow all these things to happen. For nothing occurs on earth without a cause, though many are they who understand not Thy doings.

Therefore, it was not by mere accident that Thomas was absent, when Thou camest and didst appear to Thy disciples.

No, but by Thy sure foreknowledge Thou didst purposely and graciously act thus, that great good might come therefrom.

One doubted, that many might be established in the faith. One erred, was instructed, and set right, that a vast multitude might, by his conversion and preaching, attain to a more perfect knowledge of the truth.

For he who doubts profits by inquiry, provided he heeds the words of God's Saints, and persists not in his gainsaying.

There are many things beyond the intellect

of man, which cannot be easily attained by him, because of the vast height of the Divine Counsel.

No one, therefore, when tried in the faith, should despair; let him rather firmly rest on the words of Holy Scripture. For God, to encourage a hope of Salvation, has left us many examples of Saints and great Doctors, who also doubted on various points. They returned to the truth, and profited many not a little.

The Lord Jesus is gracious; He despiseth no one; He thrusteth none aside; but he, who cometh to Him in singleness of heart, is taught by Him the true faith—never is he deceived.

But what is too high should be committed to Him, who clearly discerns all hidden things; and all, that is unknown to men, He rightly and wisely sets in order.

Therefore, let not the ignorant be troubled about matters between Jesus and His disciples; nor let him be indignant with the holy Apostle, who was so slow to believe; because, what happened to him, by God's permission, might happen to any other.

And now, O most gentle Jesu Christ, Thou Visitor of the secluded, and Upholder of the timid, Instructor of young and those of full age, visit me also in my retirement from the world; when I am alone studying and writing, or with others in Thy Courts singing and praying.

Open to me the gate of eternal Life; lighten the darkness of my mind; drive from me the evil spirits that tempt me; cast from me the many idle thoughts that assail me.

When the eyes of my body are closed, come unto me secretly, and, by Thy presence, pour into my heart peace and gladness; and, to assure me of sins forgiven, show me in spirit Thy all-sacred wounds, endured for me upon the Cross, to redeem me from eternal death. Out of pure love didst Thou die for me, and rise again. Who with the Father and the Holy Ghost liveth and reigneth, one God, world without end. Amen.

CHAPTER XIII

ON THE APPEARANCE OF CHRIST ON THE OC-
TAVE OF THE FEAST OF EASTER, WHEN ST.
THOMAS WAS PRESENT

O LORD JESU CHRIST, Author of life, Bestower of pardon, Thou that infusest grace, and promisest future glory in eternal bliss with Thy holy Angels, I bless and give Thee thanks for Thy gracious appearance a second time, to all Thy Apostles; Thomas, Thy

Apostle, as yet doubting, being now present. Adorned with the sacred marks of Thy five wounds, in memory of Thy most holy Passion for our Salvation, Thou didst, by the sight and touch of Thy glorious Body, strengthen him in a true and right faith.

I praise and honor Thee for Thy joyful salutation, and for Thine openly showing Thyself with the heavenly benediction, blessing Thine Apostles with Thy holy mouth, and, with gladdening countenance, saying unto them, "Peace be unto you, here and for ever."

"Now indeed by faith and grace, but hereafter by sight and by open vision. As the Father hath loved Me, so love I you. Continue ye in My love, hold fast to Me, and I will abide with you now and for ever."

I honor and glorify Thee, O Jesu Christ, reverend Lord and Master, for Thy friendly announcement of peace, for Thy venerable standing in the midst of Thy disciples, and for Thy preserving them from fear of the Jews.

For, as a good shepherd stands in the midst of his sheep, to defend them from devouring wolves, so didst Thou stand with Thine Apostles, in the day of trouble, strengthening them against evil, for the kingdom of Heaven's sake.

And, as a mighty king and noble leader stands armed in the midst of his people, holding a spear and shield to defend him against the darts of the enemy, and encourages his soldiers to fight bravely—to conquer or die a noble death ;

So O Jesu ! bravest Warrior against evil spirits and men perverse, so didst Thou present Thyself in the midst of Thy disciples, clothed with a robe of gladness, and the armor of immortality ; holding, as a proof of Thy being the very Crucified Jesus, the marks of Thy Passion, open piercings in the shield of Thy Body ; marks with which Thou didst vanquish the princes of this world, and the rulers of utter darkness. Thus didst Thou strengthen the Apostles, Thy soldiers, in faith, hope, and charity.

For, before they were utterly cast down. They had witnessed Thy Passion, Thy Cross, Thy Death—yea, and Thy Body buried in the firmly-closed tomb of stone.

What man, having seen upon Thee so many bands and signs of death, would have believed that Thou couldest rise again ? And, therefore, lest Thy beloved disciples, who were not yet fully confirmed in the faith, should despair, Thou didst appear openly to them, with the marks of Thy sacred and glorious Body miraculously remaining on Thee ; in proof of Thy true Resurrection, that they might believe, and not doubt of Thy appearing.

Thus didst Thou say unto them, "Handle Me and see, that I am the same Jesus Christ, who hung on the Cross for you, and, by power divine, rose again the third day, as I openly foretold to you; but ye did not then clearly understand.

"Therefore, behold now My hands, and My feet, and My side; and especially consider the five wounds of My Passion, to meditate on them day and night, and learn how great was My love for you, and how much I have endured for your eternal Salvation.

"Peace be unto you, My friends, despisers of the world, for whom, when the many dangers of this present life have passed away, I have prepared the eternal joys of heaven with the holy Angels. Fear not, doubt not; I am your reward, your crown, and your blessing. Amen."

A PRAYER TO OBTAIN THE PEACE OF MIND, WHICH CHRIST GAVE TO HIS DISCIPLES

O LORD JESU CHRIST, from whom floweth all that is sweet, King of heaven and earth, the true peace of hearts, and Comforter of those who mourn, say, I pray Thee, unto my soul, troubled and desolate as Thou fully knowest it to be, "I am thy salvation, thy peace, thy life, thy comfort, thy hope, thy light, and thy rest.

"In Me is all thy good, the true solace of the soul, every pleasant and unending joy. What more dost thou desire?"

Nothing Lord, Thee only do I desire; Thee I seek, Thee I long for, Thee I dearly love. Thee, in all things and over all things, always and everywhere, I bless and praise.

Thou rulest over all things in heaven and earth, in the sea, and in all great depths; in the mountains and in the woods; and every creature, small and great, is known to Thee, and clear before Thee.

In wisdom hast Thou made them all, and by Thy Providence are they all governed.

O peace of God, O clear knowledge of my Creator, which passeth all reason, and the understanding of men and angels! when wilt Thou come unto me, when wilt Thou fill me within and without, that I may have nothing more to desire?

O Lord God, my heart is disquieted, until it rest in Thee. My mind has no peace, until it be perfectly one with Thee in the Life eternal. O peace, how sweet and desirable is thy name in all the earth!

How joyful and how pleasant is thy voice in the heavenly country. O true, most excellent, everlasting peace with God, with the holy Angels, and with men of holy will.

Grant me peace in my heart, O Lord, that I may fully love Thee. Grant me peace in my mouth, that I may devoutly praise Thee. Grant me peace in my hand, that I may ever do all good works to Thy honor.

Say unto me, when I am in heaviness:— "Peace be unto thee, it is I, be not afraid." "Peace be unto thee," nothing more pleasant to hear. "It is I," nothing more pleasant to possess. "Be not afraid," nothing safer to rejoice in. "Lo, I am with you," nothing sweeter to enjoy.

"Always, day by day, even unto the end of the world," nothing is surer, nothing firmer to be believed, if we would obtain Life eternal.

O Lord, whatever I have, whatever I see and desire, all is nothing without Thee.

In Thee alone are all my blessings; nothing better, nothing more perfect, nothing richer, nothing more happy.

Therefore, all my hope, all that I possess, all my salvation, all my peace, is in Thee, O God, my Saviour; and in no created good, however beautiful, noble and great.

I say, therefore, and with the holy and humble Francis I pray, "My God and my all. I desire nothing more."

If at any time I shall be in trouble, and bereft of inward satisfaction and comfort, again I say and pray "My God and my all; I want nothing more." I desire nothing but Thee, my God, all in all, and over all, and before all, blessed for ever.

O Lord, grant that I may meditate intently on these things, and ever devoutly accomplish them. Amen.

CHAPTER XIV

ON THE TOUCHING OF THE SACRED WOUNDS OF CHRIST BY THE HAND OF ST. THOMAS THE APOSTLE

O LORD JESU CHRIST, Enlightener of the Faithful 'mid the darkness of this world, I bless and thank Thee for Thy great compassion shown to Thine Apostle St. Thomas, for Thy special appearance to him, and for strengthening him in the faith of Thy Resurrection; that miracle, which surpasses all human reason; and is, save by faith and divine revelation to man, incomprehensible.

Many marvellous works hast Thou done, O Lord God, from the beginning of the world; and yet doest daily in heaven and in earth, that Thou mayest declare the glory of Thy Name.

Therefore, although these things cannot be fully comprehended and searched out by men, yet to Thee are they very easy. They are chiefly done and ordered for the salvation of the Elect.

And, since this Thy beloved disciple did not wilfully hold to his opinion, nor had he, with any evil intent, declared that he would not believe unless he saw and touched Thee, therefore did he obtain mercy and favor; so that he saw Thee openly with his eyes, and verily touched Thee reverently with his hand, that he might cease from all doubting, and strengthen the faint-hearted in the faith.

Therefore, seeing Thy humanity, and in his heart believing the Divinity to be hidden in Thee, he with his mouth exclaimed, saying, with great devotion and full of faith, "My Lord and my God."

This I firmly believe, this I truly profess, this I openly declare, this I boldly preach, this I tell forth to all nations, and long to proclaim it to the ends of the earth—that all may believe in Thee and be saved.

"My Lord and my God," "my Creator and my Redeemer." This is the true and sure faith, which leadeth believers to the kingdom of Heaven.

O how plentiful is Thy goodness, O Lord, to Thy Saints and elect friends, which in this life, 'mid its troubles and temptations, Thou dost often show them; and giving them a fore-taste thereof—yea, by word and by example, Thou dost exhort them to go on and persevere.

Sometimes Thou hidest Thyself, that they may mourn and seek Thee, and long to behold Thee. Thus is it they learn, by their falling and growing slothful, how weak they are; thus have they no high thought of themselves, nor attempt they lofty flights, far above their power.

In due season Thou showest Thyself again, comforting, enlightening, and instructing the sorrowful; that, in the time of trouble, they may not despair, nor presume in the day of prosperity; but consider themselves to be mortal men and sinners, ever needing the grace and mercy of God—not Angels established in glory.

I praise and highly extol Thy compassion and tenderness, that, offering peace and granting forgiveness, Thou didst show Thyself gracious towards Thy holy Apostle Thomas, as he humbly and reverently knelt before Thee, earnestly pleading for pardon. Thou didst exhibit to him Thy holy and glorious wound-prints; of more worth than all the treasures of the world; more precious than all jewels, more beautiful than all brilliant roses, more fragrant than all spices and sweet-smelling flowers.

These shine brighter far than all the glories of the heavens; they more fully rejoice the souls of the Saints; they more ardently inflame the hearts of the Faithful; they more frequently soften the hardness of sinners; and draw from them very bitter tears of penitence.

They stir up the slothful to increased prayer; they lead the devout to salute Thee oftener; they urge the grateful to thank Thee more earnestly.

Constantly meditating on the wounds of Christ, and tenderly picturing them, Thy most zealous servants have been pierced to the very depths of the soul, and wept bitterly; clearly manifesting that they had been with Jesus.

And even yet, those five wounds, that tell of the love of Jesus, often stir the hearts of the faithful, and move the penitent to tears; when they behold Christ on the Cross, or hear preached the story of the Passion, or read and dwell thereon, to the praise of God.   Amen.

ON THE GREAT GRACE OF DEVOTION, AND THE FIRM FAITH OF THE APOSTLE ST. THOMAS

O how great the grace of devotion, which the holy Apostle Thomas obtained from the sight of Thy sacred wounds, my God! even beyond many Saints, who saw Thee living in the flesh, and believed on Thee after Thy Resurrection.

I therefore highly bless Thee and thank Thee, my Lord and my God, who, through the Apostles, hast taught me to believe aright, and to live justly; to confess the true faith without any doubting or dissimulation whatever.

For Thou hast truly said: "Whosoever shall confess Me before men, him will I confess before My Father."

Grant, therefore, O Lord, that I may constantly speak the truth, and confess the right Faith, as did St. Thomas before Thee, in the presence of the Apostles, saying: "My Lord and my God."

What is more clear, what more true, what more perfect, what more worthy of belief, than this confession? Of which the blessed John thus writes: "Thomas answered and said unto Him" (namely to Thee my Lord God), "my Lord and my God."

For many of the Faithful have spoken to Thee, and called Thee by diverse holy Names, according to their faith and devotion; and, indeed, rightly and well in accordance with Thine unspeakable dignity; which, nevertheless, far exceeds the height and praise of every creature, and every title of dignity in heaven and in earth.

Some, when praying to Thee, have said: "Jesus of Nazareth have mercy upon me"; some, "Thou Son of David"; some, "Good Master and Lord"; some, "Rabbi or Rabboni"; some, "Thou Teacher and Saviour of the world"; some, "Thou great Prophet and King of Israel"; some, "Behold the Lamb of God," as John the Baptist; some, "Thou art the Son of God," as Nathanael; some, "We have found the Messiah," as Andrew; some, "Thou art Christ, the Son of the Living God," as St. Peter and other Apostles; all speaking by the revelation of the heavenly Father.

And, in order that all the terms for designating Thy Godhead, and the words of sacred praise, may be perfectly, briefly, and faithfully included in one, and be firmly believed, St. Thomas, enlightened and fully instructed by the Holy Spirit, and established in the faith by Thy presence, O Lord, said, openly and boldly to Thee, our Lord, with a loud voice: "My Lord and my God."

In which words he briefly comprehends all that can be truly said and believed, touching Thy divine and human nature, to Thy praise, and the salvation of all Christians that believe in Thee, throughout the whole world.

Grant me, O Lord my God, firmly to hold this holy Catholic faith; that I may adorn and guard it by a holy life, and never in any way depart from the truth.   Amen.

CHAPTER XV

AN ADDRESS ON THE FIVE SACRED WOUNDS OF JESUS CHRIST

O LORD JESU CHRIST, most loving Son of God, Thou who wast crucified for the salvation of the world, I bless and thank Thee for all Thy sorrows, and all Thy sacred wounds, the greater and lesser, which Thou didst lovingly and innocently endure to purge and absolve me from my sins; and which, dying in true love and perfect obedience, Thou didst offer freely and willingly to Thy heavenly Father.

More especially I praise and glorify Thee now, and will every day of my life, with the highest thanksgiving and blessing of my mouth, from the deepest affections of my heart, and with the sweetest remembrance of Thy mercies, for Thy very great and friendly condescension, and the openly manifesting Thy five sacred wounds;

Which, after Thy blessed and glorious Resur

rection, Thou didst retain in Thy most holy and glorious Body; and didst present to Thy disciples to see with their eyes; and didst kindly and convincingly grant to St. Thomas, the Apostle, when doubting, to touch them with his hands, and so didst Thou establish him in the faith.

And, as a sign of Thy perpetual love to them, and all Thy faithful people—those devoted to Thee throughout the world, Thou didst desire these things to be announced and published, that they may earnestly love Thee, and never cease rejoicing in Thy praise.

Therefore, meet and profitable for me is it daily to call to mind Thy great love towards me; that, as these Thy five sacred wounds remained in Thy glorious body (like new and ever-abiding openings in a shield) exceeding bright above all the stars of heaven; so, also, may they remain ever fixed in my memory, and in the memory of all Thy faithful servants, on account of the innumerable benefits arising therefrom, and their power for warding off and blotting out the evils of this life; and especially for the eternal joys to be happily secured by them with Thee, O gracious Jesu.

Praise, honor, power, glory, and victory be to Thee, O Lord, for Thy sacred wounds, by which Thou hast redeemed me, purged the world, spoiled hell, opened Paradise, illuminated Heaven, and caused the Angels to rejoice.

And, that Thou mightest draw some wretched one to Thee, and reconcile him to the Father, and turn away God's anger, Thou, even when ascending into heaven, hast retained these sacred wounds; and in order always to show Thy compassion on me, and all who believe on Thee, and grieve for their sins, Thou hast borne them with Thee to the right hand of the Father; and, as a token of Thy victory over death, Thou dost present them to all the inhabitants of Heaven.

O Jesu Christ, King of Glory, Thou astonishment and joy, Thou inestimable hope of believers, Thou brightness of the Father, the honor of Thy Mother, the lustre of the Virgin, the flower of the field, the lily of the valley, the solace of the afflicted, the health of the sick, the joy of the devout, the blessedness of the Saints, the felicity of Angels!

Write, I beseech Thee, O Lord, these Thy sacred and precious wounds in my heart, with Thy precious Blood, that I may inwardly suffer with Thee, and love Thee above all things; and bear most willingly a few reproaches out of love for Thy sweet and holy Name, which is to be highly blessed above every name of men and holy Angels, for ever and ever.

In crimson forms and in circles of gold, paint these Thy wounds before my wandering eyes, that I may not behold nor think of the vanities of the world, nor give ear to rumors fitted to disquiet me, nor attend to those who speak to me of aught that relates not to Thee, O Jesu, my Lord and my God.

For vain are all things, which keep me from meditating on heavenly blessings, and from weeping over Thy sacred wounds.

Fasten, therefore, Thy sacred nails to my feet as sharp spurs, that I may tread in Thy footsteps on the rough road of bitterness and affliction. Then shall I not be elated in prosperity, nor cast down when troubles assail me.

Wound me in each foot, that I wander not further from Thee. In the left fix the nail of fear, that, dreading the future torments of hell, I may not give way to the lusts of the flesh.

In the right foot fix the nail of holy love, that I may run the way of Thy Commandments with fervid devotion, night and day serving Thee; ever joyfully giving Thee all possible thanks in hymns and heavenly praises.

Short and light is all earthly labor, and hard doing, thirst and pain of body, for Thee, my God, Who, in the flesh, suffered and was wounded; but long, yea, very long, is eternal punishment—the unceasing pains of hell.

Strike also Thy two nails into my hands, that, while there is time, I may diligently bring forth good works, and avoid that vile indolence, which is so hurtful to the soul; nay more, that I may throw mine arms around Thee, lovingly hanging on the Cross for me, full of wounds, yet pleading for Thine enemies.

Draw me therefore to Thee, from the flesh to the Cross, from earth to heaven. For I long for my departure, that I may die with Thee on the Cross, and by Thy wounds be cleansed from all my sins, and so escape death eternal.

Thou art my God, and to Thee will I confess my sins. Heal me by Thy sacred wounds, which, in my behalf, were so cruelly inflicted on Thee. For who will cleanse me from my sins and negligences, but Thou alone, O God, my Redeemer, Who, for me, wast crucified and wounded with many stripes?

Among those stripes Thy five precious wounds, made by the nails and spear, are specially eminent, of sweet odor, and brilliant like the crimson seals of the Lamb of God. They are colored with blood, and marked in with the spur of divine love; and, as the sure and sacred tokens of my eternal Redemption, never to be blotted out, full are they of all grace and sweetness; open to me and to all mankind to kiss, and to behold with the eyes of the mind; and granted to those who mourn, that they may enter into the secret things of Heaven.

Enter, O my soul, enter boldly into the tender mercies of Thy God, who is hanging on the Cross.

Enter into the deep hollows of His wounds, safe from the face of the serpent, who is everywhere secretly and openly lying in wait for thee.

Here remain in silence and in safety, as a turtle mourning in solitude, and as a dove hidden in a cleft of the hard rock; despising all the pleasures of the world, meditating on the sacred wounds of Jesus Christ, and through them looking for the eternal rewards of Heaven, by Himself to be given unto thee.

I beseech Thee, now, O most gracious Jesu Christ, speak also to my soul Thy saving word, which, as a mark of Thy great love, Thou spakest to Thy holy Apostle Thomas, strengthening him in faith, and forgiving him all his sins:

"Reach hither thy finger and behold My hands," with hard nails lovingly fixed to the Cross for thee. Reach hither thy hand and touch Me thoughtfully. Thrust it into My side, that was in tender pity opened for thee; that side, so cruelly pierced by the soldier's

spear, that blood and water flowed therefrom
freely, for the perfect remission of all sins, and
in compassion for all believers. "And be not
faithless, but believing." Not doubting, but
firm and steadfast; not over-curious, but honest
and devout; not idle, nor forgetful, but zealous,
and ever thankful to God for benefits so great.

Grant, O kind and beloved Jesus, that I may
often think and meditate on these things; that
I may believe on Thee, and cleave to Thee.
May I never doubt Thy words and the truth
eternal. In every temptation and sorrow, may
I ever turn at once for comfort to Thy Passion,
and seek for consolation in Thy sacred wounds
and suffering. Yea, may I ever find peace and
rest for my soul in Thee, Who, with the Father
and the Holy Ghost, liveth and reigneth, ever
one God, world without end. Amen.

CHAPTER XVI

ON THE ARMOR OF CHRIST; THE CROSS, NAILS, SPEAR, AND CROWN OF THORNS

O LORD JESU CHRIST, King of all
kings, I bless and give Thee thanks for
Thy triumphal and royal arms; namely, the
cross, nails, spear, crown of thorns, rod, cord,

pillar (to which Thou wast bound naked, when cruelly scourged); and for all the other instruments of torture, used during Thy sacred Passion for us vile sinners;

To vanquish the devil and the lovers of the world, with all their pomps and evil doings; to give mercy and remission of sins to all that believe in Thee, and are truly penitent;

To obtain the hope of eternal Salvation, and the glory of celestial bliss with Thy holy Angels in heaven, after the coming general Resurrection of the dead, both of the just and the unjust, according to their deeds, whether good or evil. For then will appear many signs in heaven and in earth, and the sacred wounds of Thy Passion with the standard of the Cross, and various achievements of Thine arms, to the joy and assurance of Thine Elect, but to the terror and misery of the lost.

Then will all the Elect leap for joy—the humble, the innocent, the devout and chaste, the simple and the obedient, the meek, and they who have often endured contradictions for Thy Name's sake. Yes, many a time and oft, they think sorrowfully of Thy Passion and Thy sacred wounds, as if wrought upon themselves, and devoutly thank Thee for all Thou didst endure.

Then also will they greatly fear and lament

for themselves—the proud, the covetous, the envious, the greedy, and walkers after the flesh; they who seldom or never think compassionately on Thy Cross and wounds, but rather set their thoughts on their own gains and advantages, than on Thy goodness and Thy bitter sufferings.

From these perverse and ungrateful men preserve me, O Lord; and ever unite me with the pure and innocent sheep of Thy flock, for whom Thou didst deign, out of Thy tender love, to be crucified and die, tortured by many wounds.

O gentle Jesus! endue me now with the power of Thy might, and gird me about thoroughly, everywhere and at all times, with the sacred armor of Thy most bitter Passion.   This do, for many are the snares and temptations of the evil spirit, assailing me on the right hand and on the left, by a thousand wicked schemes, and vain deceptions.

Therefore, O Lord, to Thy Passion do I humbly fly for succor; and I heartily pray Thee to comfort me, and with Thy power to uphold me.

O gracious Jesus, Helper and Defender in every temptation and trial of this frail life, raise aloft before me the royal Standard of Thy holy Cross, the sign of eternal Salvation, the sceptre of the divinity, the bow and shield of the humanity, a very strong tower, a terrible thunder, and the sharpest dart against the angry assaults of the devil;

A defence is it against the turmoil of the world, and the incitement of the flesh; against every vice and perverse thought, against the spirit of blasphemy and the abyss of despair; which are ever ready to overwhelm me, and to turn me aside, O Jesu, from the invocation of Thy most sweet Name, to blacken the life and character of Thy Saints; and, what is worse, to call me, an earnest believer, back from the right faith, and from the veneration and love of Thy holy Cross.

O Jesu! most valiant King, because of the many perils and dangers around me, be Thy holy Cross my Salvation, my peace, and my life, my shield, sword, and spear, a strong tower from the face of mine enemy; a solid defence from the fraud of the old serpent, my light at home, my leader when abroad, my safeguard within and without, above and below.

May the Cross be sweet and pleasant to me; a rest in labor, a comfort in affliction, a medicine in illness, an ointment in pain.

May it be a defence in solitude, a security in crowded gatherings, a lamp in darkness, a joy at noon; in the evening praise, honor, power, and glory.

May it be to me a fair and beautiful Cross, sweetness in my hours of bitterness, health in sickness, a firm faith in the agony of death, my only hope in the departure of the soul, a support at the day of judgment, a protection from hell, an acquittal from all punishment, a transporting by the holy Angels into the glory of Heaven.

Moreover, O patient Jesu, in sorrows apply to me the sacred nails, cruelly fixed in Thee when Thou wast hanging on the Cross; that they may be the guard of my heart, my mouth, and of all my senses, and keep me from daily and nightly terrors of evil spirits; that, when they see the signs of Thy nails, they may flee from me, as from sharp arrows, leaving me to rest in Thy peace, or, to pray and seriously to meditate on the pangs caused by those nails, when in the Body of my Lord Jesu Christ.

Nor can they dare, with their wicked delusions, to disturb me, while I am meditating on Thy sacred wounds; which, so great and so deep, Thou didst endure in Thy hands and in Thy feet.

Apply also, I pray Thee, to my side, as a guard of my heart, at all times, whether I be awake or asleep, Thy holy and sharp spear, so deeply thrust into Thee, when Thou wast dead; that I also may, with Thee, be pierced on the Cross; suffering with Thee inwardly, while outwardly eschewing all that is worldly; banishing from me all that is vain; bearing in memory only heavenly things, and Thy sacred wounds.

So wound my heart, O my God, that nothing impure may any longer be found in me.

O most excellent and ever to be loved Jesu Christ! sure hope of the faithful, the strength of them that fight, and the crown of them that conquer, the wisdom of the contemplative, the enlightener of the ignorant, show also unto me, now an exile under the burden of the flesh, Thy holy and blessed Crown of thorns; which, with derision and hard blows, was cruelly fixed and pressed down upon Thy sacred head, while on all sides, from Thy many wounds, dropped down Thy most precious Blood.

I pray Thee, that the abundant ebbings from this sacred and most bitter Crown may fully cleanse me from all my sins, draw forth from me floods of tears, and suddenly soften my dry and hardened heart.

May I have a continual remembrance, and a vivid conception of this Thy holy and blessed Crown; and may the great injury inflicted by the wounds, and prayerful meditation thereon, drive away from me and put to flight all evil things and impure thoughts; may they abolish and destroy troubles of every kind.

Enter, therefore, enter fresh sorrow, deep into my heart, for this blood-stained Crown of thorns. May that sorrow work upon every member of my body, and fill me with bitterness; blotting out all the imperfections of my soul, which, in my folly, I have been so long gathering together.

May it reduce to nothing in me every lofty desire; all I deem beautiful, to dust; everything precious, to mire; everything flourishing, to decay; everything delectable, to the bitterest wormwood; everything joyful, to lamentation; all that is amusing and witty, to derision and contempt.

O! in the great hereafter, how bright and lovely in heavenly glory will be the crown of a devout and chaste soul; which, in this world, so often and so sorrowfully thinks of the thorn-crown of Jesus; and bears in sad remembrance all His cruel wounds.

Such a soul, at the hour of death, when leaving this miserable life, will, I believe, at the last, enjoy a great hope of pardon, and a full assurance of mercy, in the remembrance of Thy sacred Passion, O Lord.

Therefore, for the sake of Thine every

wound, forgive me also all mine offences, present and past; as Thou didst, solely out of Thy mercy and grace, to St. Mary Magdalene; who greatly bewailed her sins, and mourned bitterly over the sacred wounds of Thy Passion, inflicted on Thee for our very many and grievous transgressions;

For Thy mercy and goodness, O most merciful Jesu, have overcome all our evils, new and old, through the bowels of Thy compassion, and the innumerable stripes of Thy wounds, most patiently endured from wicked men; wounds seen with their eyes by Thy holy Mother, and by the beloved Mary Magdalene, and moistened with streaming tears.

Therefore, still further vex me, O Lord, from within by Thy scourging, and tight binding with cords to the hard pillar; and that, in the presence of many scoffing and reviling. No pity, no shame was there for Thee; but, like furious dogs, they longed to tear with their teeth an innocent sheep. They added blow to blow, sorrow upon sorrow, but never once didst Thou resist, no cry was heard, "Alas! Alas! why do ye so cruelly scourge Me?"

O! how great and unspeakable Thy patience, O Lord Jesu, during such bitter affliction, Thy wounds red with issuing blood; all to make atonement for my sins.

I have sinned, O Lord, and Thou bearest the scourge for me. I have done wickedly; in many ways have I ofttimes offended, yet Thou, utterly blameless, art unjustly condemned by the ungodly.

I often in my folly laugh, but Thou art basely derided. I am well clothed, my desire is to please men, but Thou art hanging naked between thieves.

I eat and drink that which is fitting; but Thou hast, on the altar of the Cross, the bitter draught of vinegar and gall.

I sleep on a soft couch, but Thou art buried in a hard tomb, as some outcast in the world.

I often pass by the Cross, no tears bedew mine eyes; but Mary Magdalene and other holy women ceased not weeping, until, beholding Thee risen from the dead, they in adoration embraced Thy sacred feet.

Grant, O gracious Jesu, that I may meditate on these things, and, with Thy holy and most devoted ones, Mary Magdalene and Thy other disciples, may so weep that, at the last day, when the trumpet shall sound, I may be found meet to come to the glory of the Resurrection; and to enter, with all Thine Elect, into the kingdom of eternal blessedness. Amen.

May Thy most noble armor, O Lord Jesu Christ, be to me a sure protection, within and without, against all the darts of the enemy, and against whatever allurements and oppositions the world may offer me.   Amen.

CHAPTER XVII

ON THE APPEARANCE OF CHRIST TO SEVEN DISCIPLES, WHEN THEY WERE FISHING IN THE SEA OF TIBERIAS

O LORD JESU CHRIST, Who art the Maker of all things, and the Ruler of heaven and earth, of Angels and men, of high and low, of rich and poor, of those who dwell on land and those who labor in the great waters, I bless and thank Thee for openly showing Thyself, after Thy glorious Resurrection, to seven of Thy disciples, who were toiling for fish in the Sea of Tiberias, to secure, out of their honest labors, the necessaries of life, and means of support for the helpless and strangers.

All this was well pleasing to God and man; allowed to us by the law of nature, and the bountiful favor of God; for the manifold advantages arising therefrom. Idleness is avoided, and time profitably employed.

I praise and honor Thee, most gracious Jesus, Thou Visitor of them that labor, the helper in due season, by giving good counsel to them that need it; thereby graciously sustaining bodily life by land and in the waters.

I bless Thee for Thy reverend standing on the sea-shore, observing how lovingly Thy disciples were joined together, aiding one the other in their labors; how orderly they proceeded; how, after their wonted manner, without any noise or words of anger, they took up their implements of fishing, and passed to their respective posts; ready to apply themselves vigorously should some storm oblige.

Thus wisely placed, these disciples labored all the night through. They rowed, and dragged, and toiled hard, until morning, but nothing whatever did they take.

Wherefore, despairing of their labor, they were now thinking of ceasing from further fishing, unless God should provide better for them.

But this great difficulty in catching fish was permitted, that, afterwards, when Jesus, their Master and Lord, came and guided them, great might be their joy.

Because, during the past night, Jesus was not bodily present in the ship, as He had wont to be so often formerly, little or no success had they. It was as He had told them before, "Without Me ye can do nothing."

But, beloved disciples, do not despair on account of this change; for a cloudy morning often, by God's favor, turns to a bright noonday.

Wait a little, and call upon the gracious Lord Jesus, and it shall go well with you after your night's toil.

And so it came to pass. When Jesus appeared and said, " Cast the net on the right side of the ship, and ye shall find plentifully, although before, when I was absent, ye could take nothing."

I praise and glorify Thee, O Jesu, who foreseest all things, for Thy gracious discourse with these poor fishermen, who had now no sure income, no Church supplies to live on; but, by the labor of their hands, were lawfully procuring for themselves the necessaries of life, lest, by begging, they should become burdensome to others, or, by their idleness, prove an offence to the weak.

Therefore didst Thou, O good Jesus, in the time of their need, come to the aid of Thy poor ones; asking them, if they had with them anything to eat; inquiring, in a friendly manner, concerning their food, " Children, have ye any meat?" They answered, " No."

A brief reply to the Lord Omnipotent, who knoweth all things from eternity; to Whom every heart is open, and every secret; all that was in the ship, and everything that swims in the sea.

Thou didst therefore, O gracious Jesu, pity their poverty, as Thou hadst formerly compassion on the hungry multitude in the desert; speedily giving, by a single word, counsel and relief to those that were obedient to Thee.

Therefore, trusting to God rather than to their own skill, with good faith they cast the net on the right side of the ship. They obeyed the command of the Lord, Who was standing on the sea-shore; and His words were more effectual far, than oars or aught beside.

And lo! now, by the help of Jesus, their net was filled with so great a multitude of fishes, that they were not able to draw it to the shore. So vast are the gifts of God, they far exceed the powers of man.

Seeing this, so great a miracle wrought, that disciple, whom Jesus loved, said to his companions, and especially to Peter, "It is the Lord."

On hearing this, Peter rejoiced with exceeding great joy, and his heart was moved with such fervent love, that, forgetting and heedless of all left in the ship, he girt his fisher's coat unto him, and at once cast himself into the sea, and hastened to Jesus his Lord; Whom he loved above every holy name, blessed for evermore.

O with what great reverence and boldness did he approach Thee, O Lord Jesu, and bend his wet knees before Thee, adoring and honoring Thy face, which is brighter than the sun, and ever visible to the holy Angels.

That face was now, for a brief season, manifested to Peter and his companions, for their comfort; but the sight thereof is utterly denied to the mighty and rich of this world, and to all the idle lovers of luxury.

O gracious and sweet Jesus! hide not Thou Thy face from me, whatever may be my place or my calling.

Come and be near unto me, when I am singing, reading, meditating, writing, or studying.

Remember me in prosperity, and, when any trouble shall suddenly visit me; give me patience in my heart, and with my mouth ever to bless Thee, and to bear all things contentedly, for the love of Thee and of Thy honor.

Visit me in the night season, that, at the call to early prayer, I may quickly rise with my brethren, to sing the Psalms, and help them; as did those Apostles, who, throughout the whole night, toiled on together to catch fish, until the day dawned, and Thou camest and gavest a blessing.

For when Thou wast present and didst bless them, their net was filled with a multitude of great fishes.

In like manner, O Lord, I beseech Thee, that, when I pray, Thou wouldest, by Thy grace preventing and following me, vouchsafe to fill me with so great a sweetness of inner devotion, that many long Psalms may be more pleasant to me, than great fishes to him that is hungry.

For the delight of the mind is greater far than that of the flesh. The spirit revives, the flesh weighs down. The spirit purifies and gladdens, the flesh stains and makes sad.

The spirit is submissive and obedient to God, but the flesh often resists Him and does us harm. For the soul is better than the body; the living spirit more worthy than decaying flesh. The world has its sweetness, but sweeter far and more excellent above all things is God, the Creator and Ruler of all things.

Through all creation blessed be Thou, O Lord Jesu Christ, my God! who alone doest great wonders by sea and by land.

For, with Thy chosen friends Thou dost gladly eat and feast. Yea, in hymns and psalms, which are sweeter than all earthly food and pleasant drink, Thou dost prepare for them a sacred and spiritual banquet.

CHAPTER XVIII

ON THE FEASTING OF CHRIST WITH THE SAME DISCIPLES

O LORD JESU CHRIST, Thou Comforter of the afflicted, Pitier of the poor, Restorer of the hungry, and Strengthener of them that labor; I bless and give Thee thanks, for corporally feasting with Thy disciples; and for the capture of fishes so many and so great, by the hands and labor of Thy beloved disciples; made in Thy presence and through the power of Thy words, when Thou saidst unto them, " Cast the net on the right side of the ship, and ye shall find."

O the great grace of God! Thou art the Creator of all things, and dost provide for the needy and the little ones, who have no storerooms filled with food, nor bags of money hidden in chests.

Woe to those who trust to their treasureholds, whence thieves can, in one night, steal all, and wickedly squander it.

I praise and give Thee glory, most glorious Jesus, for the friendly invitation of Thy disciples, poor fishermen, to dine with Thee, after

332 Meditations on the Life of Christ

a long fast and hard fishing, saying unto them:
—" Come and dine.

"For I have prepared for you, who are
wearied and hungry, fish laid on burning coals
and bread.

"If any of you need warmth, let him come
to the fire and warm himself. If he has soiled
or wetted his clothing, let him at once wash
them, and dry them, at the fire I have Myself
made ready.

"You know well what I did to you formerly,
at the Supper, before My Passion; how I
washed your feet and wiped them. You must
well remember My discourse to you, how I ex-
horted you long, by My example, to walk in
humility and love, one with the other.

"And now, after My Resurrection, I appear
to you, admonishing you the more diligently
to discharge all such duties, and dining with
you.

"For Me there is no need of food; but I
now speak and eat with you, to show to you
the reality of My glorified Body.

"Therefore, dine with Me in love, soberly
and modestly with silence; abstaining from
all vain things, as I so often taught you, and
as ye have seen in Me and ofttimes heard.

"For from My mouth no light word ever
proceeded; but always that which was well

pleasing to My Father; and to others that heard it, it was helpful and prolific of good."

Witnesses of these things are the four Holy Gospels, scattered abroad over the world, within which is found nothing vain, nothing unseemly.

"Be content now with the few things ye see, which I have made ready for you, My children, who have said, 'We have no meat.' Desire not food that is costly and prepared with spices; fare of the luxurious, unfitted for devout brothers and sisters in Christ, who have given up this world. Be pleased rather with simple food, bread and fish, which, by God's favor, is graciously provided for you.

"These, however, may not perchance be sufficient for you, because of strangers, and poor mendicants, who come to you. Such sufferers ye must not turn away, but, according to your power, nourish and comfort them.

"Therefore, I say to you, be not cast down when ye have but little. Trusting in Me, bring of the fish, which now, with joy of heart, ye have taken so abundantly."

Hearing this, Simon Peter, in ready and prompt obedience, went up and, aided by his companions, drew the net to land full of great fishes, an hundred and fifty and three.

And they all, full of wonder, gave thanks to God the Father, and to Thee, Jesus Christ, His

Son, Whom they saw present with them, and knew by the Holy Ghost.

And therefore, no one durst ask Him, "Who art Thou, Who now standest here with us, and speakest and eatest?"

For they all knew of a truth, that it was Thou, our Lord Jesus Christ, Who didst rise again from the closed tomb, alive and immortal, and didst manifest Thyself to us.

O Lord Jesu Christ, Who art the beloved friend of all the devout, the sweet host of the soul, a cheerful companion among Thy brethren and friends, I praise and thank Thee for so good a meal and social repast; which Thou didst prepare for Thy beloved disciples, who were wearied, after long and laborious fishing. Thou didst invite them to dine, and with Thine own hand Thou didst administer to them bread blessed by Thy mouth, and also fish broiled on the fire, glowing with love; inwardly savored with spiritual sweetness.

O how pleasant was the taste of that food, which Jesus prepared—and then served at the table, for which He, as Director of the Refectory, had provided!

And what shall I say more? Truly very delightful was this feast, which Jesus held with His disciples; but O! how far more excellent, how much higher in dignity, and more joyous, is the sacred Feast of His precious Body and Blood, which is ever celebrated in His Church.

In which Jesus Himself is taken; His Passion, which He endured for us all, is remembered anew; the mind, which in itself is often arid and cold, is filled with grace, through the joy-giving presence of Jesus in the heart.

In this sacred Feast a pledge of future glory is also given to the devout soul, for the comfort and nourishment of its spiritual life, in this its pilgrimage; until Christ shall come, and take that soul to Himself, away from every labor and sorrow of its present misery, into eternal rest; to be, together with His holy disciples, ever in the house of His Father. There the Redeemed shall neither hunger nor thirst, but shall rejoice with Christ for ever.

Unwillingly am I torn from that good and joyful company of Saints, and from the sweet feast of Jesus with His disciples, on the shore of Galilee's Sea.

I desire and pray, with the deepest yearning of my heart, that, in this present life, I may be made one of the least of the beloved disciples of Jesus, through a contempt of the world, and a renouncing of all that is transitory therein;

Not by my merits and my doings, but through the grace of God, and the compassion of my Lord Jesu Christ; so that, in His kingdom to come, I may be found meet to be visited and comforted by Him, and, with all His Saints, to rejoice and be blessed in glory.   Amen.

CHAPTER XIX

ON THE LOVING DISCOURSE OF JESUS WITH ST. PETER AND ST. JOHN THE APOSTLE, CONCERNING THE LOVE OF HIM

O LORD JESU CHRIST, Thou tenderest Lover of men, and most wise Teacher of little ones, I bless and give Thee thanks, for Thy gracious discourse with St. Peter, concerning the love of Thee; chiefly, in Thy having thrice questioned him.

Vouchsafing to call him by the name of his father, making special mention thereof, to the wonder and exceeding great joy of the Apostle.

Joy indeed, because, speaking with him, Thou didst only ask concerning his inward love, saying, "Simon, son of Jonas, lovest thou Me more than these?"

I praise and glorify Thee, O most worthy Jesus, for Thine ineffable goodness and gentleness, that Thou didst not reproach St. Peter, for the grievous sin he had committed against Thee; but rather Thou didst inquire after his love for Thee, the existence of which Thou knewest full well, and so didst stir him up to greater fervor, and make that love manifest to the Brethren, there present.

Moreover, how noble and holy was Peter in Thy sight; and how tenderly Thou didst love him, even after his fall, Thou didst now declare to the whole world.

Lest, may be, some fallen creature, forgetful of his own state, should think irreverently of him, with whom Thou, O Lord, didst so lovingly talk and eat.

I praise Thee, for the right and free answer of St. Peter to Thy words. All presumptuous and careless speaking being avoided, he professed not himself, in his love for Thee, more devoted than many others; teaching me and all men to think humbly, to consider discreetly, to answer questions wisely, and to uphold the Christian Faith truly and resolutely against all opposition.

Thrice, therefore, he spake in honor of the Holy Trinity, because thrice, when in fear, he had denied Thee. Believing with his whole heart, all doubt discarded, thrice he said, "I love Thee," "I love Thee," "I love Thee." What more? "Lord, Thou knowest that I love Thee."

O St. Peter! what sayest thou, if men, who see not thine heart, believe thee not?

"I speak to my Lord, and cry aloud in the hearing of all, and steadily declare with heart and voice, 'Lord, Thou knowest all things, Thou knowest that I love Thee.'

"Lord, Thou hast searched me out, and known me; Thou knewest my downsitting, when I denied Thee; Thou knewest my uprising, when I wept bitterly and truly repented. Thou hast pardoned me, Lord, Thou hast pardoned me, wherein I have sinned against Thee.

"Thou hast pardoned all mine offences for Thy holy Name's sake, for sweet is Thy compassion; manifold are Thy mercies over all Thy works, from everlasting to everlasting."

I praise and glorify Thee, most sweet Jesus, for the faithful, loving commendation of Thy lambs and sheep to the pastoral charge of Thy devoted Apostle, St. Peter: whom Thou didst call, from catching fishes, to the care of souls; from a little ship, to a Bishop's Chair; from poor parents, to be a great Master in Thy Church.

Therefore, by a divine utterance of Thy loving voice, Thou didst carefully command Peter, and hast enjoined the same on all other Prelates, saying, "Feed My sheep, the small ones and the great, the rich and the poor, whom I have redeemed with My precious Blood."

"Remember, Peter, what thou wast, before I

called thee from the ship to the Apostolate; and what thou art now become. Even after thy threefold denial, by My special mercy and favor, I have raised thee to high honor; that thou mayest always seek not thine own glory, but Mine, and the glory of My Heavenly Father, and of the Holy Ghost."

I praise Thee, most loving Jesus, for the most excellent provision touching St. Peter and St. John, who were beloved by Thee with a special love.

For by Thee was St. Peter well instructed; by Thy example he was strengthened for the sufferings of the Cross.

But John, a youth beloved, Thou didst continue, that he might teach and write mysteries of Thy Holy Church higher and more profitable. Thou didst with a foreseeing goodness give him a longer life for the consolation of many of the faithful.

Therefore, to Peter's inquiry concerning the end of John, Thou didst briefly reply, "My will is, that he tarry thus in the body, for the instruction of My whole Church; and the special care of My Mother, commended to him by Me, when I was yet hanging on the Cross.

"My will is that he live long, and write certain sublime records concerning My Godhead, and My Incarnation, My Passion, and Resur-

rection. This he will do, according as he has
seen with his eyes, and very often heard with
his ears from My mouth; until I come in person
to him, and take him with great joy to Myself.

"What is that to thee, Peter? Follow thou
Me."

"Follow Me, bearing the Cross for My sake.
For great indeed to thee will be the honor, if
thou suffer for Me a like death on the Cross."

This being said, and all peacefully arranged,
the bodily feast is finished; but not the spiritual, which is better felt in devout meditation
and prayer, than by a lengthy recital.

Most merciful Lord Jesu Christ, Thou best
Physician of the wearied soul, I beseech Thee
now to guide me aright, through the various
troubles and changes of this my life of sorrow;
and bring me to Thy glory in the Heaven of
Heavens.

Drive far from me the blasts of pride, when
I am reading and singing in the choir with my
Brethren, albeit better men than I. And when
I am studying and writing holy treatises, grant
that I may not think highly of myself, or com-
pare myself with those who are more learned,
and by Thee more highly endowed than I. So
shall I not lose the fruit of good works here on
earth, nor, in the world to come, eternal reward
with Thee in heaven.

Preserve me also, in the strong tempest of anger, from hard thoughts against the Brethren; that I may study to bear kindly with the manners and failings of others; to excuse them, as I readily do my own shortcomings. For so didst Thou, O Lord, in wisdom teach Thy disciples, bearing with them long and often, gently guiding them to a more perfect life.

Grant me, that I may follow Thee by the way of the Cross; patiently bearing labor of body, and sorrow of heart, even unto death.

Of Thy gracious compassion, vouchsafe to me, an unworthy sinner, with honest and faithful St. Thomas, mentally to touch and rely on Thy sacred wounds; and daily to meditate thereon, at the time of the Blessed Sacrament, in my study, at my meals, at all times and in all places, for an expression of my thanksgiving, for the love of Thy holy Name, and the honor of Thy holy Cross.

Grant me also, with the Apostle St. John, to love Thee with a pure heart and body, gladly to read and hear his holy Gospel, and treasure it in my breast. Let me rest, as it were, on Thy bosom; lose all thoughts of things earthly; and, with him in the Apocalypse, contemplate the secret things of Heaven.

Be Thou merciful to me, O Lord, and defend me from all evils, that violently assail me.

Strengthen me, in all virtues and godly living, to resist the enticing but bitter delusions of Satan; so hateful to, and despised by Thee and Thy holy Angels.

Strengthen me also to root out all pride of mind, to bridle all fleshly lust, to keep the door of my heart and mouth, and have a strict guard over my other senses.

Grant me, O Son of God, with the sons of Zebedee, to drink the cup of Thy Passion for the forgiveness of my sins; and with them, and all Thy Saints, to feast together with Thee in the Kingdom of Heaven.   Amen.

CHAPTER XX

ON THE APPEARANCE OF CHRIST TO THE ELEVEN DISCIPLES ON MOUNT TABOR, IN GALILEE

I BLESS and give Thee thanks, O Lord Jesu Christ, Thou King of heaven and earth, Who weighest the mountains, and enclosest the earth in Thy hand; Who sittest above the Cherubim and Seraphim, beholding the great deeps; Who walkest above the stars of heaven, and considerest the ends of the earth; and knowest all things before they come to pass.

I bless, praise, and honor Thee, for that joyful, glorious, and noble Manifestation of Thyself to Thy eleven disciples on Mount Tabor; as before Thy Passion Thou didst openly and clearly promise them, saying, "I will smite the Shepherd, and the sheep of the flock shall be scattered abroad. But after I am risen again, I will go before you into Galilee."

First, therefore, Thou didst foretell to them two events, sad indeed and grievous for beloved friends to hear; namely, the smiting the Shepherd, meaning that Thou Thyself shouldest suffer from the Jews; then that the dispersion of the sheep—their own flight and waiting for fear of punishment and death—would speedily follow.

But lest they should despair, weighed down by the load of evils, Thou didst forthwith add two great consoling joys. Thou didst assure them of Thy glorious Resurrection on the third day; and of Thy blessed appearance at a certain place well known to them, on Mount Tabor, in Galilee. There formerly, Thou didst work many signs and wonders, in the presence of Thy disciples, and before all the people.

O Galilee! thou Holy Land! Christ's country, wherein is Nazareth, the flowery, that city which He inhabited, and made illustrious by His glorious presence; and from whence came forth to us the eternal joys of our salvation, told of in the Holy Gospels.

I praise and honor Thee, O Jesu, for Thy great goodness; because Thou didst invite Thy disciples to come apart to a holy and secret place, far away from the noise and worry of the world; fitly chosen for hearing commands divine.

On that spot, formerly, before three fitting witnesses, Peter, James, and John, the other apostles being absent, Thou wast transfigured; and, a voice coming from the Father, out of the cloud, Thou wast clothed and adorned with an exceeding brightness; there, by a secret revelation, wast Thou manifested, to strengthen the faith of Thy Apostles, before Thy Passion.

But in this most open appearance, after Thy most glorious Resurrection, Thou didst manifest Thyself in the presence of a greater number of Thy disciples; strengthening those who believed, convincing those who doubted, graciously teaching all; gladdening them by Thy presence, and by the power given to Thee by the Father, over all things in heaven and in earth.

Having heard these things from Thy mouth, those who were present justly worshipped Thee, and glorified Thy holy Name. Falling down before Thee to the ground, they rejoiced and sang with deep devotion a new hymn to Thee, our God. For they then learnt such lofty and wondrous things concerning the Holy Trinity, such as no one is able fully to express.

O glorious and delightful vision! O most exalted and divine revelation! O the great and unspeakable joy in the hearts of Thy Holy Apostles.

O sweet and gentle Jesus, I praise and glorify Thee, Thou who spakest with Thy disciples so lovingly on the Mount; revealing to them the true doctrine of the Holy Trinity, and delivering to them the right form of words to be used, when baptizing the Faithful in the river of waters, for the remission of sins, "In the name of the Father, and of the Son, and of the Holy Ghost. Amen."

In these words, verily, I believe that I was baptized by a faithful Priest, and by faithful parents instructed and brought up in the true Catholic Faith, as taught in the Holy Church.

Thanks to Thee, O Christ, from Whom cometh every good to man, together with the hope of Life eternal. To which, O Lord, vouchsafe to bring me, when my days on earth are over; deliver me, I pray Thee, from the bitter pains of eternal death!

It is for me to pray; Thine it is, in mercy, to be my Helper.

I am weak and unstable; Thou art holy and full of compassion. Thou canst deliver me from every trouble; leading me with Thee to the mountain of Thy glory.

O Jesu! Thou saving health of my countenance, and my God; to Thee I cry, for Thee I yearn, night and day I pray unto Thee. Let Thy grace alone uphold me, until I be safely with Thee for ever. Who, with the Father, and the Holy Ghost, livest and reignest, ever one God, world without end. Amen.

PART IV

ON THE ASCENSION, PENTECOST, AND CERTAIN OTHER MATTERS

CHAPTER I

ON THE ASCENSION OF OUR LORD, AND HIS APPEARANCE

I BLESS and give Thee thanks, O Lord Jesu Christ, Thou King of Glory, Creator of heaven and earth, Ruler of Angels and Saviour of men, Who hatest the proud and comfortest the humble, Who didst on this day triumph above all the heavens, and above all the stars thereof; above the Cherubim and Seraphim; above all angelic dignity, and created excellency. Yea, on this day, 'mid the songs of Angels, with the sound of the trumpet and a merry noise, Thou didst by Thine own power, in the presence of Thy disciples, ascend with a joyful countenance and glorious Body, clothed with light as with a garment.

Having overcome the prince of this world, Thou didst show the way of eternal Life and Glory to chosen and devoted friends; whom Thou didst call out of this world, and strengthen to follow Thee, along the rugged road of the Cross.

O Lord, my God, how excellent is Thy Name in all the earth! O King of Heaven! how glo-

riously didst Thou enter into the Kingdom of
Thy Father.

With what great honor and glory wast Thou
crowned above all Thy Saints, and placed in
the highest dignity, at the right hand of Thy
Father, because Thou didst pour out Thy soul
unto death. Yea, Thou didst vouchsafe to die
for the ungodly, that Thou mightest quicken
Thy people, and make them to sit down at Thy
table in Thy Kingdom; which Thou didst prepare for them from the foundation of the world.
It was not for their own merits or for any goodness that dwelleth in man, but in Thy loving kindness, and the multitude of Thy tender mercies.

O how great the dignity of man's estate, that
human nature, united to God in one Person,
should far excel every creature in heaven and
in earth.

Rightly, therefore, as a fitting act of thanksgiving and praise, all creatures, which are in
heaven, and on earth, and under the earth,
should, at Thy Name, most gracious Jesu, bow
down and bend their knees before Thy face,
and worship the presence of Thy Glory—they
should exalt and praise Thy high and holy
Name above all things for ever.

I praise and honor Thee for Thy loving visit
and last appearance before Thy disciples, as
they sat at meat, assembled in an upper room.

They were devoutly talking of Thee, and greatly longing to see Thy face; and rejoiced were they, that, during their meal, Thou didst come for their especial comfort.

For, as often as they assembled to eat together and to converse, their talking was chiefly concerning God, and the Kingdom of God; concerning peace and brotherly love; concerning virtues and the salvation of souls; but, of the meat and drink set before them they cared little—secondary were they altogether. Having all things in common, no one sought for special and choice dishes.

For the common life of Saints is rich and sufficient; but they who seek their own comforts lose blessings free to all, and rarely are inwardly content.

I more especially praise Thee, O eternal King most High, for that loving feast with these Thy poor Apostles. It was not with Rulers and Chief Priests, nor was it with the rich of this world, by whom Thou and Thy disciples, whom Thou didst choose out of the world, and separate from the company of the wicked, were utterly despised.

I thank Thee, that, before Thou didst ascend into Heaven, Thou didst visit and strengthen Thy weak and timid disciples, left to struggle amidst the waves of this life.

To them Thou didst reveal many heavenly secrets concerning things past and things to come, that, comforted by Thy words, they might not fail to endure troubles manfully for Thy Name's sake.

I praise and honor Thee, O Lord Jesu Christ, Thou Teacher that excellest all Teachers of Theology, for every word Thou spakest, whether openly or dimly, to Thy disciples, and before the multitude; for Thy many beautiful and mystical parables; and for the plain doctrines, fitted to the capacity of Thine hearers.

I praise Thee for the right interpretation and clear exposition of divine utterances in the books of Moses and the Prophets, which bear true witness of Thee, and of all the holy works and glorious miracles wrought by Thee, whilst Thou wast in the world; and by Thee ordered to be proclaimed throughout all nations.

I praise and greatly bless Thee, most loving Jesus Christ, Thou eternal Shepherd, for the tender care of Thy poor and humble flock, placed as they were in the midst of a stubborn nation, whom Thou didst, on this day, visit with gladness in an upper room.

Having instructed them, and upbraided them for the hardness of their unbelief, Thou didst lead them out of Jerusalem unto the Mount of Olives, to behold Thy public and illustrious

Ascension to the celestial Glory of Thy Father, after the long pilgrimage of this life, and the requisite and due fulfilment of all righteousness and perfect obedience.

Where, also, in the presence of Thy holy Mother, with the devout Mary Magdalene, and other women and disciples dear to Thee, Thou didst then again very earnestly address to them profitable words concerning the Kingdom of God, the contempt of the world, the expectation of future grace, and of the coming of the Holy Ghost after a few days. Thou didst also repress an over-curious questioning, on the part of some, about the end of the world, as a matter not in any way pertaining to them.

After thus speaking, having blessed them with Thy sacred hands, and bade them farewell, Thou, with a glorious Body, wast lifted up, by divine power, into the lofty habitation of the Heavens; where an innumerable company of Saints and Angels, and all the Heavenly Hosts, singing and rejoicing on the pipe and harp, came forth to meet Thee. With them were the Patriarchs, and Prophets, and holy men of old, whom Thou didst valiantly redeem from the power of the grave, and quietly seat in a Paradise of delight, even to this day.

Therefore, with this great multitude of noble and exulting Saints, Thou didst openly ascend with joy, and might, and majesty, to the royal and lofty throne in the Heaven of Heavens— the throne most worthily prepared for Thee alone, from all eternity.

I praise and heartily thank Thee, Thou only Son of God, for that heavenly and perpetual blessing, which Thou didst bestow on Thy holy Mother, and on all Thy holy Apostles, and Thy other disciples, gathered together on Mount Olivet.

Wherefore, I now, with bended knees, embracing and glorying in Thy holy Cross, adore and together praise and humbly entreat Thee, my Lord, Thou King of Glory, that I may share in Thy loving benediction, and find in Thee comfort to my heart in this my day of exile.

And, I rejoice with all Thy Saints, for this day's exceeding great joy and solemnity, such as no one before ever saw or heard of, in heaven, or on earth; because now man's nature has been raised to the right hand of the Father, in glory everlasting.   Amen.

CHAPTER II

ON THE APPEARANCE OF THE ANGELS IN WHITE APPAREL

I BLESS Thee and praise Thee, sweet Jesu Christ, and devoutly do I thank Thee, because, after Thy withdrawal from the Apostles, and Thine entrance with the Angels into Heaven, Thou didst send two Angels, clothed in white apparel, as ambassadors from the celestial Court, to comfort Thy desolate disciples, as they were looking after Thee into Heaven, but unable to follow Thee.

And the Angels said : "Ye men of Galilee, why stand ye gazing up into Heaven ? Why are ye amazed at this great and wonderful miracle, such as before was never seen ? God is omnipotent. The Incarnate God is gone up with a shout, as was prophesied in the Psalm concerning Him.

"Ye, therefore, ought to preach, and testify to others, what things ye have heard and seen, as was commanded you.

"For this same Jesus, which is taken up from you into Heaven, shall so come in like manner, as ye have seen Him go into Heaven.

"And then He, who lately appeared meek and lowly among you on earth, that He might lead His humble followers into His heavenly kingdom, shall come, with great power and glory, to judge both the quick and the dead."

O loving Jesus! I beseech Thee now, in Thy Glory, remember me, poor and helpless.

Remember and have mercy upon me, an exile and a pilgrim, an outcast in this vale of tears, sighing and wailing 'mid the various temptations and troubles of this life, which so often draw back my heart from heavenly blessings.

Draw me, therefore, after Thee, O most faithful Jesu; so that, if with the feet of my body I cannot follow Thee, I may seek Thee diligently in the steps of holy desire and fervent love.

Although I am unworthy—utterly unfit to behold Thee in the loftiness of Thy divine Majesty, I will with lowliness follow Thee in the path of Thy humility.

O blessed vision, to behold God clearly in Himself, as He is now seen perfectly in Heaven by the Angels and all the Saints!

And, now I know of a truth, that all my yearning can never be satisfied, nor wholly set at rest, by any earthly good. That will only come, when, freed from all that is evil, I am united to Thee, my God, in Heaven.

Therefore, O Jesu Christ, art Thou gone before me to the Father, to prepare the way and a place for me, where I may abide with Thee; to secure for me pardon of my sins through the scars of Thy wounds; that I may, now and for ever, have full confidence in Thy presence, through the multitude of Thy mercies, and the magnitude of Thy merits.

O good Jesu! forsake me not. Thou, who by Thy power hast done great and marvellous things, art my love, and the desire of my soul; my Saviour and my Redeemer; my hope from my youth up; my expectation and my sole trust, even unto old age.

Thanking Thee most heartily for Thine abundant mercies, I will, with all Thy Saints, so long as I am a stranger and an exile in this my pilgrimage, love Thee, and praise Thee above all things.

Come, now, my Soul, return with Mary the Mother of Jesus, and with the Apostles, from the Mount of Olives into Jerusalem; there to seek peace of heart, and rest from all the cares of the world.

Ascend then with them into the large upper room, where the old Passover ceased to be, and the new was instituted in the Holy Sacrament of the Body and Blood of Christ, given and ordained.

Therefore, seriously reflect within thyself; remaining in silence and solitude, waiting upon God in prayer and devout meditation.

And, make thyself ready for the Feast of Pentecost, now at hand; to receive with the Apostles the Holy Ghost, on a greater Festival. All earthly comfort cast aside, they are awaiting, in a secret chamber, the new joy to be sent by Christ from Heaven.

Call to mind, in the mean season, the mercies of God, from the beginning of the world until now; more especially the Incarnation of Christ, and all the sayings and doings recorded of Him in the Gospels, from the day of His birth, even unto the present day of His glorious Ascension to the Father.

CHAPTER III

ON THE SENDING OF THE HOLY GHOST UPON THE APOSTLES OF CHRIST, AT THE FEAST OF PENTECOST

I BLESS and give Thee thanks, O Lord Jesu Christ, Thou most loving Comforter of the distressed, sweet Visitor of the sick, and mighty Helper of all in trouble, for Thy faithful promise of celestial gifts, from Thy lofty habitation in the Heavens, and from the Father of Lights.

And for Thy profuse bounty, and the marvellous pouring forth of the manifold graces of the Holy Ghost upon Thy disciples, assembled in Jerusalem.

There they were together in an upper room, praying and earnestly waiting for the comfort of the Holy Ghost from Heaven; their minds far from this world. Away from the tumult of life, in quietude and silence, they cast from their hearts all earthly cares, and, intent on heavenly and eternal blessings, they prepared themselves by devout prayer for the richer gifts of grace.

I praise and glorify Thee, O blessed Jesu Christ, King of the holy Angels, for the joyous festivity of this day, and for the solemn benediction, and sacerdotal consecration of the sacred fount of Baptism, by virtue of the Holy Ghost; in which, all the Faithful, baptized in the name of the Holy Trinity, are cleansed from all their sins, and made partakers of eternal Life. Also, by the grace of the Holy Ghost, they are deemed meet to be numbered as heirs of the heavenly Kingdom, and companions of Angels.

I laud and honor Thee, Who didst adorn this most sacred day by many miracles, signs, and

gifts; and didst command it to be observed by
Thy faithful followers for ever, with cheerful
devotion.

For, on this very day, the Law of old time
was first given to Thy people Israel, by Moses
on Mount Sinai; when, freed from the heavy
burden of bondage, they had gone forth from
the land of Egypt to offer to Thee Sacrifice in
the wilderness. Then was it, Thou didst also
give for food sweet manna from heaven.

To preserve a perpetual memory of this, Thou
didst ordain that, every year on this memorable
day, a new offering of the first fruits of the
earth should be brought to Thee for a thanksgiving.

But now, under the New Testament, after
Thou hadst gone up with great power into
Heaven, far above all Angels, Thou didst dis-
tinguish, bless, and consecrate this sacred day,
by a more abundant grace and favor.

In the place of sweet manna Thou didst, by
a visible sign from Heaven, send to Thine
Apostles the Holy Ghost, with a "great sound
as of a rushing mighty wind; and there appeared unto them cloven tongues, like as of
fire, and it sat upon each of them": that they
might be inwardly fervent with love, and outwardly ready and eloquent to preach; boldly
setting forth, as the Holy Ghost inspired and

gave them utterance, all the wonderful works, wrought by Thee so gloriously in the Holy Land, for our Salvation.

For these works were very many, and with man impossible; but with God all things are possible, and very easy.

Then was fulfilled that which was foretold by the notable Prophet, Isaiah, saying: "The Law shall go forth from Zion, and the Word of the Lord from Jerusalem."

Never were such wonderful things heard, as on this day; that, on one day, so many faithful men and women received the Holy Ghost in a visible sign, and in tongues of fire; openly prophesying and understanding the Holy Scriptures, and speaking in the languages of all nations; that men, uninstructed and unlettered, should, in the School of God, be taught by the Holy Ghost so quickly and so perfectly; and, with the gift of so much knowledge, should even shine forth as workers of many miracles and wonders.

O marvellous and unspeakable power of the Holy Ghost, who makes all those whom He visits and sustains, fervid and learned, lowly and devout, joyous and strong.

For there is no delay in learning, where the Holy Ghost is present as the inward Teacher, revealing heavenly secrets to babes, as He may

see best for the furtherance of their Salvation,
and for the benefit of others.

He especially teaches His disciples and secret
friends to despise the world; not to be high-
minded, but always to condescend to men of
low estate; to be vile in their own eyes, to
avoid honors, to examine their own faults,
deplore them, and quickly amend them; and
whatever, contrary to the Holy Ghost, lies hidden in the conscience, working remorse, hon-
estly and humbly to confess the same, however
light and trivial it may appear to the worldly.

CHAPTER IV

A PRAYER OF THANKSGIVING TO CHRIST FOR
HIS INCARNATION, PASSION, RESURRECTION,
AND ASCENSION; AND FOR SENDING THE HOLY
GHOST WITH A FULLER OUTPOURING OF GIFTS

O MOST sweet Lord Jesu Christ, Thou
Lover of my eternal Salvation, I, a poor
frail man, unworthy of any comfort and benefit, together with all the Saints and Thine Elect,
bless and glorify Thy holy Name for ever.

And especially do I give thanks to Thee, my
God, that, of Thy great love and compassion,
Thou wert willing to become man for me, to

take my nature, and, beyond the course of nature, to be conceived by the Holy Ghost, wonderfully born and nourished of the Blessed Virgin Mary, to be circumcised and presented in the Temple, that Thou mightest cleanse me of all impurity of mind and body, and teach me to live a godly, righteous, and sober life.

Still more do I thank Thee, for Thy most holy and bitter Passion; and, every day and hour of my life, shall I do so; because for me Thou didst deign to suffer on the Cross, die, and to be buried; that, by Thy innocent Death, Thou mightest deliver me from eternal death, and strengthen me by Thy example to suffer adversity.

I thank Thee again most joyfully, that, for my comfort, Thou didst, on the third day, rise again from the grave, and didst appear with great joy to Thy disciples in a closed upper room, that I may not despair in my day of trouble, or in any loss and danger; but have in Thee full confidence of my deliverance from the evils of this life, and a firm hope that Thou wilt, at the last day, raise me together with Thine Elect unto eternal Life.

And, I also most devotedly thank Thee, inwardly rejoicing heart and voice, for Thy solemn procession and glorious Ascension into Heaven, in the presence of Thy holy Mother, and others Thy disciples.

Because Thou wentest before me to prepare a place, that I might be with Thyself; and to open to me, by Thy Cross and Passion, the gate of the heavenly Kingdom:

Where, with the Angels, Thou now livest and reignest in the glory of Thy Father, until Thou dost return, at the end of the world, to judge both the quick and the dead; as the two holy Angels, clothed in white raiment (token of the joyfulness of this sacred Feast), taught us, who then appeared to Thy disciples, as they were looking upwards after Thee, towards the stars of heaven.

O blessed eyes, which were permitted to see Thee in the flesh! And blessed ears, which heard Thee speaking of the Kingdom of Heaven! What more delightful to be heard? What more blissful to be enjoyed?

For me, then, Thou didst ascend into the highest Heavens, above all the orders of Angels; where is the habitation of the Blessed, who reign with Thee now in exceeding great glory.

That all my hope may tend heavenwards, and yearn towards Thee; and never rest in things earthly, nor delight therein.

For all is vain and passing, all loss and unreality, that is not my God.

Every thing, also, must be despised and cast

aside which draws me back from my God, and hinders me from devoutly praying, and meditating on heavenly things.

Therefore, I beseech Thee, O loving Jesu, King of eternal glory, in the kingdom of Thy Father, remember me, Thy poor one; and send to me now from Heaven the Holy Ghost, the Comforter, to be my true solace, with a fresh fervor, and a fuller pouring forth of the gifts of the Spirit of God. Amen.

CHAPTER V

A PRAYER CONCERNING THE GIFTS OF THE HOLY GHOST, AGAINST DIVERS DISORDERS OF THE SOUL

COME, Holy Ghost, come with all Thy gifts, and drive away from me Satan, with all his idle delusions; which often disturb me in my prayers and devout meditations.

Come, Thou sweetest wind of heaven, blow through the garden of my heart with the warmest fire of Thy love, and keep down all evil affections within me; that the fragrance of thanksgiving may flow forth, with a shower of tears, through my great sorrow for my sins, and at the sweet remembrance of all Thy blessings.

Come, Thou best of comforters, and raise me from the abyss of gloomy sadness into the brightness of inward joy, with the hope of eternal rest—a reward for but a short labor of love.

Against weariness of mind strengthen me with Thy words, in the Psalms and Hymns. Against the impulse of anger, grant unto me, O God, the shield of patience.

Against fear, strike into me a fear of death, and of eternal torment. For, who will not dread the power of Thy wrath, and the punishment that knows no end?

Against boasting and vain glory, cause me to study mine own infirmities and the virtues of others. Against idle words, teach me to observe silence.

Against wanton laughter bring me to tears and sighs. For it is better to weep bitterly, than to laugh foolishly.

Against curiosity and wandering looks, set before me Jesus, Crucified for me.

Against gay clothing, exhibit to me worms and corruption. Against the lusts of the flesh, lay open to me the graves of the dead.

Against excess of wine, give me to drink the gall and vinegar of Christ. Against the silly tattlings of the world, repeat to me heavenly discourses.

Against long stories, quickly close up mine ears, lest poison enter by their passages.

Against loitering about broad streets and places of business, bind my hands and feet with the cords of Thy fear, lest I fall into divers temptations.

Against melancholy depression and spiritual sloth, pour into me the grace of thy holy unction.

Against any unfavorable suspicion of another, move me to a higher estimation of my neighbor.

Against any wrong done to me, strengthen me to bear it, and to avoid all avenging myself; lest in Heaven I lose the crown of glory, promised to the long-suffering.

Against the many diseases of my soul, bestow on me the health-giving odors of Thy virtues, and the choicest beauties of the holy Doctors.

Against any evil habit I may have, grant that I may do violence to nature, for the sake of Life eternal.

Against the oppressiveness of work, grant that I may retain peace of mind, through devout prayer.

Against distrust during the many trials of life, give me, O loving Holy Spirit, Thou present help in trouble, full confidence in Thee through Thy perfect holiness. Amen.

CHAPTER VI

A PRAYER FOR THE GRACE OF DEVOTION IN
THE PERFORMANCE OF HOLY OFFICES, AND
ON THE CHEERFUL PRAISE OF THE ANGELS
IN HEAVEN

O HOLY SPIRIT, the Comforter, Thou
wisest Teacher of teachers, Thou most
excellent Master of all physicians! Thou
canst, by a word and in a moment, teach the
ignorant, and perfectly cure all the infirmities
of body and soul.

Be graciously present with me in every place
and season, and lovingly pour into my heart
the grace of devotion when I am praying, meditating, singing, and reading; that I may devoutly and diligently go through my daily
duties and observe my vows.

For without Thee all prayers are vain and
unfitted for the ears of God; yea, without Thee,
I can do no good thing.

In whatever, therefore, I am deficient,
through my infirmity, do Thou by Thy grace
mercifully supply me.

Against all terrors of the night, and temptations of the devil, grant me the gift of faith in

Thy Cross and Passion, and protect me thereby as with an invincible shield; lest the malicious enemy, the prowler for my soul, lying in ambush here and everywhere, prevail against me.

Against weariness in long night watches, and still longer night readings, give me grace to think, what vast rewards are laid up for the Faithful in Heaven.

To uphold self-denial in eating and drinking, vouchsafe me the power of fasting, together with health to labor, pardon for past sins, protection against future ill-doing, and the hope of peace eternal, with the Elect in God's Kingdom.

Against inattention during Divine Service, stir me with songs on the harp and psaltery; in the words of David, inspired by Thee, the Holy Ghost.

And open to me the hidden manna concealed within the arid letter; and precious spices shut up in a box of seemingly little worth.

Many secret things indeed, which are justly kept from the wandering and idle, are laid open to the soul that devoutly prayeth and well considereth.

Against drowsiness at Morning Prayer, pluck me sharply by the ear, that I may the more quickly wake up to hear what the Lord says unto me in the Holy Scriptures, in His Hymns and Canticles; to lift up my heart to my God in the Heavens, and to forget the things done on this earth below.

Drive away from me all weariness of the body, and open the ear of my heart; that, in an ecstasy of mind I may be made meet, through the Holy Spirit, to contemplate the secrets of Heaven; and to hear the voices of the holy Angels, praising God and devoutly singing Psalms to Him, seated on His exalted throne.

O that I were one of them in Heaven, there to join them in their choir and sing, "Holy, Holy, Holy!"

They never grow weary, neither do they ever cease from the praise of their Creator; but, being filled with the Holy Spirit, they burn with love, they shine in snowy whiteness, they are fragrant with the odor of spices, they sing cheerfully, continuously, sweetly.

They intone together, they support each other resolutely, they pause equally, they lovingly triumph, they rejoice with great gladness, they ineffably surpass themselves in God.

Who then could sleep in the choir through weariness, when he thinks on this great and blessed joy of the Angels in heaven?

Who would not wake up at the echoing of the celestial organs, and the harmony of the musical host, singing for ever and ever, with one heart and one voice, "Holy, Holy, Holy"?

When the doors of heaven are shaken by the mighty shout of Angels, shall vile man be silent?

When the stones of the heavenly temple cry out, and the Nine Orders make a joyful noise unto God, shall the sons of God on earth be lost in sloth?

Behold the sun and the moon serve God by giving light, and will ye sleep? God forbid!

The holy Apostle Paul says: "Awake to righteousness and sin not."

Sleep not, be not slothful, let there be no hurrying, no discord, but with all reverence and devotion stand and sing, and with one accord offer, to the praise of God, sacrifices of thanksgiving.

For the joyful praise of the lips is pleasing to God; if outwardly the voice be in harmony, and inwardly there be the attention of a pure mind.

For the highest enjoyment in social gatherings, and the greatest charm in organs and songs, is harmony of voices, with cheerfulness of countenance, and honesty of bearing.

O how beautiful and holy the society, where the Holy Spirit is present and controls; where among the brethren is found love in the heart, truth in the mouth, and piety in the life; everywhere peace without guile, and free of all deception.

True brotherhood is that which is never disturbed by strife, not injured by labor, not overcome by grievances.

Because the love of God is shed abroad in our hearts by the Holy Ghost, which is given to the humble and contrite, to the needy, the meek and the peacemakers; and to all who are ready, night and day, to do that which is good, to the praise and glory of God.

These are the works of the Holy Ghost, who still worketh many good works in His faithful people, " dividing to each one severally even as He will; " provided they prepare themselves for grace, and diligently guard their heart in every thought and deed.

Great and arduous is the labor to keep the heart from wandering in prayer, and to unite the mind to God in spiritual contemplation.

And, though our spirit often fails of that which is good, and is consumed of evil, giving heed to vanity; still, the Holy Ghost, coming again, rebukes our heart, pricks it, wounds, anoints and heals it.

He instructs and enlightens; He humbles through daily transgressions, and lifts up through inward consolations; He refreshes by frequent prayers, and purifies by bitter lamentations.

O Sanctifier, Ruler, and Guardian of all the Faithful, Pardoner of all sinners, Restorer of innocence, Consoler of the sorrowful; O God, the Holy Ghost, O Thou Lord the Comforter, Who art gracious and full of compassion, and the most tender soother of babes in Christ, turn all that is evil within me into good, and the good ever into that which is better.

Sorrow into joy; wandering into a straight path; ignorance into knowledge of the truth; lukewarmness into fervor; fear into love; every bodily good into a spiritual gift; all earthly yearnings into heavenly desires; everything transient into that which is eternal; everything human into the divine; every created and finite blessing into the highest, infinite and boundless good; for Thou art my God and my Saviour.

O my God, my true and eternal Salvation, guard me from every present evil; forgive that which is past, and deliver me from all future danger by the bounteous grace of the Holy Ghost, which Thou didst on this day pour forth, with copious blessing, into the hearts of the Apostles, that they might preach Thy Word unto all nations.   Amen.

CHAPTER VII

ON THE PREACHING OF THE APOSTLES, AND
PROCLAIMING THE HOLY NAME OF OUR LORD
JESUS CHRIST, THROUGHOUT THE WORLD, FOR
THE SALVATION OF MAN

I BLESS and give Thee thanks, O Lord Jesu
Christ of Nazareth, Thou Son of the Most
High God, eternally blessed above all Saints,
because on this day, when the Holy Ghost, sent
into the world by Thee, came in the visible
form of fire, the hearts of the Faithful were in-
visibly inflamed with the love and praise of
Thy Holy Name;

Then forthwith Thy Apostles cast away all
fear, and that Name, glorified by the Father
above all holy names, began to be publicly
preached, praised, spread abroad, and magnified. Openly was it proclaimed before all the
people of Jerusalem, and among the Gentiles,
from day to day to be exalted, honored, and
worshipped.

At length, as the number of the disciples increased, so great a devotion and brotherly love
arose among all, both men and women, that
they were one in faith and holy living; and

were all of one heart, and one soul, through
love perfected in God.

No one sought his own, but Christ's. All
private possessions were used for the common
good in the Holy Primitive Church, gathered
together in the Holy Ghost.

So great also was the joy, peace, and unity
among them, that no one called anything his
own, nor held any thing as his own; but all
rejoiced to have in God all things in common,
and to distribute to the needy.

And this holy and heavenly life, the blessed
Apostles were first taught by the Lord Jesus
Christ Himself, and afterwards were careful to
observe it. And they retained it until the end
of their days, when they died, as martyrs, for
the faith of the Lord Jesus.

I praise and bless Thee, O Holy Father,
Almighty Everlasting God, with Thine Only-
Begotten Son, and the Holy Ghost, the Comforter, for all the loving-kindnesses and spiritual gifts, which Thou didst once vouchsafe to
Thine Elect Friends, and the holy Patriarchs
and Prophets; to whom, in times past, Thou
didst by words and signs reveal, by the Holy
Ghost, the secrets of Thy wisdom, and the
judgments of Thy mouth; and more especially
the mystery of Thy glorious Incarnation.

But, after Thy coming, O holy Jesu, many

more hidden things of the Scriptures didst Thou Thyself reveal and expound more fully; and things, which the babes in Christ could not yet receive, Thou didst lovingly leave, till the sending down of the Holy Ghost.

And, what is still further wonderful and praiseworthy, Thou didst suddenly inflame the rude minds of the Apostles with the fire of the Holy Ghost. Those above the wise of the world, chosen out of its vanities and devoted to Thee, them Thou didst perfectly instruct within, and strengthen them to convert the whole world.

I praise and give Thee honor, O ever glorious Jesu Christ, all-holy Enlightener and Restorer of all mankind, for the conversion and gathering together of multitudes, whom Thou didst assemble in the unity of the Catholic Faith and Apostolic Doctrine, from all parts of the earth, and from nations of many languages. Theirs it was to honor Thy sweet and Holy Name, in hymns, and psalms, and spiritual songs; and so, to devoutly celebrate in all places and churches the sacred Festival of the Holy Ghost.

During which many marvellous things, that were done in those days, are recited in God's House, so that even the common people, together with the princes and nobles, hear the divine works, which, for the Salvation of believers, the Holy Ghost has wrought on earth from the beginning of the world, and will not cease to work, until the Day of Judgment.

For, if God be for us, who can be against us? Wherefore, in the Psalm the Holy Ghost exhorts all the Faithful, saying, " Bless ye God in the congregations, even the Lord, from the fountain of Israel." There is little Ben a-min, rapturously contemplating the things of Heaven, forsaking all that is earthly.

Blessed are those servants, who gladly hasten to sing the Lord's song, and, together with the Angels, rejoice to bless God.

Blessed are they who despise outward vanities, and wholly turn their hearts to God ; that they may receive the grace of the Holy Ghost, by which they may overcome all carnal affections, and resist Satan.

For greater far and stronger is the power and grace of the Holy Ghost to effect good, than of the spirit of darkness to work evil.

I bless and praise Thee, dearest Jesu, for the great favor and wisdom given to Thine Apostles, empowering them to preach Thy Word boldly, before all that dwell in Jerusalem, and Judæa, and in Samaria, even unto the ends of the earth.

And especially for their constancy and perseverance. They remained true to the faith, when their citizens were persecuted; rejoicing for Thy Name's sake to suffer contempt, to be imprisoned, to be scourged, to be tormented with hunger, and tortured with punishments of divers kinds.

All these trials seemed light and of small account, in comparison with the crown of eternal Life, and the greatness of the glory to be revealed; as also the blessed Paul says, "the sufferings of the present time are not worthy to be compared with the future glory, which shall be revealed in us."

Which glory, O most loving Jesus, Thou Son of God, in Thy most gracious compassion, and by the boundless love of the Holy Ghost, do Thou, after the bitter and perilous struggles in this life, deign to grant unto me.

Who with the Father and the same Holy Spirit, livest and reignest, Three Persons and One God, co-equal in glory. for ever and ever. Amen.